MW01132448

Sociolinguistic typc-- ₀ⲟ/

Sociolinguistic typology

Social determinants of linguistic complexity

PETER TRUDGILL

OXFORD
UNIVERSITY PRESS

OXFORD
UNIVERSITY PRESS

Great Clarendon Street, Oxford ox2 6DP

Oxford University Press is a department of the University of Oxford.
It furthers the University's objective of excellence in research, scholarship,
and education by publishing worldwide in

Oxford New York

Auckland Cape Town Dar es Salaam Hong Kong Karachi
Kuala Lumpur Madrid Melbourne Mexico City Nairobi
New Delhi Shanghai Taipei Toronto

With offices in

Argentina Austria Brazil Chile Czech Republic France Greece
Guatemala Hungary Italy Japan Poland Portugal Singapore
South Korea Switzerland Thailand Turkey Ukraine Vietnam

Oxford is a registered trade mark of Oxford University Press
in the UK and in certain other countries

Published in the United States
by Oxford University Press Inc., New York

British Library Cataloguing in Publication Data
Data available

Library of Congress Cataloging in Publication Data
Data available

Typeset by SPI Publisher Services, Pondicherry, India
Printed in Great Britain
on acid-free paper by
MPG Books Group, Bodmin and King's Lynn

ISBN 978–0–19–960434–0 (Hbk.)
ISBN 978–0–19–960435–7 (Pbk.)

1 3 5 7 9 10 8 6 4 2

For William Labov

Contents

Preface

This book is about sociolinguistic typology. By sociolinguistic typology I mean a form of linguistic typology which is sociolinguistically informed, asks sociolinguistic questions, and tries to supply sociolinguistic answers. My book is based on the assumption that the nature of the human language faculty is the same the world over, and has been so ever since humans became human. Here, however, I consider the possibility that, because of the influence social structure can have on language structure, this common faculty of the human mind may nevertheless produce different types of language in different places and at different moments in human history.

The book is speculative—if you read it, you will see that I have awarded myself the luxury of wondering about things. They are things I have been wondering about for quite a while—my first essay on this topic, containing in embryonic form a number of the ideas presented here, appeared in Trudgill (1983) as "Language contact and language change: on the rise of the creoloid", but was actually written in 1977, and was first presented in public at the *International Conference of Historical Linguistics* at Stanford University in March 1979, where it aroused both opposition and support—I recall discussions with Henning Andersen, C.-J. Bailey, Sally Thomason, Marianne Mithun, and other participants (see Traugott 1980).

What I have been wondering about is the extent to which different types of human society produce different types of language and, if this is the case, what this might mean for the future typology of human languages. As I wrote for my 1979 presentation, "I want to suggest that the present is in some important respects obviously very different from the past, and that these differences may have linguistic consequences" (1983: 102)—a point to which I shall return, especially in Chapter 6.

My 1979 presentation was followed by other work by linguists tackling similar issues, such as Bailey (1982), Andersen

(1988), Thurston (1989), Grace (1990), Ross (1997), Nettle (1999), Nettle and Romaine (2000), McWhorter (2007), Wray and Grace (2007), Sinnemäki (2009), and Lupyan and Dale (2010). But of course my paper was by no means the first occasion when scholars had wondered about the relationship between linguistic and social structure. It fell into a long tradition that included Schlegel (1846), Madvig (1857), Jespersen (1894), Gabelentz, (1901), Sapir (1912), Jakobson (1929), Whorf (1956), and Hymes (1974).

My legendarily sceptical friend and colleague Lyle Campbell is not impressed by this kind of work by these scholars. Campbell and Poser (2008: 358) find that the approach has little or no merit; and they tell us that their problem is that, whatever generalization workers in this tradition propose, "there are many counterexamples" (2008: 359). As far as my own proposals are concerned, I am certainly aware that it is in their very nature that there should be counterexamples. I am dealing with likelihoods, and formulating tendencies rather than strict rules of correlation. That is, I am using the word *determinant*, as it appears in the subtitle to this book, in the relatively weak sense in which it means, as the *Oxford English Dictionary* has it, "a conditioning factor".

I hope, though, that I have made some progress, as compared to earlier work, on the topic of what the social determinants of linguistic structure might be. I have done this by isolating not just one but a number of different social parameters which, when taken in combination, shed much more light than was previously the case on the sociolinguistic factors which influence linguistic typology, particularly in terms of linguistic complexity and simplicity. In this book I consider structurally different types of community from the point of view of the roles of, principally, the following social factors: community size, social networks, social stability, contact with other communities, and shared information.

I also, crucially, investigate the issue of *how* and *why* there should be links between linguistic and social structure; and I do this by proposing and examining a number of linguistic *mechanisms* which permit the social factors just listed to impinge on language. Specifically, I try to answer the *how* part of this question by looking at different types of linguistic change, since, obviously, linguistic structures at any given moment in time are to a considerable extent the result of the changes which have produced them. And then it turns out, fortunately, that attempting to answer the *how* question also gives us very considerable insight into the *why* problem. As I say in Chapter 4, it is one thing to produce data showing that there might be a structural society–language connection, and another matter altogether to explain why this should be so—but this I have attempted to do.

Whether I have succeeded in this at all will be for the reader to judge, but I am not trying to actually prove anything in this work. I have dignified some of my suggestions with the label *hypothesis*, but if readers feel that I have gone too far in using this term, I will be happy to accept their view. The book contains ideas, but no statistics. It deals with tendencies and possibilities, but there are no tests of significance. It contains data, but there is no random sampling. And I use terms such as "large" and "small" in a relative way without defining what I mean by them, because I am not actually sure about this. In the text I have also occasionally used, as I did in the previous paragraph, the word *explain*; but it will be noted that these explanations are mostly of the probabilistic sort which suggest that something tends to be "more likely" to be the case in certain situations (hence the irrelevance of counterexamples). It is true that Lass (1980: 13) reckons that probabilistic explanations are essentially "non-explanatory"—so perhaps I should have written *"explain"* rather than *explain*. But Lass does help out: what I am seeking after here is perhaps best described as he has done (1980: 158):

We might anyhow try admitting that often when we say we are providing 'explanations', what we are really doing is proposing models or 'metaphorical redescriptions' (Hesse 1966), which we think provide something woollier, but equally important: what we might, without at the moment attempting further definition, call 'insight'.

Nettle writes that "no relationships of grammatical typology to structure or social organisation have been convincingly demonstrated" but that "it seems quite plausible that some such relationship could exist" (1999: 138). "The question", he also says, "has received little rigorous scholarly attention". I am not sure that Nettle, or indeed anybody else, would agree that what follows in this book is rigorous or scholarly; but I hope they will agree that the question has received attention. And if readers find that, in Lass's terms, there are any insights at all in this book, I shall be pleased.

Acknowledgements

The first reference in print to this book is as "Trudgill (forthcoming)", in my 1986 book *Dialects in contact*. It has, in other words, been a very long time coming. In the course of the decades that it has required for the book to finally appear, very many people indeed have been of assistance to me in its writing, in various ways. I know I have not been as diligent as I should have been in keeping a record of their kindnesses, and the following list is therefore incomplete. I apologize. But I thank all the people I have inadvertently left off the list, and all those who are on it, very warmly indeed for their help, and for sharing different parts of this enterprise with me. Here is the list—it goes without saying that none of the people cited here are to blame for any of the many things which I am sure will be shown to be wrong with the book, but here I am saying it anyway:

Sasha Aikhenvald, Anders Ahlqvist, Enam Al-Wer, Henning Andersen, Lars-Gunnar Andersson, Amalia Arvaniti, Wiesław Awedyk, C.-J. Bailey, Laurie Bauer, Winifred Bauer, Allan Bell, Raphael Berthele, Kurt Braunmüller, David Britain, Keith Brown, Neil Brummage, Kate Burridge, Andy Butcher, Lyle Campbell, Andrew Carstairs-McCarthy, Jack Chambers, Magdalena Charzynska-Wójcik, Sandra Clarke, Michael Clyne, Donna Christian, Bernard Comrie, Grev Corbett, Bill Croft, Anne Cutler, Östen Dahl, Alice Davison, Rik De Busser, Gunther De Vogelaer, Bob Dixon, Yvonne Dröschel, Katarzyna Dziubalska-Kołaczyk, Jan Terje Faarlund, Małgorzata Fabiszak, Ralph Fasold, Janet Fletcher, Paul Fletcher, John Foulks, Alexander L. Francis, Mike Garman, David Gil, Elizabeth Gordon, Stephane Goyette, George Grace, Patrick Griffiths, Walter Haas, Liliane Haegeman, Eric Hamp, Jean Hannah, Ray Harlow, John Harris, Martin Harris, Martin Haspelmath, Jack Hawkins, Roger Hawkins, Junko Hibiya, Raymond Hickey, Jarich Hoekstra, Ernst Håkon Jahr, Mark Janse, Adam Jaworski, Brian Joseph, Peter Kenyon, Marcin Kilarsky, Paul Kiparsky, Jussi Klemola, Miklós Kontra, Andrew

Koontz-Garboden, Bernd Kortmann, William Labov, Stephen Laker, Randy LaPolla, Christian Lehmann, Gillian Lewis, Ken Lodge, John Lyons, Brian MacWhinney, John McWhorter, Brit Mæhlum, Didier Maillat, Jim Milroy, Lesley Milroy, Marianne Mithun, Magdalena Murawska, Daniel Nettle, Terttu Nevalainen, Michael Noonan, Thomas O'Rahilly, Robert Orr, Michael Osborne, Frank Palmer, Andreas Papapavlou, Andy Pawley, Magdalena Perdek, Lukas Pietsch, Mark Post, Dennis Preston, Andrew Radford, Mechthild Reh, Geoffrey Sampson, Klára Sándor, Nathalie Schilling-Estes, Daniel Schreier, Wolfgang Schulze, Peter Siemund, Kaius Sinnemäki, J.C. Smith, Tonya Stebbins, Jackson Sun, Sali Tagliamonte, Sally Thomason, Arne Torp, Milton Tynch, Jacques Van Keymeulen, Wim Vandenbussche, Johan Van der Auwera, Theo Vennemann, Nikos Vergis, Susanne Wagner, Alastair Walker, Søren Wichmann, David Willis, Don Winford, Ilse Wischer, Walt Wolfram, and Laura Wright. And of all the many people just listed, I would like to single out for very special thanks my wife Jean Hannah for her tolerance, guidance, support, advice, and enormously helpful constructive criticism, which I have actually acted on really rather often.

I am especially grateful to the following people, already mentioned above, who have also read the entire book in earlier versions, and supplied me with extremely helpful comments, corrections, examples, counterexamples, references—and suggestions for improvement, for which there was certainly a great need: Sasha Aikhenvald, Laurie Bauer, David Britain, Andrew Carstairs-McCarthy, Östen Dahl, Bob Dixon, Jan Terje Faarlund, Jean Hannah, Marcin Kilarsky, Lesley Milroy, Søren Wichmann, Ilse Wischer, and an anonymous reviewer for OUP. Very special thanks also go to John Davey of Oxford University Press, described by Bob Dixon as "linguistics editor *sans pareil*", a sentiment with which I heartily concur, not only for his help with and enthusiasm for this book but also for his magnificent work in promoting linguistics generally.

This book was worked on and written while I was employed in Switzerland, first as Professor of English Linguistics at the Université de Lausanne; and then as Professor of English Linguistics at the Université de Fribourg/Universität Freiburg Schweiz; while I was affiliated to the Research Centre for

Linguistic Typology at La Trobe University, Melbourne, Australia; as well as to the University of Agder in Kristiansand, Norway; and to the University of East Anglia in Norwich, England. I have also been able to work on the book while enjoying visiting professorships at the Ohio State University, Albert-Ludwigs-Universität Freiburg, the University of Vienna, and the University of Hamburg.

Peter Trudgill

University of Agder, Kristiansand, Norway
January 2011

Prologue: Social correlates of linguistic structures

In this book I suggest that there is a challenging issue to focus on which involves the relationships which might exist between societal type generally, on the one hand, and aspects of linguistic structure, on the other.

There are good reasons to explore these issues. Linguistic-typological studies have provided us with a series of insights into the range of structures available in human languages; into what the constraints on these structures might be; and into relationships between different typological characteristics. But we do not yet have explanations for why, of all the possible structures available to human languages, particular languages select particular structures and not others—except of course that it is obvious that a major role is played here by linguistic-genetic and areal influences. It is not surprising if languages which are genetically related have certain characteristics in common, having inherited them from some ancestral language. Most of the Germanic languages, such as Swedish, Dutch, and Frisian, have the "verb second" rule, e.g. *No kjem ho* 'now comes she' (Norwegian), which is not found in unrelated languages. Nor is it surprising if languages spoken in geographically adjacent areas have similarities. Indeed, "adjacent" may not be a particularly accurate term here—Holman et al. (2007) show that there is a tendency for similarity between languages to decrease with geographical distance up to a range of several thousands of kilometres.

But a legitimate sociolinguistic viewpoint would be that genetics and geography are not the whole story. Other explanations for why particular languages select particular structures and not others may be available, and some of these explanations might be social in nature; that is, the distribution of linguistic features over languages may not be totally random when viewed from a social perspective. The challenge for a sociolinguistically-informed typology, therefore, has to do with whether there are indeed any social determinants of linguistic patterning, and, if so, what these determinants might be, bearing in mind that, as I said above, the dictionary definition of *determinant* I am using here is "an influencing factor" rather than "a determining factor". The issue at hand for this sociolinguistic typology is whether it is possible to suggest that certain linguistic features are more commonly associated with certain types of society or social structure than others. Of course, these are not new questions, as mentioned earlier; and they are also questions which linguists have, quite rightly, treated with a certain amount of suspicion in the past, because of their links with mistaken notions to do with "primitive" languages and "primitive" societies. However, after many decades of academic linguists agreeing, and asserting, that there is very definitely no such thing anywhere as a primitive language, it now seems safe to consider this issue in print without this suspicion arising (see Dixon 2003b).

The "why" question

As I wrote in the Preface, this search for social explanations for linguistic structures is not new. It can be found, amongst other places, in work going back to Boas, Sapir, and Whorf (see Mathiot 1979). It is also, for example, supported by the research programme outlined more recently in Dixon (2003b; and see also Dixon 2010a: section 1.6). He also argues that the discipline of linguistics should be concerned not only with 'how?' questions, such as "how do languages differ?". He suggests that, in addition, "for every question that asks 'how', there should be a related enquiry into 'why?'". The sample of 'why' questions which he presents, and the type of answers he gives to them, are very instructive for the subject matter of this book. The sorts of questions Dixon wants us to ask would include:

(1) Why does the Tibeto-Burman language Lahu have five spatial demonstratives, including distinct forms for 'up there' and 'down there', while neighbouring Chinese, like English, has only two, 'here' and 'there'? The explanation he provides is in terms of the physical environment in which the language is

found. Lahu is spoken in mountainous country; and whether something is 'up' or 'down' with respect to the speaker is therefore as important as how near or far away it is (see also Dixon 2010b: 243).

(2) Why does Japanese have a developed system of honorific registers while, say, English does not? The answer this time lies in cultural values. Japanese society has traditionally been highly stratified, with "strict conventions of politeness", and the relative social status of the speaker and hearer determines the speech register employed (see more on Korean below).

(3) Why can the verb *wotte* 'want' in Canadian Old Order Mennonite Pennsylvania Dutch no longer be used in constructions like 'I want to come'? Here another explanation in terms of cultural values is suggested. The Mennonite community which speaks this language has strong religious beliefs which subordinate the self to the will of God, so that for an individual to want something for themselves would be inappropriate (Burridge 2002: 219).

Of all of Dixon's example questions—there are others, as we shall see below—these are the easiest to suggest answers to. The fact is that they are answerable in terms of the physical and cultural environment in which the language in question is spoken. And it is well established that a language can be influenced, on the one hand, by natural, physical factors such as the geography, climate, and terrain of the area where it is used; and, on the other hand, by cultural factors such as social values and social practices of the society which speaks it. There is already a considerable body of work which focuses on relationships between natural and cultural factors and certain aspects of language structure, and I now list a number of examples of such influence from different linguistic levels, beginning with lexis.

Lexis

Social culture and lexis

According to Givón (1979: 289) "a communicative system never rises in a sociocultural vacuum". And in terms of cultural environment, it is easy to find examples of how this may be reflected in the vocabulary of a particular language. The more different a culture is from one's own, moreover, the more likely the different vocabulary items are to strike one as exotic. For instance, Jacobson's *Yup'ik Eskimo Dictionary* cites lexis which reflects a very specific set of social values and organization:

> *tunrirtuq* 'he feels embarrassed because he is imposing on someone; beholden because of an inability to reciprocate for things someone has done for him; embarrassed by the actions of someone such as a child for whom he feels responsible'
> *qatnguq* 'half sibling through a spouse-borrowing relationship'.

One of the most obvious types of relationship between lexis and society lies in the way in which kinship terms provide a reflection of the social structure and the social roles of different kin in particular societies. We can suppose that the kinship structure of a community which speaks a language like Njamal (Australia) in which *mabidi* is a reciprocal term translatable into English by, amongst other things, *grandfather, great uncle, grandson, granddaughter, wife of grandson,* and *husband of granddaughter* (Burling 1970: 21) is very different from that of the average European community. The point is that certain Njamal kinship terms distinguish not generation, as in English, but generation distance: a man can use the same term, *maili*, for his *father's father* and his *daughter's son's wife's sister*, the person in question being two generations removed. Equally, the Njamal term *mama* signifies what for the Njamal is a single kinship relationship, but which has to be translated into English in different ways according to context: *father, uncle, male cousin of parent,* and so on: the term is used for males of the same generation as the father. A reasonable deduction would be that the distinction between *father* and *father's brother* cannot have the same importance in Njamal society as in European cultures. On the other hand, whereas English employs the term *uncle* for *father's brother* and *mother's sister's husband,* as well as for *mother's brother* and *father's sister's husband,* Njamal uses *mama* for the first pair and another term, *karna,* for the second.

This type of difference of course explains why anthropologists are interested in such terminology. On the other hand, the issue is by no means totally straightforward since it is not always clear to what extent differences of lexis truly reflect differences of social role. It would probably not be easy to deduce anything truly insightful from the fact that French distinguishes, in a way that English does not, between male and female cousins—*cousin* vs. *cousine*; nor from the fact that Danish distinguishes, in a way that English does not, between two different types of aunt—*moster* 'mother's sister', and *faster* 'father's sister'.

It is also well known that anthropologists are interested in tabooed lexis, since this will generally reflect behavioural taboos in a community more generally, and will represent a good reflection of at least part of the system of values and beliefs of the society in question (Allan and Burridge: 2006). In different parts of the world taboo words include those for the left hand, for female relations, or for certain game animals. In the English-speaking world, the most severe taboos have been traditionally associated with words connected with sex, closely followed by those connected with excretion and the Christian religion. This is a reflection of the emphasis traditionally placed on sexual morality in the culture. But now, as the English-speaking world becomes more sensitive to issues involving inegalitarian discrimination against people on the grounds of their social or physical characteristics, words such as *nigger, cripple, poof* are acquiring increased taboo-loading, and their use is becoming increasingly shocking. In other, particularly Roman Catholic, cultures the strongest taboos may also be associated with religion; and in Norway some of the most strongly tabooed expressions are concerned with the devil (Trudgill 2000).

Physical culture and lexis

Another obvious site for the study of language–society relationships is to be found, as already noted, in the reflection of aspects of a community's material and physical culture in its lexicon. The topography and climate of Norway mean that it is not surprising that Norwegian has a number of vocabulary items not found in English, in spite of the close relatedness of the two languages: *ur* (masc.) means "rain clouds over the mountains", while the coincidentally homonymous but unrelated word *ur* (fem.) means "the debris of boulders resulting from cracking and erosion of a cliff or mountain".

In fact, it is generally considered very usual that those semantic distinctions which communities need to make frequently in the course of their everyday lives should be lexicalized. It should therefore be no surprise that Sami has a large number of words for different types of reindeer; that Bedouin Arabic dialects have many words for different types of camel; and that the Eskimo languages have many different words for snow—even if we acknowledge that the concept of "word for something" is not a straightforward one.

Magga (2006) confirms and illustrates the validity of the Sami/reindeer point. Pullum (1991), on the other hand, intends to make us wary about the facts of Eskimo and snow (see also Martin 1986): according to Dixon (2010a: 65), Pullum has shouted his refutation of this thesis, in *The Great Eskimo Vocabulary Hoax,* "as loud as only he knows how". Pullum's piece is indeed powerful, but I note that Woodbury's reading (1991) of Steven Jacobson's *Yup'ik Eskimo Dictionary* (1984) suggests—to me at least—that there are perhaps seven candidate lexemes in that language:

kanerrluk	'fine snow (or rain)'
natquik	'drifting snow'
qanikcaq	'snow on the ground'
muruaneq	'deep soft snow'
nutarynek	'fresh snow'
qanisqineq	'snow floating on water'
cellallir-	'to snow heavily'

although, as Woodbury says, any decision about which of these items should actually "count" is bound to be arbitrary.[1]

An even more persuasive picture of the relationship between environment and "snow words" is painted in the work of the native Sami-speaking linguist Ole Henrik Magga (2006). He cites a large number of "snow words" and related lexical items in North Sami, as spoken in the far north of Norway, which include the following:

muohta	'snow-covered ground'
jassa	'patch of snow in summer or late spring'

[1] For further discussion on Eskimo snow vocabulary, see Krupnik and Müller-Wille (2010); and Cichocki and Kilarski (2011).

čahki	'hard lump of snow, hard snowball'
geardni	'thin crust of snow'
goahpálat	'the kind of snow-storm in which the snow falls thickly and sticks to things'
guoldu	'cloud of snow which blows up from the ground when there is a hard frost without very much wind'
luotkku	'loose snow'
moarri	'brittle crust of snow, thin frozen surface of snow (thicker than *geardni*); frozen crust of driven snow, *čearga*, which does not quite bear; thin crust of ice'
ruokŋa	'thin hard crust of ice on snow'
seaŋaš	'granular snow at the bottom of the layer of snow'
skárta	'thin (more or less ice-like) layer of snow frozen on to the ground'
skáva	'very thin layer of frozen snow'
skávvi	'crust of ice on snow, formed in the evening after the sun has thawed the top of the snow during the day'
soavli	'very wet, slushy snow, snow-slush'
vahca	'loose snow (especially new snow on the top of a layer of older snow or on a road with snow on it)'
bohkolat	'deep snow of varying depth; small (steep) snow-drift on road or where one goes' (plural: 'wave-like, steep, little snow drifts')
časttas	'hard snowdrift (smaller than *skálvi*)'
čearga	'snowdrift which is so hard that it bears; crust of drift-snow'
činus	'firm, even snow (but not firm enough to bear)'
dobádat	'sticky snow, heavy wet snow'
fáska	'snow blown together by the wind, snowdrift (of snow blown along the ground)'
joavggahat	'place where the snow lies particularly deep after a fall of snow'
lavki	'slippery going: ice covered with loose, dry snow with no foothold'
moarri	'the kind of going, surface, when the frozen snow or crust of ice breaks and cuts the legs of horses or reindeer'

muovllahat	'place where people or animals have ploughed through or plunged along in deep snow or a soft bog'
njeadgga	'ground drift' (drifting snow which gets blown up from the ground) which covers roads or tracks'
oppas	'untouched, untrodden, covering of snow (where no way or road has been made by walking or driving, or where reindeer have not grazed), deep snow, untrodden reindeer pasture in winter'
sievlla	'the state of things when the spring snow is so soft that one sinks in it'
skálvi	'big (high, steep, and usually hard) snow-drift'
spoatna	'hard, firm, snow to drive on (when there is little snow)'.

For a different sort of geographical environment, Sapir (1963 [1912]: 91) quotes the detailed lexical distinctions made in the topographical vocabulary of the desert plateau language, Paiute, of the Southwest USA. These so amazed him that he is moved to add that they "in some cases seem almost too precise to be of practical value". Paiute lexis includes terms for:

sand flat, semicircular valley, circular valley, spot of level ground in the mountains surrounded by ridges, plain valley surrounded by mountains, canyon without water, canyon with creek, slope of mountain or canyon wall receiving sunlight, shaded mountain slope or canyon wall, rolling country intersected by several small hill-ridges—and so on,

which is because "accurate reference to topography is a necessary thing to dwellers in an inhospitable semi-arid region; so purely practical a need as definitely locating a spring might well require reference to several features of topographical detail" (1963: 91).

Mithun (1999: 36) also cites many other items from Jacobson's *Yup'ik Eskimo Dictionary* which reflect a culture formed in a very specific milieu:

araq	'ash made from birch tree fungus and mixed with chewing tobacco'
caginraq	'pelt of caribou taken just after the long winter hair has been shed in spring'
partak	'spruce root stretched above water, from which to hang a line of snares just above the water's surface, to catch waterfowl'
qamigartuq	'he goes seal-hunting with a small sled and kayak during the spring'
pug'uq	'it (a fish or seal) came to the surface, emerging halfway'
qellukaq	'the flipper of an elderly seal'.

Physical environment is also mirrored in the way in which island languages may reflect, in their directional vocabulary, the locale in which they are spoken. Manam (Lichtenberk 1983: 571), an Austronesian language spoken on the island of Manam off the north coast of New Guinea, has an elaborate directional system reflecting the island habitat. In this system, "two directions are of cardinal importance: (1) the sea, (2) the interior of the island. All the other directions are related to these." The four basic directional terms are:

ilau	'seaward'
auta	'inland'
ata	'to one's right when one is facing the sea, to one's left when one is facing inland' [i.e. clockwise]
awa	'to one's left when one is facing the sea, to one's right when one is facing inland' [i.e. anticlockwise].

If greater precision is necessary, these terms can be combined[2]: *auta ata, auta awa, ata auta, awa auta, ata ilau, awa ilau, ilau ata, ilau awa,* so when facing inland, *auta* will be at 12 o'clock, *auta ata* at 11 o'clock, *ata auta* at 10 o'clock, *ata* at 9 o'clock, and so on.

There is an additional series of directionals:

elau	'over there in *ilau* direction'
eta	'over there in *auta* direction'
ene	'over there in *ata* or *awa* direction'.

---

[2] Just as with *north, northeast, east, southeast,* etc.

And compound forms are then possible, e.g. *elau* + *ilau* > *elelau* 'long way over there in the *ilau* direction and out of sight'.[3]

Interestingly, an *ata/awa*-type system has also developed during the last two centuries in at least one variety of English. In the dialect of the isolated South Atlantic island of Tristan da Cunha, uninhabited until 1815, the directional term *east* refers to travel around the (roughly circular volcanic) island in a clockwise direction, while *west* is employed for the anticlockwise direction (Schreier 2003). The only human settlement on the island is on the north coast, and so people heading off in the clockwise direction are initially of course heading east, but the directional term is actually maintained throughout the whole of any journey which starts in this direction, so that people travelling west on the south coast are actually still said to be travelling 'east'. It is not known how soon after settlement this system developed, but it was certainly well established by the 1920s (Daniel Schreier p.c.). The fact that such a system developed in the span of a few generations, at most, in a variety of English which grew out of a mixture of (mostly) British dialects, none of which had such a system, is a powerful indicator of the extent to which language reflects environment precisely because environment can influence language.

In an early paper on this topic, Haugen (1969 [1957]) makes use of two papers by the Icelandic author Einarsson, as well as of his own enquiries. He shows that the situation in Iceland is reminiscent of that on Tristan, but a great deal more complicated. He writes (1969: 332) that the details "are sometimes quite startling, as when a man travelling directly south (from Strandir) may speak of himself as going north (to Húnavatnssýsla), or conversely, a man directed to go south (from Grindavík, on the Reykanes peninsula) may find himself travelling due north (to Njarðvík)". The organizing principle of this system seems to be based ultimately on four major reference points or *orientation areas* in the west, south, east, and north of the island; on the fact that travel from a particular point on the coast is likely to be along the coast, as on Tristan, and therefore in one of only two possible directions; and on the *ultimate* goal of the travel rather than the immediate compass-point direction.[4]

---

[3] For additional material on directionals in Oceanic languages, see Bennardo (2002).

[4] There is an extensive literature on 'grammars of space' in different cultures and environments—see for example Levinson (2003); Levinson and Wilkins (2006).

This kind of relationship between society and lexis is particularly unsurprising since, as was also pointed out by Sapir, not only languages but also human individuals have bigger or smaller vocabularies relating to different semantic fields. Speakers are able to make grosser or finer distinctions in different semantic fields depending on their interests, preoccupations, and experiences. British sheep-farmers, for example, have the following lexicon for types of sheep, much of it unknown to most people who are not sheep-farmers:

ewe lamb	'female up to 12 months old'
ewe hogg	'ewe lamb after mating'
gimmer	'ewe hogg after mating in second summer, following shearing'
ewe	'gimmer after second pregnancy'
ram lamb	'non-sexually mature male'
ram	'sexually mature non-castrated male'
tupp or *tipp*	[ditto]
store lamb	'overwintered to be killed in second year'
freemartin	'twin female rendered infertile by effect of male twin's dominant hormones during pregnancy'
rigger	'half-castrated male'
shearling	'any sheep shorn once'.

Similarly, British carpenters have a lexicon which includes the following items, again normally unknown to others:

scarfe, arris, chamfer, cill, soffit, purlin, bressumer, lapping, feather-boarding, butting-up, offering-up.

Grammar

It must be admitted, however, that cultural influences on lexis are perhaps relatively uninteresting from a sociolinguistic-typological point of view, being predictable and not difficult to account for. Happily, then, it turns out that it is by no means only in lexis that we can find reflections in language of the society in which the language is spoken. It is clear that penetration of cultural and environmental factors into the grammars of languages, which is less unsurprising, and therefore more important for the subject matter of this book, also occurs.

Newman does tell us that "it is important not to overestimate the extent to which culture and grammatical structures can be directly connected" (2002: 93), but I now supply some examples which demonstrate that this is in fact a phenomenon of some significance.

Social culture and grammar

As far as social culture is concerned, much consideration has been given in the literature to a possible link between the grammars of languages, and societal values and norms in terms of the grammatical category of gender, in particular with respect to the extent to which there may be a connection between social roles, on the one hand, and the grammatical signalling of sex through grammatical gender, on the other.

Corbett (1991) notes that, in Polish plural forms, women and girls are classed together morphologically with animals and things, while male human beings constitute a separate class. Aikhenvald (2000: 341) similarly shows that Machiguenga (Peruvian Arawak) has two genders, masculine and non-masculine, which groups women together with things. Can we conclude from this, asks Corbett, that Polish society is sexist? In fact, Corbett is forced to concede that:

When we consider work with sociolinguists and sociologists, where the concern is the link between language and society, we find the problems are more challenging than expected ... it is not at all straightforward to establish links between grammatical gender and the relative status of those classified by the different genders. ... In Polish we find a distinction male human versus all others in the plural, which appears to be a particularly sexist division. Russian, which is related to Polish, has no such feature: however, this does not reflect any obvious difference in the relative status of Polish and Russian women and men (1991: 323).

Wierzbicka (1992: 323), a native Polish speaker, does on the other hand make the interesting observation, concerning unsuccessful attempts by Polish communist governments to encourage the use of the second-person plural T (familiar) pronoun *wy* instead of V (formal, cf. French *tu, vous*) forms, that "Polish courtesy stresses respect for every individual and is highly sex conscious.[5] The collectivist and *genderless* ring of the form *wy* was jarring in that tradition" [my emphasis]. Jaworski (1986, 1989), and Herbert and Nykiel-Herbert (1986), both also argue rather convincingly that Polish is in some respects structurally sexist.

Chafe (2002) points to a similar situation in Northern Iroquoian languages such as Mohawk and Oneida. In these languages "there are three genders in the singular, but only two in the dual and plural, where feminine and neuter fall together and there is only a masculine versus non-masculine distinction" (2002: 101). This is manifested very extensively throughout the language, notably in the pronominal prefix system, where "there is an obvious bias toward masculine gender paired with ambiguity and lack of distinctiveness in the expression of feminine gender" (2002: 108). Chafe then says that he wants "to suggest that the development of such a system may not be unrelated to non-linguistic culture patterns" which were operative at the time when the gender system developed, approximately 1,000 years ago (2002: 104). Chafe cites anthropological and other evidence to show that "sex roles were distributed in Iroquois society in such a way that men were conspicuous, often even flamboyant, and invested with decision-making powers" and played constantly changing, individualized roles. "It was the males who stood out as highly visible figures" whereas "women stayed in the background" in stable undifferentiated roles (2002: 106).

Chafe's reference to a social situation a millennium ago tallies with a possibility suggested by Wierzbicka (1992: 394), namely that certain linguistic features may be a reflection of aspects of culture from "the past, possibly the remote past", rather than from the present.[6] Chafe's assumption is in fact that Iroquoian society, as first described by Europeans, had not changed significantly in the relevant respects since the origins of the modern grammatical gender system; whereas Wierzbicka's suggestion is that for Polish there was, much earlier than 1,000 years ago, a set of social conditions which no longer

---

[5] On the V forms *pan/pani* see Chapter 6.

[6] Miller (1977) discusses the sexism of Indo-European society, and its role in the development of the feminine gender in Proto-Indo-European.

survive, which gave rise to the Polish gender system which itself does survive. (The long-term survival of such gender systems is further discussed in Chapter 6.)

Wierzbicka (e.g. 1986) also suggests that some features of grammar are more likely to have some connection with social culture than others. She argues that optional grammatical categories are more likely to be connected to a society's culture than obligatory ones, as are those parts of a language which have to do with the relationship between the speaker and the addressee. She then produces a convincing socio-cultural account of why Australian English favours "antidiminutives" such as *Shaz* (for Sharon) and *Tez* (for Terry) as terms of address. The explanation lies in the high value attached in Australian culture to solidarity and anti-elitism (meaning that, one supposes, diminutives might be regarded as patronizing). She outlines the way in which cultural ideas such as 'mateship', 'toughness', 'antisentimentality', and 'congenial fellowship' have found their way into the grammatical system of the language in Australia, and contrasts this with the rich system of affectionate diminutives found in Polish.

The importance of "the relationship between the speaker and the addressee" is demonstrated in all languages, since all languages have means of expressing varying degrees of politeness, or lack of it. But the point becomes particularly clear in the case of certain languages which are spoken in societies with very highly developed codes of politeness, where, in contradistinction to the point made by Wierzbicka, degrees of politeness find *compulsory* grammatical expression. For example, in Korean, grammatical honorifics play a highly important role. Honorifics or indexical politeness norms are defined by Sohn (1999: 408) as "grammatical and lexical forms encoding the speaker's socio-culturally appropriate regard towards the addressee (i.e. addressee honorification) and the referent (i.e. referent honorification)". Furthermore, "sentences cannot be uttered without the speaker's approximate knowledge of his social relationship with the addressee and/or referent in terms of age category (adult, adolescent or child), social status, kinship, and/or in- and outgroupness", i.e. grammatical coding truly is compulsory.

This is reflected, firstly, in the forms of personal pronoun and address/reference choice, as in many other languages—although the system is much more sophisticated than the simple choice between T (informal) and V (formal) second person pronouns found in most European languages (Brown and Gilman 1960), as with *tu* and *vous* in French, extending as it does in Korean to first and third persons, and to more than two terms. The first person system involves a distinction between 'humble' and 'plain' forms, whereas the second and third person forms reflect degrees of respect and intimacy:

	singular	plural
1st person		
plain	*na*	*wuli*
humble	*ce*	*ce-huy*
2nd person		
blunt	*tayk*	*tayk-tul*
intimate	*caki*	*caki-tul*
familiar	*caney*	*caney-tul*
plain	*ne*	*ne-huy*
deferential	*elusin*	*elusin-tul.*

Like many other languages (Dixon 2010b: 189), Korean has no third person pronouns as such. Rather, it has demonstrative compounds involving:

pun	'esteemed person'
salam	'person [higher]'
i	'person [lower]'
ai	'child'.

However, the highly developed code of politeness is also manifested in terms of lexical selection and, more strikingly, postnominal suffixes, postverbal suffixes, and sentence-final syntactic markers. The system is very complex (Sohn 1999: 407–18), but Sohn provides a number of striking examples including the following (1999: 414), with what would have been less humble, less honorific alternatives presented in the right-hand column:

A daughter-in law addresses her father-in-law and says:
ape-nim, eme-nim kkeyse halme-nim kkey yak ul tuli-sy-ess-sup-ni-ta
'Father, mother gave a pill to grandmother'

HONORIFIC, HUMBLE		NEUTRAL
ape	'father'	
-nim	addressee honorific suffix	*-ci*
eme	'mother'	
-nim	referent honorific suffix	*-ni*
kkeyse	nominative particle	*ka*
halme	'grandmother'	
-nim	referent honorific suffix	*-ni*
kkey	'to'	*hanthey*
yak	'pill'	
ul	accusative particle	
tuli	'give'	*cwu*
-sy	subject honorific suffix (referring to *eme*)	zero
-ess	past tense suffix	
-sup	addressee honorific (referring to *ape*)	zero
-ni	indicative suffix	zero
-ta	declarative sentence-final suffix	*-e*.

It will be seen that only six of the sixteen forms have no alternative. That the recognition of social roles, respect, and status has penetrated thus far into the grammatical structure of the language is a clear testament to how far social factors of certain types may influence language structure.

A perhaps more complex example is given by Newman (2002). He describes how, according to his interpretation, there is a grammatical reflection in Chipewyan, and other Athabaskan languages of North America, of a pervasive cultural distinction which is of great societal relevance. The distinction is between behaviours which are highly valued in the society—behaviours which are controlled, careful, deliberate, respectful, polite, considerate, and gentle; and behaviours which are uncontrolled, rough, quick, inconsiderate, careless, and uninhibited, which are stigmatized as undesirable.

Newman relates this distinction to the grammar and semantics of Chipewyan verb forms. First, for example, verbs referring to the handling of objects corresponding to English verbs such as *give, take, put, hand, bring, throw, carry*, etc. are distinguished, not in terms of the nature of the action involved in the handling, as in English, but in terms of the nature of the object being handled. Objects are classified into the following categories: animate (e.g. 'baby'), round or hard ('radio'), stick-like ('pen'), flat or flexible ('blanket'), in a closed container ('pack of cigarettes'), in an open container ('pail of water'), plural ('keys'), mushy ('porridge'), granular ('sugar'), and unspecified. Thus the verbal root *-tsir* means 'to transfer [give/throw/take etc.] a granular object' and *-xes* means 'to transfer an object in a closed container'. Secondly, verbs are also, and vitally for Newman's argument, differentiated in terms of whether they refer to "controlled" or "uncontrolled" actions. Both *-tsir* and *-xes* come into the uncontrolled category and thus mean something like 'throw at', 'dump on', etc. The corresponding form for "controlled" meanings such as 'give, hand, take' are *-dzai* for granular objects and *-ɫti* for closed-container objects: *-tsir* means 'to handle sugar [for example] in an uncontrolled way' and *-dzai* means 'to handle sugar [or something similar] in a controlled way'. "Controlled" behaviours bestow on the actor the ideal quality of *séodit'é*—the form the term takes in Bearlake, a Slave Athabaskan variety from the Canadian Northwest Territories—which "requires an individual to exhibit industriousness, generosity, personal autonomy, and restraint" (Rushforth and Chisholm 1991: 34). As Newman says (2002: 88) "the existence of a 'controlled' versus 'uncontrolled' distinction in the verb system … appears to reflect a pervasive and profound distinction in the culture at large"—though note his careful use of the phrase "appears to".

A similar though perhaps less well-known reflection of society in language can be found in systems of nominal classifiers (Aikhenvald 2000: 340–1). Nominal classifiers are "one of a set of specialised grammatical words which, in certain languages, typically or obligatorily form constituents of certain types of noun phrases, especially those containing numerals, the choice of classifiers being determined by the semantic characteristics of the head noun" (Trask 1993: 44).

A well-known example is the noun classifiers of Chinese. For example, in Cantonese (Matthews and Yip 1994: 92ff.), each noun is assigned one (or sometimes more than one) classifier out of a set of over sixty, which are based on "distinctive features of shape, natural kind and function". The choice of classifier "is often not predictable from the meaning of the noun: hence, dictionaries typically provide the appropriate classifier(s) in the entry for the noun". Particularly relevant for our purposes are the *sortal classifiers* which relate to intrinsic qualities of the nouns which they accompany. They include *jek* for animals, *go* for people, *faai* for 'flat-surfaced objects which are typically vertically oriented', *ga* for large machines, and so on. So:

yāt	*jek*	*gāi*
one	CLASS	chicken
'a chicken'		

sāam	*go*	*hohksāang*
three	CLASS	student
'three students'		

gó	*faai*	*bōlēi*
that	CLASS	window pane
'that window pane'.		

Which classifiers, i.e. which noun classes, such languages possess may to a certain extent reflect aspects of the cultural environment in which they are spoken. Aikhenvald (2000: 288) says that if a language has more than one classifier for humans, one possibility is that they will be involved in classifying people "according to their social function and status".

Changes in classifier systems may thus reflect cultural changes. Aikhenvald (2000: 349) describes how in Setswana "a number of ethnonyms for strange or unusual groups such as Chinese or Bushmen" belonged to a noun class which also included substances such as earth or clay and abstract nouns. Happily, in Modern Setswana the official recommendation is that groups like the Bushmen (San) should now be assigned to the human class. Similarly, in traditional Dyirbal culture, birds were believed to be the spirits of dead human females and were therefore assigned to the feminine class. Once that belief had vanished, the assignation was to the class of non-human animates.

Physical culture and grammar

Classifiers can also reflect aspects of the physical culture in which a language is spoken. As Aikhenvald (2000: 341) points out, "if a language has a classifier for 'domesticated animals', people must be familiar with the domestication of animals, and, consequently, are unlikely to be nomadic hunters and gatherers"; and one would not expect people living in a desert environment to have a classifier for 'canoes'. From the above, it is clear that the Cantonese-speaking community is a society familiar with large machines, for example; and it is not surprising that a special numeral classifier for chopsticks is found in Korean rather than, say, in Australian languages. The Uto-Aztecan language Cahuilla has a classifier for 'fruit to be picked' (Seiler 1977). And many Mon-Khmer languages have numeral classifiers for deities (Adams 1989). We can, rather obviously, conclude that fruit-picking is important to the Cahuilla, and that the Mon-Khmer people are (or were) polytheistic.

It is further interesting to note that deep penetration of social factors into grammar may occur in that the physical environment in which languages are spoken can also be reflected not just in the directional lexis as we saw above but even in their deictic grammatical systems (Frei 1944; Bowden 1992: 57). As Dixon says, "the geographical terrain in which a language is spoken may be reflected in its grammar" (2010a: 15). The reflection of a mountainous environment in the Lahu system of five spatial demonstratives, including distinct forms for 'up there' and 'down there', as mentioned above, is paralleled in many other languages by directional morphemes.

LaPolla (2003: 124) cites the example of the Tibeto-Burman language of the Qiang people of Sichuan, China, who live on the sides of mountains along river valleys. Qiang has "a complex system of direction prefixes including prefixes marking 'up-river' versus 'down-river' and 'up the mountain' versus 'down the mountain'", witness the following forms derived from ʁue:

təʁu	'throw up the mountain'
ɦiaʁu	'throw down the mountain'
səʁu	'throw down-river'
nəʁu	'throw up-river'
zəʁu	'throw towards the speaker'
daʁu	'throw away from the speaker'

əʁu   'throw inside'
haʁu   'throw outside'.

As LaPolla says, the fact that these prefixes occur in a language spoken on mountainsides "is no coincidence".

Post (2010) introduces the term *topographical deixis* for this sort of phenomenon, which is widespread in the Tibeto-Burman languages. In the Tani languages of Arunachal Pradesh, India, he reports that "referents' locations or trajectories are identified in spatial terms, as being *upward of, downward of* or *on the same (or an unknown) level as* a shifting 'deictic' centre (often, though not always, the place of speaking)" (2010: 141). The source of these deictic systems is "human interaction with a topographic-ally varied environment"; in this particular case the environ-mental factor, as with Qiang, is that the communities live on sloping hillsides at altitudes of between 500 and 2,000 metres (1,600–6,500 feet) in the Eastern Himalayas. Interestingly, this upward/downward system can also be secondarily extended in two ways. Firstly, it can be extended into the riverine domain, such that "upward" terms can also be interpreted as "upriver" and "downward" as "downriver"; and, secondly, it can be extended into compass orientation, such that "upward" can mean "north", "downward" = "south", and "on the same level" = "east or west". As Post says, it is obvious why these developments have occurred: "just as it is the case that altitude decreases in this area as one moves southward—but remains, overall, more or less the same as one moves from east to west—it is also (necessarily, therefore) the case that all Arunachali rivers ultimately flow from north to south" (2010: 143). In the Galo language investigated by Post, this kind of topographical deixis can be encoded on both verbs and demonstratives. For example, the verb root *càa-* has the function of signifying motion UP-WARD/UPRIVER/NORTHWARD and is glossed by Post as 'ascend', while *áa-* has the function of signifying motion AT THE SAME LEVEL/EASTWARD OR WESTWARD and is glossed as 'come, enter, move laterally'.

Similarly, the Australian language Dyirbal (Dixon 2003a: 94) has a single nominal demonstrative which, however, can be optionally followed by forms from two different sets of spatial indicators. The first set consists of the following:

-bayji	'short distance downhill'
-bayja	'medium distance downhill'
-bayju	'long distance downhill'
-balbala	'medium distance downriver'
-balbalu	'long distance downriver'
-dayi	'short distance uphill'
-daya	'medium distance uphill'
-dayu	'long distance uphill'
-dawala	'medium distance upriver'
-dawulu	'long distance upriver'
-guya	'across the river'
-bawa	'long distance (in any direction)'.

A member of this set can optionally be followed by a member of another set:

-gala	'up vertically'
-gali	'down vertically'
-galu	'out in front (of speaker or actor)'.

Much more dramatic illustrations of this point are provided by systems like that of Kwakwala (Kwakiutl) (Boas 1947: 301–77; Mithun 1999: 148) which, like other languages of the Wakashan family of British Columbia, has hundreds of spatial verb suffixes, very many of which also, as Mithun says, "reflect the natural environment in which the language is spoken". These include:

-amala	'along the bank of a river'
-atus	'downriver'
-xs	'in a canoe'
-usdes	'up from the beach'
-dzod	'on a flat thing'
-siu	'at the mouth of a river'
-xta	'seaward'.

Examples include:

la'sdes	'go up from the beach'
hand'zo'd	'put the kettle on'
la'xt'a	'go out to sea'.

According to Bowden (1992: 69), the grammaticalization of 'sea' and 'land' as directionals, "and the existence of grammaticalised terms for UPRIVER and DOWNRIVER point to [the] ability for culture and geography to determine what can be linguistically significant".

Phonological systems

A rather different candidate for consideration in an investigation of the influence of societal factors on language structure comes from phonology. There was of course something of a history of earlier generations of philologists attempting to relate, in what it is now clear was a nonsensical way, the nature of sound changes and sound systems to factors such as climate and topography. I do not of course wish to associate myself with claims such as that the Second German Sound Shift was due to the mountainous terrain in which speakers were living.

The work of Butcher (2006), however, gives us reason to consider possible effects on phonology of a rather different type. It is well known that the phonological systems of the indigenous languages of Australia are very unusual. In a remarkable observation, Butcher cautiously speculates as to whether an explanation might be available for this eccentricity.

The typical Australian vowel system is very small, often consisting of only three members. The typical consonant system has no voicing contrast, and no fricatives or affricates, i.e. it has very few manners of articulation. It does, on the other hand, make use of an unusually large number of places of articulation. These "long flat" systems employ the bilabial, dental, alveolar, retroflex, palatal, and velar places of articulation, and have a single oral stop, plus a nasal, at each of these places. The canonical system then has a lateral at all positions other than velar and bilabial, and three approximants /w/, /r/, and /j/. Thus a consonantal phoneme chart for a typical Australian language "has more columns and fewer rows than most languages elsewhere in the world" (Butcher 2006: 189). It is also the case that there is a far higher proportion of sonorants—nasals, laterals, and approximants—than usual. According to Butcher (2006: 190):

These languages have as rich a system of sonorant contrasts as any language in the world—and richer than most. This means that these systems have precisely the opposite proportion of obstruents to sonorants to that proposed as the normal tendency amongst the languages of the world (Lindblom & Maddieson 1988). A typical Australian inventory may consist of 70% sonorants and only 30% obstruents. This implies that the perception of opposition within Australian phonological systems is heavily reliant on systematic differences in formant transition patterns at vowel-consonant boundaries.

This combination of vowel and consonant systems would appear to be unique amongst the world's languages. So, Butcher asks: what motivates and perpetuates the unusual phonemic inventories? He hypothesises that they may not be unconnected with the fact that chronic middle-ear infections develop in almost all Aboriginal infants, at a hugely greater rate than in any other population in the world, within a few weeks of birth, and that as a result about 70% of children have significant hearing loss. This loss affects the lower end of the frequency scale, but may also affect the upper end. Voicing contrasts rely on low frequency acoustic cues, and friction and aspiration rely on cues at the high frequency end of the spectrum. But Australian languages "are rich in contrasts which depend on rapid spectral changes in the middle of the frequency range" (2006: 205), which is precisely the range which is most likely to remain intact after chronic middle-ear infection. If such infections have been the norm for many generations, this would indeed provide a very plausible explanation for these unique phonological systems.

Unanswered questions

So far we have simply provided a brief set of indications that answers may be available to some of the sorts of questions which Dixon would like us to ask, in terms of reasonably obvious extra-linguistic factors such as natural environment, kinship structure, beliefs and value systems, politeness practices, and medical conditions.

But Dixon also has other questions, for which he has no answers, which cannot be answered in these ways and for which, indeed, the answers are not immediately obvious. For example:

(4) Unlike Lahu, many other languages which are also spoken in mountainous terrain do not include specifications for 'up' and 'down' in their demonstrative systems. Why not?

(5) Why does the Amazonian language Jarawara have three past tenses, while Russian has only one?

(6) Why does Igbo have a small closed class of eight adjectives, while very many other languages have large open classes?

I might as well admit here and now that, even by the end of this book, I will not be able to answer these specific questions—maybe they do not have answers. But in the following chapter I move on to discuss to what extent explanations based on social factors may also perhaps be possible for at least certain questions of this type, where there is no obvious, straightforward connection between language and culture or material and physical environment.

1

Sociolinguistic typology and the speed of change

The Prologue to this book focused on the clear links which exist between aspects of a language's lexis and grammar, and aspects of the society in which it is spoken. Explanations for the occurrence of features of linguistic structure in terms of physical culture, cultural values, and other societal phenomena, although by no means always uncomplicated, can obviously be helpful. They seem, however, to be only scratching the surface of the problem. They do not really answer the question posed at the beginning of this book concerning the overall distribution of typological characteristics over the world's languages. They work well enough in terms of answering questions such as those of Dixon, cited above as (1), (2), and (3) (e.g. *why can't Pennsylvania Dutch* wotte *be used in constructions like* 'I want to come'). But they are no help at all with questions of the type of (4), (5), and (6) above (e.g. *why does Igbo have a small closed class of eight adjectives?*).

In the rest of this work, concentrating on phonology, morphology, and morphosyntax, I therefore tackle the question of whether it may be fruitful to look at other aspects of human societies in an attempt to get to better grips with Dixon's "why" question. The fact that questions of types (1), (2), and (3) can be answered by reference to social factors gives us some confidence that perhaps at least some questions of types (4), (5), and (6) may be susceptible to social answers also, albeit in a less straightforward and less obvious way. A decision therefore has to be taken as to what other societal features it might be promising to look at in our search for explanations for why certain languages select certain structures and not others.

An obvious place to look for connections between language and society is, of course, in the work of sociolinguists. It is true that much work in many forms of sociolinguistics is actually directed to answering questions which have little or no connection with linguistic structure, as such. However, there have been very large amounts of successful and important sociolinguistic research in recent decades which have been directly aimed at the study of the linguistic-structural issue of linguistic change (e.g. Labov 1994). I suggest therefore that in attempting to answer the question posed at the beginning of this book, we may be able to learn a lot from what is already known about the sociolinguistics of language change. This is particularly legitimate since, obviously, the structure of any language is to an extent the result of changes which have taken place at earlier stages of that language. Explanations for types of change will therefore give us explanations for types of structure.

Speed of linguistic change

It is therefore encouraging to note that one of the lessons which we have learnt about linguistic change from work in sociolinguistics, and perhaps especially from sociohistorical linguistics, is that societal factors can be strongly involved in determining or influencing the *speed* of linguistic change. A promising preliminary avenue for this research may well reside therefore in an examination of differences in the speed of linguistic change between different types of society.

Before we look at this issue in more detail, however, it has to be acknowledged that there is a complication here, in that change proceeds at different rates at different levels of language structure: it is widely agreed that syntactic change proceeds more slowly than lexical change, for instance. Phonological change proceeds relatively rapidly—to the extent, indeed, that it may actually be remarked on by speakers: older adults in England can currently be heard commenting overtly on the prevalence of TH-fronting (the substitution of the interdental fricatives by /f/ and /v/) in the English of younger speakers, and even on the fronting of the vowel of the lexical set of GOOSE (Wells 1982).

And even within linguistic levels there can be striking differences in speed of change. In an impressive and helpful statistical account derived from the *World Atlas of Language Structures (WALS)*, Wichmann and Holman (2009) present data from around the world showing that, for example, indefinite pronouns are "very stable" while definite articles are "very unstable". One generalization they make is that basic structural features tend to be stable, whereas pragmatically sensitive features such as politeness phenomena and evidentials tend to be unstable.

In his study of linguistic change in sixteen Polynesian languages, Pawley (1970: 355) gives a detailed example:

Certain kinds of grammatical markers have been much more persistent than others. The Proto-Polynesian tense-aspect markers, direction particles, position markers, the complement pronoun *ai, and the causative prefix *faka- have been particularly stable. The passive-transitive suffix, the number prefixes *toko-, *taki- and *tua-, the reciprocal prefix *fe-, and the postposed conjunction *foki have been somewhat persistent. Conjunctions, manner particles and certain other affixes have been least stable. The morpheme alternants associated with the passive-transitive suffix ... have proved quite persistent. ... As might be expected, the semantic categories associated with grammatical markers, and distributional relations between the forms manifesting these categories, have been the most stable features of the verb phrase. The most fluid area ... has been the way in which 'manner' modification of the verb is formally marked.

Differences between languages and dialects

Leaving this complication aside, however, one helpful factor that we can take note of is that, while linguistic change obviously affects all living language varieties, it seems to affect some varieties more than others: rate of change is not constant across languages and dialects.

Consider the Scandinavian languages. If we suppose that 1,200 years ago the North Germanic ancestor of the modern Scandinavian languages was a relatively unified language, then we can point to the fact that Danish and Icelandic, having descended from a common ancestor, Old Norse, today differ considerably from one another to the point where they are not mutually intelligible, because of changes which have taken place in the last 1,000 years. The crucial point here, however, is that it is clear that *more of these changes have taken place in Danish than in Icelandic.* Icelandic has undergone fewer changes and thus preserved more of the structure of Old Norse than its continental counterparts. Within the context of the Indo-European language family, Icelandic and Faroese are often described as being "conservative" or "archaic" varieties, while the continental Scandinavian languages Swedish, Norwegian and—especially—Danish are said to be relatively "innovating" (see Braunmüller 2000).

This is obviously by no means an isolated example. Pawley (1970: 355) states that his study of the verb phrase in sixteen languages shows that the different Polynesian languages "have varied a good deal in the rate at which they have changed their (surface) grammar".

Given that insular and continental Scandinavian were originally dialects of the same language, it is not surprising that rate of change also differs as between dialects of a single language. For example, the English dialects of the southeast of England are in most, although not entirely all respects, considerably more innovating than those of northeastern England and Scotland where, for instance, pre-Great Vowel Shift Middle English-style monophthongal forms such as *out* /uːt/ and *house* /huːs/ can still be heard, although they disappeared from the south of the country via the innovation of diphthongization several centuries ago (Trudgill 1999a). Middle English *o:* and *ou*, which have for centuries been merged in most varieties of English including RP (Received Pronunciation) and the central dialects of England, remain distinct as in *moan* and *mown* in East Anglia and South Wales. Similarly, the distinction between /m/ and /w/ has been lost in nearly all of England, including in the RP accent, but it still survives as in *witch* vs. *which* in northeastern England, Scotland, and Ireland (Trudgill 1999c).

Modern Greek dialects also illustrate very nicely the thesis that some dialects may be more conservative than others (Trudgill 2004b). For example, most varieties of Greek lost the classical distinction between geminate and non-geminate consonants probably as early as the first century AD, so that for example Ancient Greek /gramma/ 'letter' is now Modern

Greek /ɣrama/. Remarkably, however, 2,000 years on, geminates are still retained, according to Newton (1968), in the Greek dialects of southern Italy, the Dodecanese islands, the island of Chios, Cappadocia in central Asia Minor, and Cyprus.

Explanations

Why would this be? Why would some languages and dialects change faster than others? As Blust says, "sound change proceeds at very different rates in different languages" (2007: 40), and although "given enough time, language change is inevitable ... this inevitability does not explain radical differences in rates of change within any given language family" (2007: 1).

Blust's paper then helps to shed some light on this problem. Blust cites cases of languages which in terms of linguistic change are widely considered to have "run wild", such as Armenian within the Indo-European family—noting that Armenian *erku, erekh* are cognate with English *two, three*—and French amongst the Romance languages. (It does not require massive computational skills to appreciate that French *août* /u(t)/ has diverged further from Latin *augustum* than has Italian /agosto/.)

But Blust's focus is on what he calls "hot spots" of phonological change, with particular reference to the Austronesian languages of Borneo. His observation is that north-central Borneo south of Sabah is a phonological "hot spot" within the Austronesian language family: "a wide swath of languages extending across northern Sarawak far into Kalimantan show an exuberant efflorescence of phonological innovations" (2007: 2); and they are characterized by "more disfiguring types of sound change" (p. 4), i.e. changes which are so extensive that they totally conceal the etymological origin of the items in question. For example, Proto-Malayo Polynesian **duha* 'two' has given rise to forms in the languages of the Philippines such as *dua* and *duah*, while in the relevant "hotspot" area of Borneo reflexes are found such as *ba, lugwa,* and *wëh*.

Then, having linked the rapid linguistic change that has occurred in these contiguous areas of North Sarawak to the sociolinguistic-typological insight that, in areas such as this, "some small but not insignificant subset of sound changes may be driven by social forces" as opposed to being "the products of phonetic or phonological causation" (2007: 2), Blust proceeds towards an explanation. He suggests that "contact may have played a role" in the genesis of this phenomenon. Contact, then, is in his view a key factor, with higher levels of contact leading to faster rates of change.

It is not difficult to find supporting examples for this claim. The contrast between the continental and insular Scandinavian languages that we discussed above makes the point very nicely. The Faroe Islands and Iceland lie far out into the Atlantic Ocean, away from the European mainstream, and have experienced relatively low levels of contact, while the continental Scandinavian languages experienced considerable levels of contact, notably with the Low German of the Hanseatic League: Jahr (1995, 2001) talks of the "heavy influence of language contact between Norwegian and Low German" (2001: 100). Similarly, the more conservative northern English dialects mentioned above are clearly geographically more peripheral than the innovating southeastern dialects. And the conservative Greek dialects cited by Newton as having retained geminates all come from geographically peripheral areas of the Greek-speaking world such as Italy, the eastern Aegean, central Turkey, and Cyprus.

Many other examples of related languages and dialects being more or less conservative as a result of differential levels of contact could be given. If we consider individual Norwegian dialects, for instance, one thing that we can note is that the most conservative dialects of Norwegian are by general consent those found in relatively remote inland valleys and other non-coastal areas, while the most innovating are those in the well-trafficked southern coastal areas. The latter have, for example, lost the marking of the dative case on nouns, while the former have retained it. According to Haugen (1976), the dative was probably lost in all of mainland Scandinavia by 1400 in indefinite nouns in the singular and by 1500 in the plural. It survived longer in the definite form of nouns, but has now disappeared from most varieties of mainland Scandinavian, except in some fossilized phrases. However, several centuries later, the dative is still alive and well in definites in the dialects of central

Norwegian districts. The Toten dialect of Norwegian (Faarlund 2000), for example, includes forms such as the following:

Han kom frå *butikka*	[nom./acc. *butikken*]
he came from *shop-the*	'He came from the shop.'
Hu bor hos mor *sinne*	[nom./acc. *si*]
she lives with mother *her*	
'She lives with her mother.'	
Je gav *hestom* vatn	[nom./acc. *hesta*]
I gave *horse-the (pl.)* water	
'I gave the horses water.'	

It is also important to note that in the Toten dialect the dative case is not a fossilized peripheral grammatical category. It is well established and has a number of complex functions. It not only occurs with indirect objects and after many prepositions but also with direct objects in the case of certain verbs with benefactive or anti-benefactive meaning (e.g. 'help' or 'bother'):

Hu lærde *gutta* å synge	[nom./acc. *gutten*]
she taught *boy-the* to sing	
'She taught the boy to sing.'	

The dative is also found after verbs which have to do with politeness and respect—*rose* 'praise', *takke* 'thank'—as well as verbs having to do with being together with or accompanying someone—*møte* 'meet', *besøke* 'visit'. And this is by no means an exhaustive list.

Similar forms occur in other central areas of Norway such as Hedmark, Hallingdal, Setesdal, and Voss, and the adjacent Swedish dialects of Härjedalen, Jämtland, and upper Dalarna, as well as in Västerbotten and Norrbotten. In all these areas, inflected forms of the dative still survive in the definite form of nouns and in pronouns (Haugen 1976: 293; Skjekkeland 1997: 151–4).

The link here between these conservative Norwegian and Swedish dialects, on the one hand, and conservative Faroese and Icelandic, on the other, is clearly relative geographical isolation. The conservative varieties of Norwegian and Swedish have traditionally been more isolated than the more innovating communities, and have therefore experienced less contact.

The importance of the role of peripherality vs. contact is also supported for Arabic by Ingham (1982: 33), who writes that "comparison of the dialects of inner Arabia with those of the outer fringe, namely Mesopotamia and the Gulf, reveals a marked generalisation: that the outer dialects, and more particularly those of Mesopotamia, have reduced a number of contrasts still extant in the dialects of the interior". He continues: "in the main it is more accurate to regard the process as one of simplification"; and, crucially, he observes (1982: 34) that simplification in the dialects of Mesopotamia and the Gulf appears to correlate with contact.

This type of differential geographical distribution received considerable attention in the work of the school of linguistics arising out of research by Bartoli (e.g. 1945) known as "Neo-linguistics" or "Spatial Linguistics" (Bonfante 1947). The work of this school was based in part on areal principles, which included:

(1) If, of two linguistic forms, one is found in isolated areas and the other in areas more accessible, then the former is the older.
(2) If, of two linguistic forms, one is found in peripheral areas and the other in central areas, then the former is the older.

The concept of geographically peripheral "relic areas" is also one of considerable antiquity in dialectology (see Chambers and Trudgill 1980: 109).

Differences between chronological periods

If rates of change differ as between particular languages and dialects, it is also clear that *within* particular languages and dialects the rate of linguistic change is not constant chronologically either: there are big differences between rates of change at different periods in the history of individual varieties.

In a remarkable claim, for example, Jackson argues that nearly all the sound changes which converted Brittonic/Brythonic into Welsh, Cornish, and Breton took place between the middle of the 5th and the end of the 6th century, and that evolution was so rapid that "we can be fairly sure that Vortigern around

450 could not have understood Aneirin around 600" (Jackson 1953: 690). The linguistic changes which occurred in British were to "alter its whole appearance" and "to modify fundamentally its syntax" (1953: 691).

O'Rahilly (1976: 248–9) similarly describes an extremely rapid series of linguistic changes in the transition from Middle Irish to Early Modern Irish. He says that "the fifth and sixth centuries are known to have been a period of unusually rapid development in the Irish language" (1946: 495). And Beaken (1996: 166) also suggests for English that 1350–1500 was a period of unusually rapid change: he points out, for instance, that the class of modal verbs in English developed very suddenly in the years around 1400.

Explanations

Why should this be—why should languages change faster at some periods of their history than at others?

In fact, it is intuitively rather obvious what one of the major social factors involved here probably is. As Labov says (1994: 24), "it is well known that catastrophic events have played a major role in the history of all languages, primarily in the form of population dislocations: migrations, invasions, conquests, and massive immigrations". If we take the Brittonic example described by Jackson (1953), it is rather clear what happened. We can suppose that it is not a coincidence that the massive changes in Brittonic—rapid to the extent that Jackson hypothesizes putative loss of mutual intelligibility across a few generations— occurred precisely when they did. After the Anglo-Saxon invasions of eastern England, much of 6th-century Celtic Britain was a socially very unstable place indeed. There were battles, murder, destruction, flight, migration, emigration, enslavement, land- taking—in other words very considerable upheaval indeed. This is certainly Jackson's interpretation of the relationship between the social and linguistic events: he says (1953: 690) that "periods of unusually marked linguistic corruption [sic] are sometimes associated with great social upheavals, or with invasion and conquest".

And for Beaken (1996), we can suggest that 14th-century England was also a very unstable place. He points out that, while the English Revolution did not occur until the 1640s, "the events that led to the overthrow of this old order were shaped long before the Revolution itself. The key period may have been 1350–1500, the late Middle Ages" (1996: 166). In this period there occurred the Hundred Years War, when the English monarchy lost most of its French possessions; and from 1348 onwards the Black Death led to enormous population losses, and "loosened the ties of the feudal order and led to increased social mobility and a shortage of labour". The counter-reaction of the upper classes then led to the Peasants' Revolt (1381), and the ultimate destruction of the old feudal order. Beaken then suggests that it is plausible that there was a connection between this "social turmoil and revolution" and the "dramatic series of changes in the language" (1996: 166).

Mæhlum (2000) also outlines a theory well-known amongst Norwegian scholars that the period during and after the Black Death, which raged in Norway from 1349 to 1350, was a period of enormous social upheaval which coincided with the rather rapid conversion of the highly synthetic Old Norse linguistic system into a more analytic structure.[1]

Some linguistically more detailed examples can also be given. For instance, Raumolin-Brunberg (1998) discusses the linguistic consequences of the English Civil War, which was fought from 1642 to 1649. This was a period of very considerable turmoil, with tens of thousands of men under arms, and most areas of the country seeing some armed conflict involving very large numbers of casualties: more than 80,000 combatants and 100,000 non-combatants lost their lives, representing a higher proportion of deaths to the size of population than that suffered by England in the First World War—and these all on home soil. Raumolin-Brunberg examines four changes in the English pronominal system that were occurring at that time, and produces quantitative evidence for the influence of the upheaval from an extensive corpus of contemporary letters (*The Corpus of Early English Correspondence*). The pronominal changes are:

---

[1] Mæhlum herself actually questions this argument: "I'm not at all convinced of these intimate connections between linguistic and extra-linguistic factors which have been maintained within the Norwegian tradition" (2000: 93). She suggests that an optimal explanation for what happened remains to be found.

(a) the development of the third person singular possessive pronoun *its*, replacing earlier *his*
(b) the replacement of the object relative pronoun *whom* by *who*
(c) the development of *somebody, anybody, everybody, nobody* as fully grammaticalized indefinite pronouns
(d) the development of *someone, anyone, everyone, no one* as fully grammaticalized indefinite pronouns.

Raumolin-Brunberg's quantitative analyses of these developments suggest that the rate of change involving these changes did indeed accelerate as a consequence of—or at least during and immediately after—the Civil War.

The role of social upheaval is further stressed by Bailey et al. (1996), who also discuss the relationship between linguistic change and catastrophic events. These authors address the consequences of such events by examining the effects of the Second World War in Texas and Oklahoma in terms of linguistic developments. According to them (1996: 435), the key factors involved in producing marked and rapid linguistic change in these two neighbouring states of the USA appear to have been

rapid acceleration in urban growth, a dramatic expansion of the industrial base, the construction of a large number of military posts (and an influx of federal dollars), and the alteration of patterns of migration which had carried massive numbers of Southerners northward and westward for half a century.

They conclude that "the population dislocations caused by World War II have had significant linguistic consequences in Texas and Oklahoma, but the consequences are quite complex" (1996: 449). Using apparent-time studies comparing the speech of informants from different age groups, they show that the steepest rise in the rate of the linguistic changes they investigated coincided with the period during and immediately after the war. These changes are of three major types; they include:

(1) an increase in the use of some Southern features such as: the use of the semi-modal *fixin to* as a way of indicating the near future—*She's fixin to go.*

(2) the introduction and growth of non-local features such as:
- rhoticity (the use of non-prevocalic /r/ as in *car, cart*);
- yod-dropping after /t, d, n/, as in *Tuesday*;
- the merger of the vowels of LOT and THOUGHT (Wells 1982) such that *hock, hawk* are homophonous.

(3) internally generated changes such as:
the merger of the vowels of KIT and FLEECE, DRESS and FACE, and FOOT and GOOSE before /l/, such that *field=filled, bell=bale, pull=pool*.

The linguistic geography of the area was also significantly altered as a result of the military, political, social, demographic, and economic events of the 1940s: the area of eastern Texas that belongs to the Lower South dialect area, and which thus aligns itself with neighbouring Louisiana and the other southern coastal states, shrank during the relevant period, with the major isoglosses receding towards the Louisiana border.

In a non-European-language example, Kato argued in his 1983 article "A study of six age groups in Tokyo" that the denasalization of the velar nasal (/ŋ/ > /g/) in Tokyo Japanese accelerated during the Second World War. Hibiya (1996) argues against Kato's thesis, but her explanation for what happened is equally founded on the role of social upheaval. Her empirical work shows that the change started much earlier than suggested by Kato—she relates the loss of the velar nasal to the period of the Meiji Restoration (1868). The "Black Ships" of the American Commodore Matthew Perry arrived in Japan in 1853, and Perry negotiated a treaty allowing trade with America, thus ending the 200-year isolation of Japan from the rest of the world—two centuries during which no one was allowed to enter or leave the country. The end of the Shogunate and the restoration of the emperor, which occurred as a direct response to the pressure exerted by Perry for the opening up of Japan, led to enormous changes in the political, social, and cultural structure of the country. In particular, Hibiya stresses that the movement of newly powerful clans into Tokyo after the restoration drastically changed the make-up of the population, and made for a period of very high levels of dialect contact.

Explanations involving such social disturbances have been elevated to a general principle by Dixon (1997) with his proposal of the *punctuated equilibrium* model, a suggestion which provides a more sophisticated interpretation of the role of social upheavals in linguistic change. The model proposes that languages exist in a state of *equilibrium* with relatively little change occurring for long, perhaps very long periods, until something happens to disturb that equilibrium. Dixon refers to such a period of disturbance as *punctuation*. The punctuation is triggered by "some cataclysmic event" (1997: 68), which may be a natural event such as a flood or volcanic eruption; or some kind of social disturbance (such as the Anglo-Saxon invasions of England, the English Civil War, or the Second World War); or some "striking technical innovation"; or just movement into new territory. "After the events which caused the punctuation have run their course, a new state of equilibrium will come into being" (1997: 68).

The correct generalization, then, seems to be that social upheavals of various sorts help to accelerate the rate of linguistic change—for reasons which we will examine further in subsequent chapters.

Conclusion

In sum, we have noted two promising major social factors that would appear to be implicated in producing different rates of linguistic change in ways which remain to be explored in later chapters. We have observed a role for:

(1) the relative degree of contact vs. isolation of speech communities as illustrated by a number of cases, such as the contrast between Faroese and Icelandic, on the one hand, and the continental Scandinavian languages, on the other; and

(2) the relative social stability vs. instability of communities, which we have just illustrated through a number of examples of social upheaval from different periods and continents.

There is considerable evidence, that is, to suggest that conservative language varieties tend generally also to be those which are relatively more geographically isolated, and relatively more stable socially, than the more innovating language varieties.

In the following chapters, we turn to a discussion of each of these two factors, plus a number of others, and their relevance for sociolinguistic typology.

2

Complexification, simplification, and two types of contact

We now begin a more detailed examination of social factors which appear to be linked to linguistic change, starting in this chapter and the one which follows with the first of the social factors we have now pinpointed, namely *contact vs. isolation*. As we saw above, there is a very good case to be made for arguing that contact is linked to a higher velocity of language change. The interesting sociolinguistic-typological question is now therefore: to what extent does the available literature suggest that contact might also be linked to the presence and absence of particular *structural characteristics* of languages?

There is in fact considerable agreement in the literature that language contact is indeed associated with a very particular linguistic process, namely *simplification*, and thus with a very particular characteristic, namely *relative simplicity of structure*. This is the view which is quite naturally espoused by linguists in pidgin and creole studies: pidgins and creoles are all widely and uncontroversially agreed to owe their relative structural simplicity to language contact. These linguists, that is, do not espouse the hypothesis that has variously been called *the invariance of linguistic complexity hypothesis* and *the equicomplexity hypothesis* (Sampson et al., 2009)—namely that not only are all languages complex but that they are all equally complex, as illustrated in Hockett's (1958: 180–1): "the total grammatical complexity of any language, counting both morphology and syntax, is about the same as any other".

If simplification occurs, it obviously then follows, as I argued in Trudgill (1983), that a language must be more complex before simplification than after it; and if some languages are more or less complex at different stages of their history, then different languages can be more or less complex than others. Of course, there has been something of a tradition for linguists, when addressing non-linguists, to stress that "all languages are equally complex". But obviously this was a propaganda ploy that was vital for combating the "some languages/dialects are primitive/ inadequate" view that has been widespread in our society. In a book aimed at schoolteachers (Trudgill 1975: 25), I myself wrote that "it appears to linguists that all languages are equally complex and structured". In fact, however, many of us, at least amongst ourselves, have been prepared to acknowledge that this was not true. To take just two examples, Rice (1999: 392) writes that "the Navajo verb is legendary for its complexity"; and Aronoff (1994: 89) says of the noun class systems of Yimas and Arapesh that "the complexity of these systems is startling".

Of course, the variable complexity claim would not be true if simplification in one part of a language were automatically compensated for by complexification elsewhere, as seems to be suggested by the Hockett quotation above. I do not consider syntax at all in this book,[1] but Dahl (2009) demonstrates convincingly that Hockett's argument about the relationship between morphological and syntactic complexity does not hold. He is supported in this argument by Sampson (2009), and in particular by the work of Shosted (2006), who does not succeed in demonstrating the validity of this *negative correlation hypothesis*, as he calls it: it is not the case that if one component of language, e.g. morphology, is simplified, then another, e.g. syntax, must necessarily be elaborated to compensate in terms of the overall level of complexity.

Moreover, agreement about the role of contact in producing simplification more generally, in languages other than pidgins and creoles, is also widespread in other areas of linguistics, notably sociolinguistics and dialectology. For example, in Trudgill (1986) I suggested that dialect-contact induced koinés are simpler than their non-koinéized relatives; and I have argued the same point with respect to creoloids[2] (Trudgill 1978, 1983, 1996b). Thurston (1989), too, says that languages which are characterized by exeterogeny, i.e. which are open for acquisi-

---

[1] I do not, either, consider semantic complexity (Kuteva 2009).
[2] For an account of this term, see Chapter 3.

tion by non-native speakers, are likely to be simpler than those which are not. And Clackson and Horrocks (2007: 276) have suggested of the Romance languages, that it is possible

to relate the change to analyticity to the spread of Latin as a second language [in the Roman Empire]. Given the choice between a synthetic construction with complex (and often irregular) morphology and an analytic construction which can be generalised across the board, language learners tend to prefer the latter option.

The Norwegian linguist Hans Vogt (1948: 39), quoted in Harris and Campbell (1995: 133), also says that "we can often note that a language loses formal distinctions in circumstances which make it rather natural to hypothesise that they result from foreign influence" [my translation].[3] And Sankoff (2002: 657) notes that, according to Bokamba (1993), multilingual language contact situations "may result in morphological simplification" where a language is used as a lingua franca.

Milroy (1992a: 203) writes of the trend towards simplification in the transition from Old English to Middle English that "it seems clear that such a sweeping change is at least to some extent associated with *language contact*". LaPolla (2005: 481) gives an extended example of the kind of development in English which Milroy is referring to. He presents Old English examples from the words corresponding to Modern English *stone, gift, hunter*. These items came in many different forms (see Quirk and Wrenn 1957):

	singular			plural		
nom.	*stan*	*giefu*	*hunta*	*stanas*	*giefa*	*huntan*
acc.	*stan*	*giefe*	*huntan*	*stanas*	*giefa*	*huntan*
gen.	*stanes*	*giefe*	*huntan*	*stana*	*giefa*	*huntena*
dat.	*stane*	*giefe*	*huntan*	*stanum*	*giefum*	*huntum*

The adjective corresponding to *good* had the following strong, or definite, forms:

	masc.	fem.	neut.	pl.
nom.	*god*	*god*	*god*	*gode*
acc.	*godne*	*gode*	*god*	*gode*

---

[3] "On observe souvent qu'une langue … perd des distinctions formelles, dans des circonstances qui rendent l'hypothèse d'influence étrangère assez naturelle."

| gen. | *godes* | *godre* | *godes* | *godra* |
| dat. | *godum* | *godre* | *godum* | *godum* |

There is also a separate system of weak forms for adjectives (see Blakeley 1964) as follows:

	masc.	fem.	neut.	pl.
nom.	*goda*	*gode*	*gode*	*godan*
acc.	*godan*	*godan*	*gode*	*godan*
gen.	*godan*	*godan*	*godan*	*godena*
dat.	*godan*	*godan*	*godan*	*godum*

The corresponding modern system consists of two forms each for the nouns and one form for the adjective. And as LaPolla says, "we do okay with this simple system" (2005: 482).

Jespersen (1922: 332–3) makes a similar point about English:

English *had* carries the day over the Gothic form ... it unites in one short form everything expressed by the Gothic *habaida habaidedu habaidedum habaides habaideduts habaideduþ habaida habaidedun habaidedjau habaidedeiwa habaidedeima habaidedeis habiadedeits habaidedeiþ habaidedi habaidedeina*—separate forms for two or three persons in three numbers in two distinct moods! It is clear, therefore, that the English form saves a considerable amount of brain work to all English-speaking people, and especially to every child learning the language. Someone will, perhaps, say that on the other hand English people are obliged always to join personal pronouns to their verbal forms, and that this is a drawback counterbalancing the advantage, so that the net result is six of one and half a dozen of the other. This is, however, not entirely the case. In the first place, the personal pronouns are the same for all tenses and moods, but the endings are not. Secondly, the possession of endings does not exempt the Goths from having separate personal pronouns; and whenever these are used, the verbal endings which indicate persons are superfluous. They are no less superfluous in those extremely numerous cases in which the subject is either separately expressed by a noun or is understood from the preceding proposition. So that, altogether, the numerous endings of the older languages must be considered uneconomical. ... I need hardly point out that growing regularity in a language means a considerable gain to all those who learn it or speak it.

More recently the link between contact and simplification has been very ably demonstrated quantitatively by Kusters (2003). Kusters examines the history of degrees of complexity and simplicity in verbal inflectional morphology in Quechua, Swahili, Arabic, and the Scandinavian languages. He measures simplification in varieties of Arabic, for example, in terms of the degree to which different varieties have undergone developments such as *loss of dual number* and *decrease in allomorphy* (see further below). His highly detailed quantitative analyses lead him to conclude that "the level of [linguistic] complexity is related to the type of speech community" (2003: 359) in that language varieties with a history of higher contact also tend to demonstrate higher degrees of simplification.

Kusters also discusses the much greater simplification, notably deflexion, which has been undergone by the continental Scandinavian languages as opposed to the insular Scandinavian languages. He ascribes this, as many others have done before him, to the heavy and prolonged contact of the continental Scandinavian languages with the Low German of the Hanseatic League. As we saw above, Jahr (2001) has argued for the role of language contact with Low German in producing the relative simplification of Danish, Swedish, and Norwegian (as compared to Icelandic and Faroese), a view which has been shared by others including Pedersen (1999) and Askedal (2005). Askedal observes that Icelandic and Faroese have "retained most or at least a fair amount of the morphological characteristics of Old Norse", whereas the continental languages "have gone through a process of morphological change (simplification)" (2005: 1872).

Norde (2001) illustrates this type of change in terms of nominal deflexion in Swedish. She talks of the "devastating effects" (2001: 242) of loss of inflection, and contrasts the morphology of the Old Swedish masculine noun *fisker* 'fish' with its Modern Swedish equivalent *fisk* (cf. Wessén 1958: 85, 105):

OLD SWEDISH

	indefinite		definite	
	sg.	pl.	sg.	pl.
nom.	*fisker*	*fiskar*	*fiskerin*	*fiskanir*
gen.	*fisks*	*fiska*	*fisksins*	*fiskanna*
dat.	*fisk(i)*	*fiskom*	*fiskinum*	*fiskomin*
acc.	*fisk*	*fiska*	*fiskin*	*fiskana*

MODERN SWEDISH

	indefinite		definite
sg.	pl.	sg.	pl.
fisk	*fiskar*	*fisken*	*fiskarna*

In Old Swedish, the noun had 15 different forms, while in Modern Swedish it has only four.

Consider also the contrast between the nominal morphology of Icelandic and Norwegian Bokmål. I supply just one typical example:

'rich' (adj.)

ICELANDIC		NORWEGIAN
rika	f.acc.sg.; masc.acc.pl.; wk.masc./neut.acc./gen. /dat.sg.; wk.fem.nom.sg.	*rik* masc./fem.sg. *rike* pl.;wk. *rikt* neut.sg.
rikan	masc.acc.sg.	
rikar	fem.nom./acc. pl.	
rikri	fem.dat.sg.	
riki	wk.masc.nom.sg.	
rikir	masc.nom.pl.	
rikt	neut.nom./acc.sg.	
rikur	masc.nom.sg.	
rik	fem.nom.sg.; neut.pl.	
riku	wk.fem.acc./gen./dat.sg.; wk.pl.	
rikum	masc./neut.dat.sg.; dat. pl.	
riks	masc./neut.gen.sg.	
rikrar	fem.gen.sg.	
rikra	gen.pl.	

The contrast is very striking. The adjective has three different forms in Norwegian, but 14 in Icelandic. Compared to Icelandic, we can surely say that Norwegian has undergone considerable loss of morphological complexity.

Simplification

Simplification is, paradoxically, a complex notion, and other linguists will no doubt have different approaches to the topic. However, in this book I adopt the approach I outlined in Trudgill (1996b) which attempts to derive insights about simplification from studies of pidgins, creoles, and pidginization. Following Mühlhäusler's pioneering work (1977), and earlier important work such as that of Ferguson (1959, 1971), it argues that there are three crucial components of the simplification process:

(1) the *regularization* of irregularities (Sasse 2001). Irregularity diminishes—for example in irregular verbs and irregular plurals—as in the development in English of *helped* rather than *holp* as the preterite of *help*, and the replacement of *kine* by *cows* as the plural of *cow*.

(2) an increase in lexical and morphological *transparency,* where there is a higher degree of correspondence between a semantic or grammatical category and its expression (see Haiman 1980; Bauer 1988: 189–91): for example, forms such as *twice, seldom, optician,* and *went* are less transparent than *two times, not often, eye-doctor* and *did go*; any (partial or complete) replacement of the former by the latter would represent simplification. Loss of allomorphy, as described by Kusters, will also lead to an increase in transparency.

Of course categories (1) and (2) are often linked. Regular forms such as *cows* are also without allomorphic complications and more transparent, analytic (Sasse 2001: 1671), and iconic than forms like *kine*. A good example is provided by the present tense forms of strong verbs in Modern Norwegian. In Old Norse, such verb forms were monosyllabic and were derived from the base form by i-umlaut. This type of system survives in most Norwegian dialects today, where irregular forms such as *komme—kjem* 'to come—come(s)', *sove—søv* 'to sleep— sleep(s)', and *grave—grev* 'to dig—dig(s)' are usual. However, in the populous area around Oslo and along the well-trafficked southern coast, regularization has taken place, as in Swedish and Danish. In these areas, simpler more regular present tense forms such as *kommer, sover,* and *graver* are found instead. Notice, too, that they are also more transparent, in the sense that they are easily analysable into a verb stem and the present tense morpheme *-er*. The outcome is a verb morphology which is much more regular, and where as a result of there being identical stems in all forms, transparency is greatly increased.

(3) the loss of *redundancy*. All languages contain redundancy, which seems to be necessary for successful communication, especially in less than perfect, i.e. normal, circumstances—"information is repeated and this facilitates the hearer's task" (Corbett 2006: 274). But it is probable that some languages have more redundancy than others—and Dahl (2004) discusses the way in which redundancy can vary in a single language over time.

Redundancy, and therefore loss of redundancy, takes two major forms. The first occurs in the form of *repetition of information*, or syntagmatic redundancy (Trudgill 1978), as for example in grammatical agreement, where there is more than one signal that, say, a noun phrase is feminine; or in obligatory tense marking, as for example when all verbs in a past tense narrative are marked for past tense. This form of redundancy is an example of what Dahl calls *verbosity*, i.e. "containing more material than would be necessary" (2004: 53).

The second type of redundancy is paradigmatic redundancy, or the *morphological expression of grammatical categories* (Dressler 1988). Although there is no total agreement about what the major "grammatical categories" are, or about exact terminology, they would appear by relatively common consent (see, for example, Jespersen 1922; Bloomfield 1933; Lyons 1977; Bybee 1985) to include at least: number, case, tense, aspect, voice, mood, person, and gender. Some of these categories are more frequent in the world's languages than others: all the languages of the world have the category *person*, but languages differ in the extent to which the other categories are absent, optional, or obligatory. There are also, crucially for our purposes, important differences in how the categories may be expressed, the most obvious difference being between morphological (or synthetic) expression, on the one hand, and syntactic or analytic expression, on the other.

This distinction between syntagmatic and paradigmatic redundancy is important because the two types are affected differently in various types of sociolinguistic situation. In language-death situations, for instance, there is evidence that syntagmatic redundancy is lost before paradigmatic redundancy. In the Arvanitika (Albanian) spoken in the Attica and

Boeotia areas of Greece, for example, language shift and loss
are occurring (see Trudgill 1983: 155ff.). The language, however, does not demonstrate any loss of paradigmatic redundancy. The three genders remain distinct, as do the different
declensions and conjugations. But a number of instances of
loss of syntagmatic redundancy are apparent if one compares
the speech of older, more fluent speakers with that of younger
speakers. For instance, future verb forms such as /do të jap/ 'I
shall give', where /do/ is the future marker and /të/ the (redundant) subordinator, have become /do jap/ etc. in all but the
speech of the very elderly.

Simplification of the *reduction in syntagmatic redundancy*
type will take the form of reduction of the number of repetitions,
as in the loss of grammatical agreement. For example, adjectives
do not receive a plural ending when used predicatively in the
Norwegian dialect of Bergen, the major town on Norway's west
coast, e.g. *vi er trøtt* 'we are tired' as opposed to plural *trøtte* in
other dialects. Jahr (1998) points out that this system of adjective inflection is simpler than in most other Norwegian dialects
which do have plural marking on predicative adjectives; and
since simplification of the grammar is one of the possible
outcomes of contact, he argues that it is likely that this change
in the agreement system, involving loss of redundancy, is due to
intensive contact with Low German, which Bergen experienced
more than any other area of Norway.

Simplification of the *reduction in paradigmatic redundancy*
type, on the other hand, will take the form of the loss of
morphologically-expressed grammatical categories. The same
language can at different points in its history change with
regard not only to the way in which categories are expressed
but also as to which categories it actually possesses. Old English, for example, expressed case almost entirely morphologically (high paradigmatic redundancy), whereas Modern English
expresses it to a considerable extent syntactically (by word
order). Loss of morphological categories may be compensated
for by the use of more analytical structures, such as the usage
in Modern English of prepositions instead of the dative case
of Old English: *godum huntan* > *to a good hunter*. Or there
may be no compensation at all—sometimes loss is just loss, as
with the disappearance of the dual number in Arabic referred

to by Kusters. A good example of this latter type is the loss in English of grammatical gender—grammatical gender disappeared from English without, apparently, this loss having any compensatory structural consequences whatsoever (see further Chapter 6). Paradigmatic redundancy loss can thus take the form either of moves from less to more analytical structures for the expression of grammatical categories; or the loss of such categories altogether.

Dahl points out that many linguistic phenomena are *cross-linguistically dispensable*, i.e. there are languages which do not have them. The presence of cross-linguistically dispensable features in a language is a form of *verbosity* (see above). (This point is reinforced by the fascinating work of David Gil—see for example Gil (2009). Gil argues that human language is "hugely dysfunctional" (2009: 33) and that much of linguistic complexity is superfluous.[4]) The loss of grammatical gender from English is obviously an example of the loss of a cross-linguistically dispensable category.

A certain amount of gender loss has also occurred in Scandinavian languages: Haugen (1976: 288) points out that the three grammatical genders masculine, feminine, and neuter are preserved "in the overwhelming majority of Scandinavian dialects down to the present", but a number of varieties have reduced the number of genders to two. These are Standard Danish and Swedish, and a number of Danish and Swedish dialects, as well as Bergen Norwegian. The dating of this development is quite well known. For example, Mørck says that in the plural of the definite article "the gender distinction was lost in Old Danish, and the same happened during the 15th century in Swedish and Norwegian" (2005: 1137). Pedersen (1999) goes on to say that in Copenhagen the masculine–feminine distinction was totally lost, and the three genders became two, during the period 1450–1600.

A number of writers have ascribed this simplification to language and/or dialect contact: Dahl points out that reduction in gender systems "appears to be highly correlated with the degree of external contacts" (2004: 200). Pedersen (1999)

---

[4] Kusters (2003: 95) also suggests that "languages are full of non-functionalities, and there are no obvious omni-present forces that reduce languages to more functionality".

suggests that the loss of the distinction between masculine and feminine in Copenhagen, and hence in Standard Danish, is due to contact between the dialects of Zealand and (the now Swedish) Scania, and, at the time of the supremacy of the Hanseatic League, Low German—which would at that time perhaps have been reasonably intelligible with Scandinavian.

We can see why this might have happened. For example, in the three varieties involved, eight different forms of the first person singular possessive pronoun, which were all phonologically very similar, would have been found in the dialect contact situation. However, the masculine–feminine distinction was effected in different ways in the different varieties, and not at all in the dialects of Scania, though these did have masculine and feminine as distinct categories—for example, there were three distinct definite adjectival endings. The situation was even further complicated by the three different case forms in Low German.

The eventual new Copenhagen dialect outcome represents a kind of simplified compromise where the masculine–feminine distinction has gone missing:

	masc.	*fem.*
Zealand	min	meːn
Scania	miːn	miːn
Low Germ.		
nom.	miːn	miːne
acc.	miːnen	miːne
dat.	miːnem	miːner

OUTCOME: **miːn**

A similar development can be seen in the case of the indefinite article:

	masc.	*fem.*
Zealand	in	en
Scania	in	en
Low Germ.		
nom.	eːn	eːn
acc.	enen	ene
dat.	enem	ener

OUTCOME: **en**

Jahr (1995, 2001) arrives at the same conclusion concerning the loss of the masculine–feminine distinction in Bergen—but nowhere else in Norway apart from areas of Sami–Norwegian language contact: it is the result of "heavy influence of language contact between Norwegian and Low German" (2001: 100). As already noted, he ascribes the entire typological split between the continental and the still highly fusional insular Scandinavian languages—Askedal (2005: 1872) says "the modern languages represent two distinct typological groups"—to the absence of Low German contact with Faroese and, especially, Icelandic; and Haugen (1976: 313) does the same. Braunmüller (2001: 76) adds that a comparison of Faroese with other Germanic languages, on the basis of Hawkins' (1998) morphological typology, shows that Faroese lies precisely at the level of morphological complexity of Old High German, Old Saxon, and Old English.

Notice that many of the changes that took place during the periods of very rapid change outlined in Chapter 1 also fit very nicely into this simplification pattern. The period of very rapid change in Brittonic, as described by Jackson (1953), is a case in point. The rapid changes that Brittonic went through are described by Jackson as having drastic effects which totally altered the character of the language, and actually involved, more than anything else, the loss of morphological case. Similarly, the rapid change in Norwegian which is ascribed by some writers to the consequences of the Black Death involved a move from synthetic to analytic structures. And the changes discussed by Raumolin-Brunberg as coinciding with the English Civil War also involve simplification, albeit on a smaller scale: the loss of the distinction between the two forms of the relative pronoun, *whom* and *who*, is obviously a simplification.

Complexification

Having argued that the role of contact in producing linguistic simplification is securely established in the literature, I now have to acknowledge that this represents only part of the picture: we cannot simply suggest that simplification is a totally predictable outcome of contact. On the contrary, the linguistic-typological literature is notable for the widespread acceptance of a view which is totally and diametrically opposed to the point of view espoused by sociolinguists: the typologists' view is very strongly to the effect that contact leads to complexification (Kuteva 2008).[5]

Nichols (1992: 192), for instance, asserts that contact between "languages fosters complexity, or, put differently, diversity among neighbouring languages fosters complexity in each of the languages". Aikhenvald (2002) cites numerous examples of contact-induced complexification in Amazonia. Vanhove (2001) discusses language contact with its resultant complexification in the history of Maltese. And a study of the relevant literature shows that many other examples could be given.

The sort of complexification that typologists are referring to occurs as a result of the transfer of features from one language to another: Dahl (2004: 127) refers to "contact-induced change" as including the spread of grammatical elements across languages. This is a very particular type of transfer, of course. If a language replaces an original feature with a new feature borrowed from another language, no complexification occurs. The sort of change being referred to by Nichols as complexification has necessarily to be *additive* borrowing, in which new features derived from neighbouring languages do not replace existing features but are acquired in addition to them. So according to the typologists, a sociolinguistic-typological consequence of language contact is that languages which have experienced relatively high degrees of contact are more likely to demonstrate relatively higher degrees of this type of additive complexity than languages which have not.

Nichols (1992) examined, amongst a number of other phenomena, morphological complexity in 174 different languages from all parts of the world and from a very wide range of language families. Morphological complexity for Nichols has to do with morphological marking of syntactic relations: "any form of inflection, affixation, cliticisation, or other overt morphological variation that signals some relevant relation, function, or meaning" (p. 48). Marking may consist of:

---

[5] Acknowledgement of complexification as a process obviously also implies rejection of the equicomplexity hypothesis.

- *indexing*—e.g. marking of person and number of the subject on the verb;
- *coding*—e.g. cases on nouns marking functions such as subject;
- *registering*—i.e. marking the presence of another word without indexing its features, e.g. the definite conjugation of Hungarian verbs, which registers the presence of an object.

Nichols outlines a working definition of morphological complexity which relies on a count of the degree to which a language has *dependent* marking, *head* marking, and *detachment* ("free" marking), as opposed to *zero* marking. (Head marking might be, for example, the marking of a possessive construction on the item possessed, while dependent marking would mark it on the possessor, and detachment is the use of independent forms such as clitics or pronouns. All of these would give a count of 1, as opposed to zero marking, which would involve e.g. simple juxtaposition of the possessed and the possessor, and which would score 0.) Given these three marking possibilities, and the nine categories[6] which Nichols examines, scores in principle range from 0 to 27 (Nichols 1992: 64), but in Nichols's large sample of languages, actual scores go only from 2 to 15.

It is interesting to note that the languages in the sample with the highest degrees of complexity scored in this way (14–15), are the (unrelated) ancient languages of the Near East, Sumerian and Akkadian; the Northern Australian languages, Mangarayi and Djingili; Basque; and the North American Utian language Southern Sierra Miwok. There are no languages from Nichols's Oceanic area category among the top 27 most complex languages.

The least complex languages using this scoring system (2–3) are the Khoisan language !Kung; the North America isolates Chitimacha (a now extinct language of Louisiana) and Zuni (New Mexico); the North Asian isolate Gilyak/Nivkh (Sakhalin and Amur, Russian Far East); Central American Mixtec; the (possibly) Nilo-Saharan Songhai (spoken in Mali); and

---

[6] Noun possessor, pronoun possessor and modifying adjective in NPs; noun subject, direct object and indirect object in clauses; pronoun subject, direct object and indirect object in clauses.

Southeast Asian Miao/Hmong and Mandarin Chinese. There are no languages from Nichols's Australian or Ancient Near Eastern categories among the top 26 least complex languages.

According to Nichols, this measure of complexity "correlates with overall morphological complexity and hence can be used as an index of something real". But Nichols concedes that it "overlooks a good deal of the actual morphological complexity of languages, both in omitting categories commonly signalled by morphology (e.g. tense and aspect on verbs) and in considering where and whether something is marked but not how (e.g. by inflection, agglutination, cliticisation, or incorporation)" (1992: 64). This latter "how" point, which seems to me to be of more consequence than Nichols perhaps accords it, will be discussed further below.

Nichols also examines the characteristics of languages which occur in sub-continental *spread zones* as opposed to those which occur in *residual zones*. Spread zones show little genetic diversity, low structural diversity, "shallow" language families, a history of rapid spreading of languages; they typically have an innovating centre and a conservative periphery, and lingua franca use of spreading languages, with no long-term increase in diversity. Such zones include western Europe (Indo-European), central Australia (Pama-Nyungan), interior North America (Algonquian and Siouan), and central Oceania (Austronesian).

Residual zones have high genetic diversity, high structural diversity, "deep" language families, no appreciable spread of languages or families, no obvious innovation centre, a long-term increase in diversity, and no widespread lingua franca. Examples are the Caucasus, the Pacific North West of the USA and Canada, the Balkans, and New Guinea. Residual zones are often to be found on the periphery of spread zones.

The crucial point for our discussion of additive complexity is the fact that, as Nichols writes (1992: 192), "spread zones show lower complexity relative to their continents" while residual zones show higher complexity. Crucially, "independently of whether they are in residual or spread zones, however, almost all these high-complexity languages are in areas of considerable linguistic diversity and contact. It can be concluded that contact among languages fosters complexity, or, put differently, diversity among neighbouring languages fosters complexity in each of the languages" (p. 192).

An excellent example of this kind of phenomenon, which supports Nichols's claim, is provided by the work of Aikhenvald in Amazonia (Dixon and Aikhenvald (eds.) 1999; Aikhenvald 1996, 1999, 2001, 2003a, 2003b). In the Vaupés river basin area of northwest Amazonia on the borders of Brazil and Colombia, "obligatory multilingualism" is the norm, "dictated by the principles of linguistic exogamy (one has to marry someone who speaks a different language)" (Aikhenvald 2003a: 1). Tariana is the only member of the Arawak language family spoken in the area, where it has been in long-term contact with languages of the East Tucano branch of the Tucano language family. As a result, there are many signs of Tucano influence on Tariana, some of which, crucially, is additive. For example, the consequences of contact for complexification are apparent in Aikhenvald's information that "Tariana is one of the very few Arawak languages with case marking for core syntactic functions" and that "it developed the case marking under Tucano influence" (2003a: 3; see also p. 139).

Similarly, considerable additive influence from the Tucano languages can be seen in the Tariana 5-way system of evidentials (see further Chapter 6). As in many other languages, there is a grammatical requirement in Tariana to state explicitly the source of one's information. The evidential system intersects with the three tenses, with two lacunae, to give 13 different enclitic markers. Aikhenvald states that while the "reported" evidential was probably inherited from Proto-Arawak, the other evidentials are found in Tariana because of contact—"as a result of areal diffusion from Tucano languages" (2003: 293).

Very many other examples could be given. For example, Foley (1986) discusses the relationship between the neighbouring but genetically unrelated Papuan languages Yimas, Alamblak, and Enga. He suggests, amongst a number of other candidates for contact-induced morphological category-addition, that switch reference[7] systems and morphemes may have spread from

---

[7] Switch reference most typically refers to morphological marking on a verb indicating that its subject is not identical with the subject of an adjacent clause.

one language to another. Yimas does not have a switch reference system, but the other two languages do. Foley suggests that because "different-actor dependent verb forms are not very common in the Sepik area languages, diffusion of this feature from Enga into Alamblak is possible" (1986: 267). Tariana, too, seems to have acquired switch reference as a result of contact: "since switch reference is not found in any other Arawak languages of the Upper Negro River area and is widespread in east Tucano languages, it is likely to have entered Tariana as the result of areal diffusion" (Aikhenvald 2003a: 515).

In other examples, the Arawak language Mawayana, spoken in the southern Guyanas, has, amongst other categories, acquired past tense marking on nominals (to indicate, for example, former possessions) from neighbouring Cariban languages such as Waiwai (Carlin 2007). And Sun (2007) shows that Khalong Tibetan in Sichuan has acquired a complicating ablaut process in the formation of perfective verb stems, which is not found in any of its close relatives, as a result of contact with neighbouring rGyalrong, a Tibeto-Burman language but one not closely related to Khalong Tibetan (the perfective forms are innovative):

imp.	perf.	
ptsal	*ptsel*	'to seek'
vzhar	*vzher*	'to shave'
pci	*pce*	'to do'
ptsu	*ptsi*	'to sell'
tet	*tit*	'to drive cattle'
ʃkol	*ʃkel*	'to boil'

Such vowel alternations are extremely widespread in rGyalrong, e.g. the verb 'to approach' has two stems *rni* and *rne*.

It is clear, then, that language contact can lead to borrowing of an additive as well as replacive type; and, to the extent that borrowing is additive, we can suppose that languages spoken in communities with high degrees of contact with other communities will tend to have more such additive features than those which do not. We thus have to take seriously the sociolinguistic-typological hypothesis that languages spoken in high-contact societies are relatively more likely to have relatively more complexity.

The conundrum

We are now faced, then, with a puzzle. It would clearly be a mistake to suggest that language contact causes *either* simplification, as claimed by sociolinguists and others *or* complexification, as claimed by typologists. It clearly produces *both*.

Interestingly, this conflict between the two opposing sets of claims, as made by sociolinguists and typologists, has not been much noticed in the different camps. For instance, in a paper where he asks "what happens to inflectional morphology in cases of language contact?", Comrie (2008) does not even mention the development which sociolinguists routinely point to as being particularly likely to occur in such situations, namely a reduction in, or total loss of, inflectional morphology.

This lack of awareness has caused considerable bewilderment in the literature, including in my own writing from the sociolinguistic perspective. For example, Heine and Kuteva (2005: 258) oppose my claims (Trudgill 1983) about contact leading to simplification, as in pidginization, and they write that the contact situations they have investigated "tend to lead not to the reduction and loss of existing grammatical categories, but rather to diversification and to the creation of new grammatical categories", i.e. to additive change as studied by Nichols. And they write of pidgin and creoles that "it may seem surprising that pidgins and creoles did not figure more prominently in the present work".

Equally, in Trudgill (1983) I do not acknowledge that contact can lead to complexification. In that paper, I discussed the development of double-definite marking in Norwegian and Swedish, as in Norwegian

> *den store bok-a*
> 'the big book-the'

as an instance of the sort of development which is typical of the redundancy which does not develop in high-contact languages like creoles (which is correct), while Dahl (2004: 282) maintains that it is precisely "a prime example of a contact phenomenon in that it shows up in the intersection of two spread areas, one of the preposed and one of the suffixed article".

Thomason, however, is not bewildered. (After all, Thomason and Kaufman (1988) had already shed more light on this issue than anybody else hitherto.) Thomason simply notes that there is a common proposal in the literature that "contact-induced change leads to simplification, not complication (2001: 64) but that "the opposite claim has also been made— namely, that interference always complicates the system" (p. 65). She points out that Givón (1979) claims that contact-induced change simplifies grammar, while Bailey (1977) claims that "interference always complicates the grammar" (Thomason 2001: 96). Harris and Campbell (1995: 133), too, note the "structural simplification" claim, but also say that "there are clear counterexamples". In an agreeably wry summary, Thomason points out that "all the examples that support the claim that interference leads to simplification are of course counterexamples to the opposite claim" (2001: 65).

The 'critical threshold'

Obviously, then, there is no question of simply deciding which of the two views is correct: both the sociolinguistic-dialectological and the linguistic-typological claims about the consequences of contact have a very secure basis in linguistic fact. Rather, the basic sociolinguistic-typological conundrum is that we have to determine what are the circumstances in which contact leads to simplification, and what are the circumstances when it leads to complexification: we have to gain some insight into which language-contact-linked societal factors lead to the one and which to the other. As Thomason and Kaufman say (1988: 212) "the major determinants of contact-induced language change are the social facts of particular contact situations".

This is actually not too difficult to do. The key lies in the nature of language learning and acquisition. In Trudgill (2010a) I suggested, from the point of view of sociolinguistic typology, that contact can indeed have two totally opposed outcomes, and that this is likely to be due to the fact that they involve two different types of contact in terms of the sociolinguistic matrices in which they occur.

I make the not very startling suggestion that simplification is most likely to occur in situations involving language learning by adults, particularly short-term contact—the most extreme of these being situations which lead to the emergence of pidgins (Mühlhäusler 2001).

Correspondingly, complexification is most likely to occur in long-term co-territorial contact situations involving child bilingualism. The most extreme of these latter situations are probably those involving Sprachbünde/linguistic areas such as the Balkans (Feuillet 2001). For example, Dixon and Aikhenvald (1999) discuss the linguistic area formed by the languages of Amazonia, specifically the Amazon and Orinoco basins, which has at least ten major language families and many more smaller ones. Here, the vast majority of the languages, regardless of language family membership, have come over the centuries to share a large number of features. Dixon and Aikhenvald (1999: 8–9) give a non-exhaustive list of 15 features which are common to most or all of the languages of this vast region, including the expression of verbal categories through optional suffixes, and the formation of subordinate clauses through verb nominalization.

The contrast between the two different types of contact becomes particularly clear if we compare Comrie (2008) with Kusters (2003); it can readily be seen that they are looking at two very different types of social situation. Comrie discusses the way in which contact led to the growth of mixed languages such as Michif, which is a French-Cree mixed or intertwined language with considerable morphological complexity (Bakker 1997), and says that it is clear that the generation which developed this language must have had a high degree of fluency in both French and Cree or some other form of Algonquian. Kusters, on the other hand, relates simplification in e.g. Arabic to the acquisition of Arabic by adult non-native speakers (see below).

Anttila says that "language-learning situations, in general, are responsible for various simplifications" (1989: 189); and Clackson and Horrocks (2007), as quoted above, suppose that language learners "prefer analyticity". But it turns out that it is very much a matter of *who does the learning, and under what circumstances.* In Trudgill (1983: 106) I argued that "it is legitimate to suggest that some languages actually are easier for adults to learn, in an absolute sense, than others". This is a point agreed with by, for example, Dauenhauer and Dauenhauer (1998: 81) who say, in the context of reversing language shift in Tlingit, Haida, and Tsimshian, that "the languages of Southeast Alaska are intrinsically more difficult to learn than Maori or Hawaiian because of their more complex grammars and phonologies". I also argued that the 'easier' languages are those which are highly analytical, often because they have experienced more contact.

The clue to our conundrum lies in the phrase: "easier for adults to learn". The point is that whenever adults and post-adolescents learn a new language (Trudgill 1996b), *pidginization* can be said to occur; and pidginization includes as a crucial component the process of simplification.[8] (Note that pidginization is a common process which only very rarely, and in very unusual circumstances, leads to the development of an actual pidgin language—see Trudgill 1996b; 2000). This in turn—although other factors such as motivation may be involved—is due to the difficulty human adults face in learning new languages perfectly.

This inability is due to the fact that adult and adolescent humans are speakers who have passed the *critical threshold* (Lenneberg 1967) for language acquisition. This loss of language learning ability is the most fundamental instrumental mechanism involved in pidginization, and it has to be considered to play an important part in our understanding of language contact phenomena. Lenneberg's term refers to the well-known fact, obvious to anyone who has been alive and present in normal human societies for a couple of decades or so, that while small children learn languages perfectly, the vast majority of adults do not, especially in untutored situations.

Surprisingly, some linguists have been a little cautious about accepting this common-sense (and indeed experimentally demonstrated) position: Anderson and Lightfoot are simply

---

[8] The other major components are *reduction* and *admixture* (Trudgill, 1996b)—see Chapter 3.

willing to say (2002: 209) that "whatever we learn after the period of normal first-language acquisition, we learn in a different way". And, beginning in the 1970s, there were even more strongly dissenting voices, both from Second Language Acquisition studies and formal linguistics. (A recent example is Mark Hale (2007: 44), who says that "I do not believe in what is sometimes called the Critical Age Hypothesis".) Swan (2007) has argued, in a somewhat different context, that this kind of reluctance on the part of some linguists to accept the obvious was explicable in terms of the linguistic-ideological position taken by some linguists who were "concerned to show, in accordance with the new orthodoxy of the time, that all language development was driven by unconscious mechanisms whose operation was similar, if not identical, for both L1 and L2" and that any position which was not compatible with this view "needed to be discredited".

More mainstream are views such as those of Dahl (2004: 101), who writes of "children's ability to learn large amounts of low-level facts about language". He also claims (2004: 294) that "human children indeed seem to have an advantage compared to ... adult members of their own species"—children reveal a genetically inherited capacity for the acquisition of linguistic complexity. As Trask (1999: 63) has it, "young children learn perfectly any language to which they are adequately exposed ... [while] few adults can perform the same feat". Trask then goes on to say (1999: 64) that "strong support for Lenneberg's hypothesis comes from the observation of feral children who ... have been denied normal access to language in early life" and who fail to learn language after being first exposed to human contact as teenagers. There is also excellent evidence for this same phenomenon from the deaf community, with age of exposure to Sign Language being closely related to success in its acquisition (Hyltenstam 1992). There is, too, very persuasive evidence from empirical studies in Second Language Acquisition, notably Johnson and Newport's (1989) study of critical period effects in second language learning.

The view from sociolinguistics (e.g. Labov 1972) is also that children acquire new dialects and languages more or less perfectly up to the age of about eight, and that there is no or very little chance of them learning a language variety perfectly after the age of about fourteen. What happens between eight and fourteen will depend very much on the circumstances and on the individual. Although it must be the case that socio-logical and sociopsychological factors are also partly respon-sible for the relatively poor language-learning abilities of adults in natural acquisition situations, developmental factors play an obvious and vital role.

One might not, of course, accept that 'threshold' is the most appropriate metaphor here for what is most likely a gradual tailing off in ability: Johnson and Newport found "a linear decline in performance up through puberty" (1989: 97). In-deed Johnson and Newport report that their "results are most naturally accommodated by some type of maturational ac-count, in which there is a gradual decline in language learning skills over the period of on-going maturational growth and a stabilization of language learning skills at a low but variable level of performance at the final mature state". As they say, this leaves open the issue of whether there is a maturational change in a specific "language acquisition device" (Lenneberg 1967) or whether there are more general maturational, cognitive changes. But this is not at all crucial for my argument here.

The role of the age of the learner, and of the critical thresh-old—or "critical period" if one prefers to avoid Lenneberg's metaphor—in producing simplification is supported by Kus-ters (2003: 21), who in making the point that inflectional or fusional morphology is implicated in complexity, crucially specifies that it is "outsider complexity" he is referring to. Here an "outsider" is "a *second language learner*, who is not acquainted with the speech community of which s/he is learn-ing the language, and who wants to use the language to transmit meaningful messages" (2003: 6 [my italics]). And of course it is the fact that we are dealing here with post-threshold *adult* second language outsider-learners that is the crucial one.

L2-difficulty

Dahl describes simplification as a "sub-optimal transmission" effect (2004: 274) and introduces the term "L2-difficult" (2004: 294). This is a very helpful term. Its relevance can be judged by returning to Rice's (1999) appraisal of the "legendary" complexity of Navajo, as mentioned above. Rice explains at some length what it is that is complex about the verb in this language. The verb consists of a morphological template which takes the form: outer prefixes + distributive plural prefix + object prefix + inner prefixes + subject prefix + classifier + verb stem, different prefixes within a class interacting with each other phonologically. Any learner of the language, however, has to master not only this structure but much more besides (Rice 1999: 392):

First, the form of the verb must be determined. This is in itself a complex task, as the form of the stem varies across different modes (imperfective, perfective, future, progressive, optative). Second, the choice of the so-called classifier must be learned. Third, any lexical prefixes, either outer or inner, must be recognized. Fourth, the transitivity of the verb must be stated. Fifth, each verb has a conjugation, or pattern of forms that the verb exhibits in different modes. Finally, it is necessary to learn three further types of information, rules of combination, the form of the subject prefixes in the different modes, and vocabulary principles.

More details are given in Mithun (1999), who devotes many pages to the structure of the verb in Athabaskan languages generally. She tells us (1999: 363) that in Tanaina (southern Alaska) "the verbal morphology consists of stem preceded by nearly 20 prefix positions", with each stem having imperfective, perfective, and progressive forms.

Contrast this—or the Gothic forms of the verb *to have* cited above—with the verb in the English-lexifier creole Sranan of Surinam. According to Winford and Migge (2004), the structure of the verb here is very easily outlined. Sranan verbs are formally completely invariant but can optionally be preceded by tense and aspect particles: *ben* PAST, *o* FUTURE, *de* IMPERFECTIVE; and there is also an optional postposed COMPLETIVE marker *kaba*—and that's it.[9] Other meanings which would be associated with the Navajo verb are expressed lexically in Sranan, or not at all.

At this point we may return again to the approach of Nichols. As we have seen, Nichols argues that her morphological complexity index "correlates with overall morphological

---

[9] I concede of course that there is much more actually to be said about the Sranan verb than just this.

complexity and hence can be used as an index of something real". But it will be remembered that she concedes that it "overlooks a good deal of the actual morphological complexity of languages ... in considering where and whether something is marked but not how (e.g., by inflection, agglutination, cliticisation, or incorporation)" (1992: 64).

It is obviously the case that absence of marking, scoring 0 in Nichols's system, represents maximum simplicity, as with the loss of English gender. However, marking by inflection as opposed to marking by agglutination or detached marking (e.g. pronouns, clitics), although both scoring 1 according to Nichols, actually differ in terms of their complexity: inflexional marking is the more complex because it is less transparent.

Indeed, Kuspers cites Clahsen and Muysken (1996) and Meisel (1997) as demonstrating that L2 learners have serious problems with inflection, and that this is a point where "adults have clearly more learning difficulties than L1 learners" (2003: 48). Eubank (1996) also argues that the capacity to learn inflection in language is innate, but that for adults and adolescents this capacity is no longer accessible. And Dahl describes inflection as the archetypical exemplar of a "mature" linguistic phenomenon (see further Chapter 6) and writes that "there is a significant overlap between the mature features ... and those linguistic features that are most recalcitrant in second language learning" (Dahl 2004: 286).

Kusters then goes on to adduce (2003: 21) three simplicity principles of inflection, in connection with verbal morphological complexity, which are relevant to this discussion and which help to elucidate why inflection is so "recalcitrant". The first is the *Economy Principle*, which states that "as few semantic categories or category combinations as possible should be expressed morphologically". The *Transparency Principle* "demands that the relation between form and meaning is as transparent as possible". The highest level of transparency or analyticity is when "every single meaning is expressed in a separate form". And the *Isomorphy Principle* states that the affix order should be "isomorphic to the order of meaning elements".

It is clear then that agglutinating languages are less complex than fusional languages in terms of "outsider complexity" for post-threshold learners in that, at least, these languages adhere to the transparency principle much more closely than fusional languages, and are more analytic. To take a text-book example, Steinbergs (1996: 381) says that an agglutinating language "has words which can contain several morphemes, but the words are easily divided into their component parts. ... Each affix is clearly identifiable and typically represents a single grammatical category or meaning". In Turkish, for example, the form *adam-lar-dan* 'from the men' can readily be segmented as *man*-PLURAL-ABLATIVE. However, in a fusional language, affixes "often mark several categories simultaneously"—they have "several simultaneous functions". For example, Latin *homini-bus* 'from the men' also represents the ablative plural of the Latin noun for *man*, but clear segmentation is not possible. According to Anderson, inflectional languages "have internally complex words which cannot easily be segmented into an exhaustive and non-overlapping string of formatives" (Anderson 1985: 8). And as Andersson[10] asserts (2005: 46):

in absolute terms one could say that analytic languages are easier than synthetic languages, and there are two arguments for this claim. Firstly, children always learn a more analytic version of their native language; inflectional and derivative suffixes are learned later on. Secondly, pidgin languages from around the world are typically analytic.

Two types of contact

Now the picture becomes clearer. Simplification in language contact does not result from non-native language learning as such, but from post-critical threshold—or if one prefers, simply adult—non-native language learning. As Labov (2007: 382) says of contact phenomena he has studied, they "share the common marker of adult language learning: the loss of linguistic configurations that are reliably transmitted only by the child language learner". Simplification will occur in sociolinguistic contact situations only to the extent that untutored, especially short-term, *adult* second language learning occurs, and not only occurs but dominates.

---

[10] For anyone reading this in low light conditions, let me point out that I am quoting here from both Stephen R. Anderson and Lars-Gunnar Andersson.

If we define linguistic complexity as being identical with the difficulty of acquisition of a language, or a subsystem of a language, for adolescent and adult learners (see further Chapter 3), then it is clear why simplification takes the form it does (Trudgill 2009). Andersson (2005: 40) says:

The terms simple and complex rather refer to structural aspects of the language: a simple language has fewer rules, paradigms and grammatical forms than a complex one. Furthermore, a simple language (in this structural sense) is easier to learn (in terms of time and effort) than a complex language.

Post-threshold learners have less difficulty in coping with regularity and transparency than irregularity and opacity; and loss of redundancy reduces the burden for learner speakers. Highly irregular and non-transparent features are harder to learn and remember—they are, in Carstairs-McCarthy's nice phrase, "cognitive irritants" (2010: 120). And arbitrariness in grammar produces material which has to be learned without any generalizations being possible. As Jespersen (1922: 332) says, "if Gothic, Latin and Greek burden the memory by the number of their flexional endings, they do so even more by the many irregularities in the formation of these endings". And high redundancy means that there is more to learn (see Bakker 2003). "As is well known, second-language learners have great problems with grammatical gender, both learning to apply agreement rules and learning the gender of individual words" (Dahl 2004: 200).

In his discussion of complexity vs. cost and difficulty, Dahl (2004: 39) prefers to suppose that complexity and L2 difficulty are not actually identical but simply "related". But in any case, it seems sensible to suppose that speech communities which have frequent contacts with other societies involving adult dialect or language acquisition are relatively more likely to produce languages and dialects which demonstrate simplification, the most extreme though least usual cases typologically being pidgins and creoles. Changes such as a move from synthetic to analytic structure, reduction in morphological categories, reduction in grammatical agreement and other repetitions, increase in regularity, and increase in transparency, all make for greater ease of adult learnability. As the Danish scholar Madvig (1857) pointed out, simplification in linguistic structure makes languages easier to learn "for foreigners" (cited in Jespersen 1922: 324).[11]

This now, in turn, helps us to appreciate under which circumstances contact will lead to the reverse process, complexification. Contact leading to complexification will also be of a particular but different type. We can expect to see additive complexity developing in long-term, co-territorial contact situations which involve childhood—and therefore pre-threshold and proficient—bilingualism where young speakers know two or more languages natively or at least extremely well. Note too that our second social factor, *stability*, will obviously also be an important prerequisite for this kind of long-term development to take place.

It is this kind of situation which gives rise to the phenomenon of the Sprachbund. "Strong linguistic areas are typically characterised by large numbers of small linguistic communities *on good social terms*. Their members are in frequent contact and often become multilingual" (Mithun 1999: 314; [my italics]). Van Coetsem (2000), too, describes linguistic areas in terms of long-term, stable bilingualism.

The length of time that may be involved in this kind of co-territorial contact and bilingualism, sometimes stretching back thousands of years, is illustrated in what Mithun has to say in connection with her work on Californian languages (2007: 146):

California is home to tremendous genetic diversity. The most ambitious reductive hypotheses have grouped the languages into seven possible genetic units. ... Yet we see striking parallelisms in abstract grammatical structure which cross-cut genetic lines. The languages are characterized by pervasive, often elaborate sets of means/manner prefixes and locative/directional suffixes, structures that are relatively rare outside of the area. The situation is strongly suggestive of transfer through language contact. Relatively little is known for certain of the prehistory of the California groups before their contact with Europeans, but it is clear that there was an extensive period of intense social contact, multilingualism, and intermarriage in this area.

The situation of the Vaupés Amazonian Indians described earlier is of the same close-contact type. Jackson (1974) describes

---

[11] This does not necessarily mean that simplification occurs *only* in high contact situations—Dahl writes "it is unlikely that those [simplifying] changes can all depend on language contact" (2004: 283). As I said in the Preface, it is a matter of tendencies and probabilities.

how people live in longhouses consisting of up to eight nuclear families per house. There are around twenty different languages in the area, but there is a shared culture in which all people who are native speakers of the same language are regarded as siblings, and therefore cannot marry. A man therefore chooses a wife from a longhouse with a different native language, and she comes to live with him in his. In the longhouse, children therefore grow up surrounded by male speakers of the father's language and female speakers of a number of other different languages, and childhood multilingualism is the norm. Strenuous, overt efforts are made to keep the languages apart in speech—code-mixing does not occur—but these efforts focus on lexis, and so grammatical convergence and borrowing can occur, with consequences such as those described above.

It is clearly also this type of (very) long-term contact that Heine and Kuteva are mainly interested in in their book *Language contact and grammatical change*: they write (2005: 5) that "contact-induced language change is a complex process that not infrequently extends over centuries, or even millennia". And it is also this kind of situation which occurs in Nichols's residual zones, where complexification as a result of additive borrowing is very typical. As we saw, Nichols cites as being residual zones areas such as: the Pacific North West, which includes the Clear Lake Miwok language discussed by Mithun (see above) as being considerably more complex than related languages; and the Caucasus—Haudricourt (1961) cites the (now extinct) Caucasian language Ubykh as having an enormously complex phoneme inventory including 78 consonants, while Vogt (1963) gives the number of consonants as 80.

Case Study: simplification and complexification in Arabic

Where, then, language contact situations produce linguistically different types of outcome, we interpret this as being due to the fact that the contact situations were of sociolinguistically different types. As far as the issue of simplification vs. complexification is concerned, we have established that there are two different, major types of contact situation. Of course, in real life things will be much more complicated than a simple dichotomy; but the major distinction for the purposes of this discussion is between short-term adult contact situations, and those involving long-term child contact.

This claim that the two different types of contact will have two different types of linguistic consequence can be very nicely illustrated by comparing varieties of a single language, Arabic. Arabic provides a perfect laboratory for a demonstration of our sociolinguistic-typological thesis: the language is spoken over a very wide geographical area, and it has experienced many different types of contact situation in different locations and at different periods of its history.

First, there is considerable evidence that Arabic has experienced contact of the type which leads to simplification. The clearest cases are, as one would expect, the Arabic-based pidgins and creoles, as outlined in Owens (1997). The Nubi Arabic creole of southern Sudan/northern Uganda has received particular attention (Heine 1982; Musa-Wellens 1994; Owens 1985, 1991, 2001). Nubi has relatively high morphological transparency compared to other varieties of Arabic, and it has experienced a "radical loss of morphology" (Kusters 2003: 149), having only eight inflectional categories as opposed, for example, to 45 in Western Sudanese Arabic (Owens 2001: 366).

Owens (2001: 349) illustrates the simplification that has occurred in Nubi with a number of examples, including the structure of imperfect verb forms. Unlike other varieties of Arabic, Nubi has no person, gender, or number marking, and a total absence of ablaut in these forms. The effects of simplification can be seen very clearly by comparing the Nubi imperfect verb paradigm with that of Eastern Libyan Arabic:

		E. Libyan	Nubi
'I write'		?a- ktub	ana gi-katifu
'you (sg.) write'	(m.)	ti- ktib	ita gi-katifu
"	(f.)	ti- kitb-i	
'he writes'		yi- ktib	uwo gi-katifu
'she writes'		ti- ktib	ina gi-katifu
'you (pl.) write'	(m.)	ni- kitb-u	itakum gi-katifu
"	(f.)	ti- kitb-an	
'they write'	(m.)	yi- kitb-u	umwon gi-katifu
"	(f.)	yi- kitb-an	

As can be seen, simplification has the consequence that the Nubi verb form is invariant throughout, with person and number indicated solely by pronoun subjects and gender not marked at all. (The invariant *gi-* prefix is a progressive (durative) marker.)

It is well known that Nubi arose as a result of massive language contact, and a break in normal transgenerational transition. According to Owens (1997) and Kusters (2003), Nubi originated in a pidgin Arabic which developed, in the second half of the 19th century in the southern Sudan, out of interaction between speakers of local, non-mutually intelligible Niger-Congo and Nilo-Saharan languages, in camps housing defeated troops from an Egyptian-led army which had been attempting a conquest of southern Sudan.

As far as the non-creole/non-pidgin varieties of Arabic are concerned, the role of contact-induced simplification in their development has been a somewhat controversial topic. Versteegh's (1984) suggestion that contact-induced simplification had occurred in Arabic generally did not by any means meet with immediate approval from other scholars (see Holes 1995). In the light of Kusters (2003) and McWhorter (2007), however, the fact that contact has been responsible for some of the simplifications which Arabic has undergone would now seem to be incontrovertibly established. These would have resulted from contact of a less dramatic type than that involved in the growth of Nubi which followed on from the expansion of Arabic out of the Arabian peninsula, with language shift from local languages to Arabic in North Africa and the Middle East. The assumption is that the relatively rapid acquisition of Arabic by large numbers of adults in contact situations, followed in subsequent generations by the loss of the local Semitic and Berber languages as well as others such as Greek and Persian and a total shift to the new colonial language, was the main mechanism involved.

The work of Kusters is especially persuasive in this respect. In his work, the link between contact and simplification is very ably demonstrated, in detail and quantitatively. He examines the history of degrees of complexity and simplicity in verbal inflectional morphology in Quechua, Swahili, and the Scandinavian languages as well as Arabic. For Arabic, he measures simplification in three different varieties in terms of the degree to which they have undergone developments such as *loss of dual number*—the loss of a morphological category—and *decrease in allomorphy*—an increase in transparency. His highly detailed quantitative analyses lead him to conclude that "the level of [linguistic] complexity is related to the type of speech community" (2003: 59) in that language varieties with a history of higher contact also tend to demonstrate higher degrees of simplification. He shows that all forms of Modern Arabic demonstrate at least some simplification as compared to Classical Arabic, but that some have undergone much more contact than others, and therefore have much more simplification.

In addition to Nubi, Kusters also discusses the Najdi Arabic of central Saudi Arabia (Ingham 1994a), and Moroccan Arabic (Caubet 1993; Holes 1995). Just as Moroccan Arabic has more complexity than Nubi, so Kusters shows that Najdi has more complexity than Moroccan, giving quantitative confirmation to the kind of observation made by Ingham (1982), where "reductional changes" in the Arabic of Mesopotamia and the Gulf are contrasted with "non-reductional" changes in Najdi dialects. According to Kusters, this is because, although Moroccan Arabic has a continuous tradition of maintenance by native speakers and normal transgenerational transmission, it has also experienced considerable contact. First, dialect contact took place as a result of the migrations to Morocco from different parts of the Arabian peninsula and Egypt in the 7th and then again in the 10th centuries, with speakers of different regional dialects coming into contact in the new location. Secondly, there was very considerable language contact in Morocco, most especially with speakers of the different indigenous Berber languages. In the case of Najdi, however, there has been no migration, and relatively little contact. The conclusion is that different degrees of simplification have occurred in different Arabic varieties to the extent that adult language and dialect contact have also occurred.

It is not the case, however, that contact in the history of Arabic has led *only* to simplification. As the hypothesis outlined above would lead us to expect, in other types of sociolinguistic situation complexification has taken place. One example of this is provided by Maltese. Malta is only approximately 50 miles/90 kilometres from Sicily, and the two islands were united politically for over 400 years, from 1090 to 1530; contacts then remained close after that. It is therefore not surprising that, as is well known, Sicilian influence on Maltese has been very considerable, notably on the lexis (Aquilina 1959). But Heine and Kuteva (2005: 151–2) suggest that Maltese has also experienced grammatical influence from southern Romance. In particular, Heine and Kuteva suggest that Maltese did indeed acquire additional contact-induced complexity through the addition of a new morphological marker which is lacking in other Western Arabic varieties. (Although Maltese is sociolinguistically no longer a variety of Arabic, linguistically it is very clearly a Western Arabic dialect (Hoberman and Aronoff 2003).)

Following Borg and Mifsud (2002: 34), Heine and Kuteva show that Maltese marks human definite direct objects with the indirect object marker, translated below as 'to', while inanimate objects receive no object marking. The examples they cite are:

Il-tifel   ra   lil   Marija
'The-boy   saw (to) Mary'

compared to

Marija   qabdet   il-ballun
'Mary   caught   the-ball'

This parallels the familiar Spanish distinction of:

El   chico vió a   María
'The   boy   saw (to) Mary'

compared to

María   cogió   la   pelota
'Mary   caught the ball'

Heine and Kuteva tell us of Western Romance that "in a vast area stretching from Portuguese and Spanish through popular French to southern Italian, instances of direct object marking can be found, involving the preposition 'to' and being involved with animate and definite participants (Borg and Mifsud 2002: 42)". The area involved also includes Sardinian (Floricic 2003). Crucially, in Old Sicilian, constructions such as

Truvau   a   Micheli
'He-found   to   Michael'

were usual.

As noted above, this Maltese phenomenon does not occur in any of the western dialects of Arabic to which Maltese is closely related, and Borg and Mifsud therefore suggest that its occurrence in Maltese may well be due to influence from southern Romance. Heine and Kuteva concur that it is very likely that it developed as a result of "intense language contact with Romance languages". And of course the most obvious source is Sicilian.

A similar kind of process can be seen in the Arabic of Cyprus, as described in his work on the dialect of the village of Kormataki by Borg (1985). Kormataki Cypriot Arabic, like Maltese, has been spoken in close contact with another language, in this case Cypriot Greek, for very many centuries, and has remained sociolinguistically beyond the influence of mainstream Arabic. As a result, it shows very considerable influence from Cypriot Greek, some of which involves additive borrowing. According to Borg (1985: 143), a striking additive development has been the growth of a new system of locational deictics—"the evolution of an elaborate set of locational adverbs"—as a result of influence from Cypriot Greek, which has a similar system. The forms are:

(a) *anaxok*   'up here'   *axxok*   'up there'
     anataxt   'down here'   *antaxt*   'down there'
     anaxost   'in here'   *axxost*   'in there'

(b) *awnaxok*   'up here'   *awnkaxok*   'up there'
     awnataxt 'down here'   *awnkataxt* 'down there'
     awnaxost 'in here'   *awnkaxost* 'in there'

Borg says that the "exact nature of the semantic opposition implemented by these paired sets [(a) and (b)] has yet to be fully elaborated" but the forms under (a) "appear to refer to specific locations within the speaker's range of vision" while the (b) forms "refer to indefinitely specified locations" (1985: 144). He gives as examples:

anaxok   'up here where I'm standing' vs.
awnaxok   'up here somewhere'

Even more telling examples of this same type of phenomenon come from Central Asian Arabic. The first Arabic speakers migrated to the area of what is now Uzbekistan, Tajikistan, and northern Afghanistan in the 8th century, during the Muslim expansion. It is important for our purposes that speakers of the language have therefore been in contact with speakers of the Turkic language Uzbek and the Indo-Iranian language Tajik for more than 1,200 years—Ingham (1994b) stresses that "this area is in fact one of considerable linguistic diversity" which is "on the border of the Indo-European and Altaic language areas". As a consequence, there was very considerable influence from these languages, particularly Tajik, on the local Arabic (Versteegh 1984–6).

According to the thesis being considered here, this type of prolonged co-territorial contact should have led to complexification, and indeed this does seem to be the case. Ingham shows that, crucially, some of the borrowing from the other languages which Afghan Arabic has experienced is of the additive type: Arabic acquired features from its co-territorial neighbours while maintaining original Arabic features. Notable examples of this kind of complexification are:

(1) The pattern *relative clause + noun* occurs "alongside the original Arabic *noun + relative clause*" (Owen 2001: 355). That is, Central Asian Arabic has two relative clause structures, to mainstream Arabic's one.

(2) Similarly, we see "the construction *possessor + possessed* occurring alongside the Arabic *possessed + possessor*" (Owen 2001: 355). Again there are two structures as opposed to the original single structure.

(3) An interrogative suffix *-mi* is attached to verbs to perform the function of question-formation, which is "presumably identical with the Turkish suffix *-mi* of the same function" (Ingham 1994b). Ingham supplies the following examples:

hint battīxa kalinnak-mi   *Have you eaten the watermelon?*
sōɣ amōn hastinnak-mi   *Are you healthy and well?*

(4) Ingham also informs us that "postpositions which occur in Turkish but not in Persian are represented in Afghan Arabic". Those which Ingham recorded are *-jimiʾ* 'with, together with'; *-xilā (f)* 'after', and *-giddām* 'before':

faras-jim'	*by horse, with horses*
'ašar daqīqa-xilā (f)	*in ten minutes*
min nayamān -giddām	*before sleeping*

There is, then, clear evidence from Arabic that the two different types of language contact have indeed given rise to two different kinds of outcome in terms of complexification and simplification.

Case study: Old English

The sociolinguistic-typological proposal concerning the two different types of language contact can also be used to attempt to provide insight into certain historical linguistic puzzles. One such concerns contact effects in Old English.

Old English was typologically very different from Middle English. It was highly fusional and inflecting, while Middle English showed a marked move towards a more isolating type of morphology. It is clear, as Milroy (1992a: 177) says, that what happened represented "a trend towards simplification in Middle English". Milroy then goes on to say, as quoted above, that "it seems clear that such a sweeping change is at least to some extent associated with *language contact*" (1992a: 203).

The interesting question then is: if simplification in English occurred, as our above discussion leads us to suppose, as a result of adult contact between Old English and some other language, which language was it? Was it the Brittonic Celtic language of the indigenous inhabitants which was the ancestor of Cornish and Modern Welsh? Or was it the Old Norse of the Vikings?[12] Here the contrast we have just established between the two different types of contact may help us to decide.

The case for Old Norse has been argued for by many writers, and there is a widespread consensus about its importance. Kroch et al. (2000) accept this case, as does McWhorter (2007: 90ff.). However, an alternative thesis, that it was contact

---

[12] For a rejection of the possibility that Norman French might have been involved, see Trudgill (2010c).

between Old English and the Celtic Brittonic language which was the determining factor, is currently gaining ground (e.g. Vennemann 2002). That there was contact between the ancestors of Modern English and Welsh is indisputable. However, to argue the case in favour of the role of Celtic, it has been necessary for its supporters to explain away two rather obvious factors which seem to speak against it. First, it has generally been thought that there was rather little contact between Old English and Brittonic because the Celts either ran away from the invaders or were rapidly exterminated or absorbed by the incomers. Secondly, the chronology is not right, because the simplification did not happen until many centuries after the Brittonic Late British had died out in England and the relevant areas of Scotland.

The first factor has now been argued against by writers who produce evidence that Late British survived for much longer than had originally been thought, to the extent that there must have been extended contact with Old English. Schrijver (2006) argues that Late British survived at least until the 10th century in Highland Britain—the whole of the English counties of Cornwall, Devon, Herefordshire, Cheshire, Derbyshire, Lancashire, Westmoreland, and Cumberland, in addition to parts of neighbouring counties and the whole of Wales, plus much of Scotland. Tristram (2004) suggests that in some areas of the Midlands and Northern zone, speakers of the post-conquest Anglian and Mercian dialects ruled the native population of the Britons as their slaves. These continued to speak Brittonic, their native language, for perhaps as many as six or seven generations, before they shifted to Old English.

As far as the second factor, timing, is concerned, Tristram (2004) argues for the persistence of a written/spoken diglossia in Anglo-Saxon England. Her thesis is that simplification occurred in Old English much earlier than has usually been thought, at a time when contact with Celtic would have provided a very reasonable explanation. These fundamental changes occurred in the spoken language but did not make their way into the written language. The written evidence which has survived, and which is the only evidence we have, came from a small upper-class elite who had preserved a knowledge of how Old English was supposed to be written,

long after the original morphological complexity had disappeared from everyday speech (rather in the way that knowledge of how Latin was written survived, even though linguistic
change had produced a situation where what everyone actually
spoke in the relevant areas was one of the Romance languages).
Evidence of simplification appeared in writing only after the
social breakdown—of the type discussed in Chapter 1—which
resulted from the Norman Conquest, led to the disappearance
of the diglossia and produced the first evidence of changes
which had actually occurred several centuries earlier. As Vennemann (2009) indicates, a similar point was made earlier by
Wagner (1959: 151) who wrote:

> That Germanic was preserved in Anglo-Saxon England rather well
> for several centuries is connected to the existence of an Anglo-Saxon
> aristocracy and an Anglo-Saxon written and poetic language. The
> Norman conquest broke the supremacy of this ruling class and
> paved the way for the development of a British language. (Transla-
> tion by Vennemann 2009: 327)

So what can our posited contrast between short-term adult
contact and long-term co-territorial communal contact suggest
as an answer to this question of Old Norse versus Celtic
influence?

As far as Old Norse is concerned, it is known that, after the
initial Viking raids, contact between Old English and Nordic
speakers in northern England turned into a situation of long-
term co-territorial co-habitation and intermarriage. Townend
sees the significance of "Anglo-Scandinavian integration and
the continued practice of mixed marriage" (2002: 204). And
Laing and Laing (1979: 185) speak of "the cultural fusion of
Angle and Dane in the north". Linguistically, we know that
large numbers of words made their way from Old Norse into
English. Crucially, however, as a very persuasive piece of linguistic evidence of the intensity of the long-term contact, the
English third person plural pronominal forms *they, them,
their, theirs* were borrowed from Old Norse, as is well known.

Borrowing pronouns from one language to another is a rare
type of development which is never, I would suggest, seen
in short-term adult contact situations—only in long-term
co-territorial contact of the child-bilingualism type which is

typical of linguistic areas, as discussed above. Matras (2009: 208) has it that "pronouns may be borrowable in principle" but in practice "they show very low borrowability". It is true that pronoun borrowing is not located at the very bottom of the borrowing scale developed by Thomason and Kaufman (1988: 74–8),[13] but this form of borrowing occurs, according to them, only under intense contact. Campbell (1997a) and Thomason and Everett (2005) list a number of cases where the borrowing of pronominal forms from one language to another has occurred—and all of these cases involve long-term contact and proficient bilingualism (Trudgill 2010a). According to Nichols and Peterson (1998: 242), the "borrowing of pronouns points to *unusually close contact*" [my italics].

The fact that the contact was "unusually close", and sufficiently intimate and long-term that pronouns could be borrowed, would seem to make the thesis that it was contact with Old Norse which led to simplification in Late Old English much less tenable. Contact between Old Norse and Old English was not of the sociolinguistic type that makes for simplification. Old Norse and Old English "were roughly adstratal in Viking Age England" (Townend 2002: 204), the term adstratum being used to refer to situations where two groups of roughly equal status come into contact with one another and exert mutual influence on one another's languages (Trudgill 2003).[14]

The intensity and co-territoriality of the Old Norse–Old English contact makes it much more likely that the simplification that occurred in Old English was due to contact with speakers of Late British. Crucially, in those Highland areas where Late British survived the West Germanic invasion in the long term, its speakers were in a very different type of contact situation with Old English speakers. Late British was in a substratal, not adstratal relationship with Old English

---

[13] Curnow (2001: 434) is doubtful about the whole exercise of the development of borrowing scales: "It is possible that a variety of constraints on borrowing in particular contexts can be developed. But the attempt to develop any universal hierarchy of borrowing should perhaps be abandoned."

[14] Unsurprisingly, a substratum effect is one which results from a community abandoning their native language for another belonging to a community more powerful than themselves, and carrying over features from their original language in so doing; while a superstratum effect is the reverse of this. For a critique of the value of substratum etc. theory, see Thomason and Kaufman (1988: 118).

(Tristram 2004; 2006), and sociologically there was probably something like a caste system. The Britons were often slaves, a point made by Lutz (2009) among others. And a number of writers (see Woolf 2007) have actually described the situation as being one of "apartheid". So the two linguistic groups were hardly "on good terms", in Mithun's phrase. "From the textual evidence we have, the social barriers between the free and land-holding elite of Anglo-Saxon society and their dependents were perhaps fairly stable until the advent of the Normans" (Tristram 2004: 202).

Linguistically, then, as Tristram (2004: 101) has it,

> if we assume that the native Britons in the South West, the Midlands and the North slowly shifted to Old English in the course of two to four centuries (fifth to ninth), the type of linguistic contact and of language acquisition would have had to be that of the adult learner type.

She suggests that for Britons acquiring Old English, especially perhaps in the Highland zone, the first step was that of un-structured adult acquisition of the Old English target dialects as an L2 (Tristram 2006: 201):

> Perhaps, initially, there may have been only a small stable group of adult bilinguals who mediated between the speakers of Late British and the Old English dialects. Social segregation ... may have gen-erally kept the two population groups apart. As long as the social barrier lasted, this scenario will have meant for adult bilinguals a native-like acquisition of the lexicon but transfer on the level of phonology and morphosyntax because of their unconscious, imper-fect replication of the target language.

In any case, the pidginized[15] form of Old English hypothe-sized by Tristram would have been increasingly passed on to subsequent generations: "children would have learned the imperfectly acquired L2 from their parents as their L1 and subsequently passed on their linguistic knowledge of the mod-ified target language to their own children" (Tristram 2004: 202); and the simplified version of the language eventually became the dominant variety.

---

[15] I repeat the point made above that the fact that a variety is pidginized does not necessarily—indeed does not usually—mean that it is a pidgin.

The scenario would have resembled the one in which the colonial Dutch of South Africa, while maintaining a continuous tradition of transmission from one generation of native speakers to another, underwent considerable simplification even in the version spoken by native speakers, as witnessed by Modern Afrikaans, as a result of widespread language contact and non-native acquisition. In the Highland zone of Britain, it was the pidginized form of Old English which came to dominate, and it is therefore not surprising that it is in the north of England that evidence of linguistic simplification first appears in the historical record.

Our sociolinguistic-typological insights from earlier in this chapter suggest rather strongly (see further Trudgill 2010a; 2010b), then, that it was contact between a minority of Old English and a majority of socially inferior Late British speakers, in northern England, that set the process of simplification going, as the Britons shifted to (their form of) English, and Late British was eventually lost.

Demography and transmission

To conclude this chapter, I note that Campbell and Poser (2008: 362) have posed an important question about my approach to contact and simplification. In a long, if footnoted, discussion of my work they ask: if I am right about simplification being a consequence of adult language contact, then why has German, a language which has a long history of being learned as an L2 and of being used as a lingua franca, not been simplified like the mainland Scandinavian languages that I point to as having been affected by contact in this way?

My first reaction is that it is not exactly true that German does "not demonstrate simplification" (Campbell and Poser 2008: 362). Hawkins (1998, 2004), as referred to above, measures morphological complexity in terms of case, number, and gender distinctions in third person nominal systems in the Germanic languages. Out of a possible total of 18 (3 genders × 3 cases[16] × 2 numbers), Modern Icelandic has a system of 13 distinctive

---

[16] Hawkins does not consider the genitive. On why genitive is not strictly speaking a case, see Dixon (2010a: 45).

items, and Old High German has an 11-item system, while Modern German shows considerable simplification to an 8-item system. Low German, the variety which was implicated in the Hanseatic League contact scenarios which led to the simplification of mainland Scandinavian, has undergone even further simplification, to a 6-item system (Durrell 1990). Faroese, in contrast, still has an 11-item system (Thrainsson et al. 2004), on a par with Old High German, and is in this respect considerably more complex than Modern German rather than "very similar" to it, as Campbell and Poser maintain (2008: 362).

Campbell and Poser's question, however, remains a significant one. But it is not, I think, the right question. The question should not so much be why the acquisition of German by non-native speakers has not led to simplification. This is absolutely not a surprise. After all, in a situation where a continuous native-speaker tradition is maintained (Thomason & Kaufmann 1988), why would it? When pidgins develop, this is because there is an intergenerational break in transmission, and the result is effectively a new language. We readily understand why Nubi is radically simplified compared to (other types of) Arabic.

But where native speakers transmit their language from one generation to another in the normal way, as has happened with German, the fact that there may also be non-natives around who are speaking simplified versions of the language will normally have no effect on this transmission whatsoever. No language is currently used more by non-native speakers than English, but the mainstream native varieties of English—in the British Isles, for instance—are currently showing no serious signs of large-scale, ongoing, new simplification.

The real question is the reverse of Campbell and Poser's question. Since they mention Scandinavian, consider the Norwegian of Bergen. It has been argued by a number of writers, as we saw above, that a certain amount of simplification occurred in Bergen as a result of contact with Low German speakers. But how did this work? How are we to unpack the phrase "as a result of"? It would be no surprise if the Norwegian spoken by native speakers of Low German was simplified—undoubtedly it was. But the big question is: why should this simplification have spread to the speech of native Norwegians, and thus to subsequent generations? Equally, why should Old English have been influenced by the simplified version of their language spoken as an L2 by native Celtic speakers?

Again, the focus has to be refined, as I have been arguing throughout this chapter, onto the *type* of contact we are dealing with—it makes no sense simply to refer to "contact" as an undifferentiated concept. The answer to the Bergen/Old English question must lie in two factors central to contact processes, demography and transmission. As far as *demography* is concerned, we have some information about the case of Bergen. According to Rambø (2008), who quotes also from Nesse (2001), the population of Bergen in the 1400s may have been around 7,000. Of these perhaps 2,000 were Germans, with that number rising to perhaps 4,000 (then out of 9,000) in the summer months. There were also other foreigners, including Dutch, English, and Scottish. Elsewhere, Blomkvist (1979) says that in the 100 years from 1250 between a third and a half of the population of Kalmar, Sweden, were German. And Dahlbäck (1998) shows that in 1460 Stockholm had a population that was one third German.

Although there was a very long-term presence of these foreign communities in Bergen and other Scandinavian cities, the non-Norwegians did not typically settle, as individuals, in Bergen or elsewhere for the long term. They formed large but relatively transient and predominantly male populations, and so we are not dealing here with genuine long-term contact, nor child contact. In short-term contact, which is what this must have been for individual adults, we know that dialect mixture and dialect levelling occur as a result of contact via accommodation in face-to face interaction (Trudgill 1986). In the Bergen case, if Low German and Norwegian were mutually intelligible, as they may have been at this time, we can count Low German–Norwegian interactions as instances of dialect contact. If they were not intelligible, then we can also suppose that there was dialect contact of a different kind, between native Bergen Norwegian and the non-native Norwegian of Low German speakers.

My suggestion is that when the proportion of non-native speakers becomes as close to 50% as this—the proportion of non-native speakers of Norwegian in Bergen was certainly very high (4,000 out of 9,000)—the number of face-to-face dialect-contact-type interactions, and therefore potential instances of accommodation (Trudgill 1986), would have reached a threshold level at which some aspects of the non-native variety could transfer to the native. If the demography is right, natives can and will accommodate, to different extents, to non-natives. And the point about "different extents" is important: simplification in Bergen Norwegian is actually rather slight.

As another example, native-speaker English in the United States now has some features which were originally found only in non-native usage (Trudgill 2004a: 2)—American English *I like to swim* vs. English English *I like swimming* might be an example. And something similar seems currently to be happening in inner-city areas of a number of European cities with a high proportion of immigrants. For example, Rinkebys-venska is an immigrant-influenced variety of urban Swedish (Kotsinas 1990) which has been much referred to, though it is perhaps too early to decide what consequences this will have for the varieties spoken by subsequent generations in the areas in question. And Cheshire et al. (2008) describe a similar ongoing process in inner-city areas of London.

Trudgill (2010c) also argues that the 16th-century East Anglian English dialect of the city of Norwich was modified as a result of massive influence from the non-native speech of a very large population of Protestant refugees from the Low Countries—about one-third of the population were Dutch or French speakers by 1600. I then further argue that this modification was subsequently diffused geographically out from Norwich, the most important central place in the region (Christaller 1933), to the rest of East Anglia. The same reasoning would apply to the diffusion of simplifying innovations outwards from Copenhagen, Stockholm, and certain other Scandinavian cities.

As far as *transmission* is concerned, consider the case of Afrikaans as a form of Dutch that underwent simplification as a result of contact. Afrikaans is not a pidgin.[17] There has been

---

[17] Afrikaans is a actually a *creoloid*—see Chapter 3.

a continuous native-speaker tradition throughout its history, and the Dutch/Afrikaans language has been transmitted from one generation to another in the normal way since the arrival of Dutch/Flemish speakers in southern Africa in the 1600s. Many modern Afrikaans native speakers are the direct genetic as well as cultural descendants of earlier generations of Dutch speakers, in a way that, say, Nubi speakers are not genetically descended from earlier generations of Arabic speakers: Nubi speakers are descended from speakers of Niger-Congo and Nilo-Saharan languages who went through a process of language shift.

So how did non-native features, on a rather wide scale, make it into native Dutch/Afrikaans? Demography will again have been relevant. According to Combrink (1978), the population of Cape Town in 1795 was about 1,500, and about 1,000 of these were "slaves that had come from Guinea, Mozambique, and the far East" and "people of Khoin extraction, most of whom had given up their mother tongue and could speak only the Cape Dutch" (Combrink 1978: 77). Dutch was acquired by very large numbers of non-native speakers, initially speakers of the indigenous Khoi and San languages, and then by speakers of Bantu languages, and immigrant speakers of German, French, the Scandinavian languages, Portuguese, Malagasy, Malay, Indonesian languages, and others. There was much racial mixing and intermarriage, as the current "Coloured" population of South Africa shows. Wives in particular were quite likely to be native speakers of some language other than Dutch. This led to a situation where the nature of transmission became crucial. So many people initially acquired and used Dutch as an L2 that, in later generations, children were born who became, as it were, native speakers of non-native Dutch. A non-native variety became nativized and in time the dominant, and subsequently only, variety.

Dialect contact was also important, as is often the case in colonial situations (Trudgill 2004a), and as it undoubtedly was in Copenhagen and Bergen too. Combrink (1978) compares the present tense inflectional endings of Standard Dutch and Afrikaans:

'to work'

	Dutch		Afrikaans	
	singular	plural	singular	plural
1.	werk	werken	werk	werk
2.	werkt	werken/werkt	werk	werk
3.	werkt	werken	werk	werk

It is certain that language contact was involved in this kind of simplification. But Combrink's argument for dialect contact as well in this case is that, in the Dutch dialects that were taken to the Cape from the 17th century onwards, there were 23 different systems of present tense indicative verb morphology. In North Holland, South Holland, and Utrecht alone there were five (shown here for the singular only):

	A	B	C	D	E
1.	-	-t	-	-	-
2.	-	-t	-t	-	-e
3.	-	-t	-t	-t	-t

He says (1978: 75): "imagine the amount of noise via inflections versus the amount of communication via stems, if 73% of the Dutch Cape settlers used five of these systems and the other 27% something like eighteen other systems!"; and he ascribes this development in colonial Dutch (later Afrikaans) to "interdialectal noise deletion".

The answer, then, to Campbell and Poser's question is the following. Contact between German and other languages has many times led to simplified forms of German being used by non-native speakers—20th-century "Gastarbeiterdeutsch" (Keim 1978) is just one example. But unlike in the big Scandinavian cities such as Bergen, or in the 18th-century South African Cape, this had no consequences for the mainstream language of native speakers because the contact situation was different— the demographic and transmission factors were not right: the proportion of non-native speakers was nothing like high enough.

Conclusion

In this chapter I have proposed a dichotomy between two different kinds of contact. This is itself, of course, a serious simplification of what actually happens on the ground in real-life situations. Obvious complicating factors include the following:

- one type of contact can chronologically be succeeded by the other in the same location;
- the two types of contact can overlap chronologically, and the proportions of speakers of different ages will be very relevant;
- the degree of contact may vary considerably between different situations;
- the terms "long-term" and "short-term" are very vague with, for example, "long-term" covering periods from thousands of years down to much shorter periods;
- linguistic factors are not irrelevant—for instance, the degree of relatedness of the languages in contact may be important, since this will have implications for ease of L2 learning.

But we do seem to be justified in proceeding, as I now shall, on the basis of an understanding that contact can give rise to two very different types of linguistic outcome, depending on what kind of contact it is. In the words of Dahl (2004: 40), when it comes to learning difficulty, "the distinction between first and second language acquisition is evident".

We have also in this chapter noted an important role for the factor of social stability: both *type of contact* and *degree of stability* appear to be relevant in influencing aspects of linguistic structure, notably aspects of structure which have to do with simplicity and complexity. Much of the rest of this book will therefore be concerned precisely with this topic: linguistic complexity.

3

Isolation and complexification

It will be recalled that the view of simplification adopted in this book is that it consists of the following sub-processes:

- regularization of irregularities
- increase in morphological transparency
- reduction in syntagmatic redundancy, e.g. grammatical agreement
- loss of morphological categories.

Like simplification, complexification is a complicated notion; and different writers take different views of what exactly complexity is (see Sampson et al. 2009). I therefore make no claim that what I am here calling "complexification" is necessarily the whole story—in particular I have nothing to say about syntactic complexity (on that topic, see for example, Sampson et al, 2009).[1] However, in what follows I will take the approach of assuming that, for my purposes, if simplification can be characterized by the above four sub-processes, then it follows that complexification consists of the reverse processes:

- irregularization
- increase in opacity
- increase in syntagmatic redundancy
- addition of morphological categories.

My view is that, as noted in Chapter 2, other things being equal, complexity is identical to L2 difficulty, or at least closely related to it. I say "other things being equal" because, as Dahl (2004) has pointed out, difficulties of L2 acquisition are not

---

[1] I will observe, though, that some syntactic features have been suggested to be more L2-difficult than others—the Germanic verb-second rule is one example which, however, has been disputed (Bohnacker 2005).

unrelated to where the second language learner is starting from, in the obvious sense that French speakers will find Spanish easier to learn than Dutch, whereas for German speakers it will be the other way round.

If we now move on to examine the four sub-processes which, as I argue, are involved in complexification, we can note that the complexification discussed by Nichols—and as illustrated from Arabic, for example, at the end of the previous chapter—consists of only *one* of these processes. In Nichols's data, there are no irregularizations, no increases in opacity, and no increases in syntagmatic redundancy. The complexification described by typologists such as Nichols consists solely of *the addition of morphological categories*—indeed, Nichols computes complexity in terms of numbers of morphological markers—and, moreover, it is a very particular type of addition. The cases studied by Aikhenvald (2002), which are quite typical, are all instances of morphological categories being acquired by one language *from another language* with which it is in contact—and, crucially, being acquired in addition to categories which it already has. That is, we are dealing, as we noted in Chapter 2, with *additive borrowing* as opposed to *replacive borrowing*.

The interesting question therefore arises as to the origins of the other forms of complexity—of complexification which is the precise antithesis to the simplification which can lead to pidgins. If simplification occurs in short-term, adult contact situations, and additive complexification in long-term child contact situations, then what exactly are the sociolinguistic conditions which give rise to irregularization, increase in opacity, increase in syntagmatic redundancy, and to the *spontaneous* addition of morphological categories, i.e. categories which are not borrowed from other languages? As Thurston (1994: 603) says, what we need to be able to do is "to explain how complexity arose in languages in the first place".

Language in isolation

It is clear that we cannot look for the development of these types of complexification in any type of contact situation. As discussed in the previous chapter, short-term adult (post-critical threshold) contact tends to favour simplification, and long-term co-territorial pre-threshold contact tends to favour only additive complexification, so we must surely seek the locus of non-additive complexification in languages which have experienced low levels of language contact of any sort.

Certainly, it does seem to be the case that, in general, languages spoken in low-contact societies tend to demonstrate the *preservation* of existing complexity: Andersen (1988: 61) has pointed out that isolated dialects show "a more faithful transmission of morphological irregularity". This is one of the major points made by the authors quoted above who dealt with simplification in the Nordic languages: not only is it the case that the continental Scandinavian languages have undergone simplification, it is also true that the insular languages, Icelandic and Faroese, have preserved a very great deal of the complexity that was present in Old Norse.

It is therefore worth pursuing the hypothesis that it is in low-contact communities that we are most likely to find not only the preservation of complexity but also an *increase* in complexity, i.e. irregularity, opacity, syntagmatic redundancy, and non-borrowed morphological categories. This suggestion fits in with the observation of Werner (1984: 219):

unsere germ. Sprachen zeigen, dass eine kleine, weitgehend isolierte, sozial homogene Sprechergemeinschaft (wie etwa auf Island) am ehesten bereit ist, Akkumulationen an Komprimierung and Komplikation weiterwachen zu lassen.[2]

Wray and Grace (2007) similarly argue that languages that are used mainly for esoteric, i.e. intra-group, communication tend to have features that are more complex than those of languages used for exoteric or intergroup communication, which thereby become more regular and transparent.

This idea also receives support from the work on Arabic by Ingham (1982) cited earlier, who observes not only that non-reductional changes have occurred in the more isolated central North Najdi dialects of Arabic but also that in some cases they result "in an increase in complexity" (1982: 63), where com-

---

[2] 'Our Germanic languages show that a small, mainly isolated, socially homogeneous speech community (as for example in Iceland) is most likely to be willing to allow the continuation of an accumulation of fusion and complexity.'

plexity is equivalent to there being "more forms to be learnt" (1982: 75). For example, North Najdi has developed (and note that this is *developed*, not preserved) a greater amount of allomorphy in object pronominal suffixes compared to the less isolated Central Najdi (1982: 76):

	N. Najdi	C. Najdi
1st sg. obj.	*-an/-nan*	*-ni*
3rd m.sg. obj.	*-uh/-w/-h*	*-ih/-h*
3rd f.sg. obj.	*-ah/-h*	*-ha*
3rd f.sg. subj.	*-eih/-at*	*-at*
3rd f.pl. nom.	*-a:y/-a:t*	*-a:t*

Further Arabic support for the isolation-complexification thesis may be provided by a suggestion made by Owens:

it is assumed that case-marking in Semitic is a younger trait than nominals lacking case marking on the basis of the Afroasiatic evidence ... (2006: 115)

since caseless forms can be comparatively reconstructed at least as early as the seventh/eighth centuries, from the time of the Arabic diaspora, they are minimally as old as the case-Arabic described by Sibawaih, and hence can be projected into proto-Arabic as well. (2006: 116)

Given that Classical Arabic had case-marking, the inference has to be that late proto-Arabic gradually developed case-marking, at a time when the language was spoken by a rather small number of speakers, and most likely in a sparsely populated, low-contact area of the Arabian peninsula.

In search of complexification

There seems then to be a good case for thinking that we should look for the growth of complexity in situations which are the opposite in every respect, including degree of contact, to those in which pidgins develop. But if it is the case that non-additive complexification typically occurs, or occurs more often, in low-contact situations (see Trudgill 2002), then even generally high-contact varieties like English will permit us to explore this type of linguistic change, by doing so comparatively. We can, easily and helpfully, compare low-contact and high-contact varieties of English and of other languages with one another.

Traditional-dialects

For low-contact varieties, it is clear that what we will have to examine, in English and other similar major languages, are the *traditional-dialects*. According to Wells (1982), his term *trad-itional-dialects* applies as far as English is concerned to varieties which are equivalent to varieties of other languages which have labels such as German *Mundarten* and French *patois*. Such varieties of English are increasingly hard to find. They occur only in parts of England, especially those further away from London; in southern and eastern Scotland, and parts of Northern Ireland; and in Newfoundland in those areas settled more or less entirely from the southwest of England (see below).[3] By way of illustration, these are varieties where, rather than General English forms such as *she's not coming, she isn't coming,* or *she ain't comin,* we find forms such as *she bain't a-comin, hoo inno comin,* or *her idden comin* (Trudgill, 1999: 5).

The importance of traditional-dialects for this research comes from the fact that they are the only varieties which do not obviously result from contact. Given that this is so, we can check to see if the relatively low-contact linguistic situations in which they grew up really have led to the development of features which represent the reverse of simplification: expansion in irregularity, increase in opacity, increase in repetition of information, and the growth of morphological categories.

Moreover, traditional-dialects are especially important because it is the sociolinguistic situations in which these varieties developed over the centuries which most closely resemble the situations in which most language varieties have developed over the past tens of thousands of years of human linguistic history. As Plank argues, dialects may be "in stark contrast to a standard", and "a bias in favour of standards would deprive typology of much of its subject matter" (2006: 451).

High-contact varieties

The other varieties of English—*General English* in Wells's terms— are colonial and/or urban and/or shift and/or standardized

---

[3] A case could also perhaps be made for suggesting that some of the varieties spoken in the Appalachians in the USA are also traditional-dialects.

varieties which have a considerable history of dialect and/or language contact, and therefore show very many signs of simplification. If my hypothesis is correct, we would therefore not expect them to show many signs of spontaneous complexification.

Colonial varieties have resulted from dialect contact, as speakers from all over the British Isles came together in, for example, New Zealand (Trudgill, 2004), bringing their different dialects with them. Many colonial varieties, too, like North American English, also experienced language contact—with indigenous languages and other colonial languages in the new location. Urban dialects have also more often than not resulted from dialect contact, brought about by in-migration from surrounding areas. And shift varieties have resulted from language contact, as in the case of the development of Welsh English out of contact between English and Welsh.

As far as standard varieties are concerned, most of the major standard language varieties in Europe today, like Standard English, are especially unsuitable for the study of complexity development. This is because they are all relatively high-contact *koinés* and *creoloids* which are the result of simplification resulting from dialect and language contact.

Koinés and creoloids A brief account of what the two terms *koiné* and *creoloid* mean must begin by noting that a *pidgin* is a stable contact language, without native speakers, which is the outcome of the pidginization—simplification (see above), admixture, and reduction—of some source language, where reduction means that there is simply less of a language as compared to the form in which it is spoken by native speakers: the vocabulary is smaller, and there are fewer syntactic structures, a narrower range of styles, and so on. Pidginization has also occurred to such a degree that mutual intelligibility with the source language is no longer possible.

If then a pidgin language, as a lingua franca, becomes the only viable shared language of a community, it may be subject to expansion, so that it can be used in a wider range of functions and meet the linguistic needs of native speakers. The result is a *creole* language, which is thus a pidgin which has acquired native speakers and undergone *non-contact-induced expansion,* where the expansion process "repairs" the reduction which occurred during pidginization: a creole language is a language which, relative to its lexifier, is simplified and mixed, but not reduced.

The next possible chronological stage is decreolization. If a creole comes into renewed contact with its source language, it may begin to change back in the direction of this language. Such a change will involve a partial reversal of the effects of admixture and simplification, so that *post-creoles*—partially decreolized creoles—will show different degrees of simplification and admixture relative to the source language.

Interestingly, there are also many varieties of language in the world which look like post-creoles but which actually are not. Varieties like this have relatively undramatic admixture and simplification relative to a source language, but are known to have no pidgin history behind them. Such languages can be called *creoloids* (Trudgill 1983: 102). The process of creoloidisation thus consists of admixture and simplification. Unlike creoles, however, creoloids have not experienced a history of reduction which has been "repaired" by expansion: creoloids were never reduced in the first place, and have maintained a continuous native-speaker tradition. The difference between a creoloid and a partially decreolised creole is thus a historical one, and is not apparent from synchronic inspection. A good example of a creoloid is Afrikaans, as discussed in Chapter 2, which is a creoloid relative to Dutch.

Similar simplification outcomes can also occur in the case of dialect contact. In the long term, dialect contact may lead to the development of a *koiné* through the process of new-dialect formation (Trudgill 1986; 2004a). Compared to pidgin formation, there are two obvious major differences. There is no single source variety: the outcome is the result of contact between two or more dialects. And dialect contact does not normally lead to reduction. Because of the mutual intelligibility of the varieties in contact, there is normal transmission from one generation to another, and restriction in function does not result. However, both admixture and simplification can be observed to occur. Typically, new dialects resulting from dialect contact contain a mixture of forms from the different contributing dialects. Interestingly, though, they may also demonstrate a greater degree of regularity, i.e. simplification, than was present in any of the original dialects.

Standard English   Modern Standard English, then, is a koiné which is the outcome of very considerable dialect contact indeed: it was subject to the processes involved with dialect mixture over a period which lasted for several centuries. This fact is rather well known, and there is considerable evidence of it. For example, Wyld (1936: 50) describes the language of the Proclamation of Henry III, a text written in 1258 in the precursor of Modern Standard English, as demonstrating a "characteristic blending of Midland elements with those which are typically southern". He then writes, of similar texts from the period 1300 to 1325, that the "Southern element is still considerable but the Midland element is larger" than before (1936: 51); and he then goes on to say (1936: 52), of the 14th-century standardized English of the time of Chaucer, that "London English had by this time settled down into a definite blending of the various dialectal elements". This mixture, however, was in a state of flux for many generations. For example, "Chaucer's poetry contains more purely Southern and South-eastern elements than his prose" (1936: 52); and "the precise regional dialect constituents of London English were not finally fixed in their present proportion and distribution during the 15th century, nor indeed for some time after the beginning of the following century" (1936: 97). The language of Wycliffe, for example, is very Midland in origin; it has hardly any purely Southern features, but it does have some specifically East Midland features, together with "some indication of Northern influence" (1936: 59).

Hope (2000: 50), too, says of the London speech which became standard that "it is tempting to ask what dialects were *not* present in this Londonish–East Midlandish–Northenish–Southernish 'single' ancestor" of Standard English. Strang extends Wyld's period of flux a good deal further when she writes that "in London circles during the 16c and 17c many different usages … were jostled together" (1970: 165). And Lass adds that "the modern standard has a heterogeneous dialect base" (2000: 91). This picture of long-term mixture and flux is not at all surprising when we note from Keene (2000: 109) that "most adult Londoners were born outside the city" and that "in the 18th century the outsiders may have been as many as two-thirds of the total".

As a consequence, Standard English has undergone considerable simplification. For example, the disappearance of the second person pronoun forms *thou/thee/thy/thine* represents the clear loss of a morphological category—the distinction between singular and plural is no longer operative in the second person.

A further example is provided by the phenomenon of multiple negation, as in *I couldn't find none nowhere.* Another label for multiple negation is *negative concord* or *negative agreement*; and Standard English, as is well known, has lost this form of agreement—a good example of reduction of repetition of information, i.e. simplification. It is true that the loss of multiple negation is often ascribed to the successful efforts of 18th-century prescriptivists to exercise normative pressures against it, based on peculiar ideas about logic. However, Auer and Gonzalez Diaz (2005) cite empirical evidence from the history of English which shows that there is a "danger of overestimating the explanatory potential of prescriptivism". For instance, in the case of the loss of double comparatives such as *more nicer* from Standard English, they show that prescriptivism "can only be considered a mere reinforcing factor of a process that was set in motion earlier".

So it is very relevant that Rissanen (2000) has shown that the decline of multiple negation in written English started well before the period in which prescriptivism became operative—it began at the latest in the 15th and 16th centuries (see also Nevalainen and Raumolin-Brunberg 2003; Nevalainen 2006). It is probable, then, that what actually set this process "in motion" was the considerable degree of contact to which pre-Standard English had been subjected. This is somewhat speculative, of course, because if all the regional dialects that were in contact had identical forms of multiple negation, this simplification would have been unlikely to happen; so this presupposes that the different dialects had different negation mechanisms. But this seems perfectly possible. To take just one potential example, it was at this time—from the 1500s at least—that the functional use of *do* in negative sentences was beginning to establish itself (Lightfoot 1979); and of course while this change was taking place, over a number of generations and at different times in different places, there would have been considerable inter-dialectal variability in upper-class London speech, involving as it did a mixture of the different innovating and conservative regional varieties of the many in-migrants, as well as those of the minority of locals.

Low-contact varieties   To return now to low-contact varieties, the argument that communities of this type favour complexification receives initial support in the case of English from the important corpus and survey-based work of Kortmann and Szmrecsanyi (2009). They provide comparative analyses of about fifty varieties of English from around the world, applying cleverly devised complexity metrics to pidgins such as Ghanaian Pidgin English, creoles such as Belizean Creole, Second Language Englishes such as East African English, high-contact mother-tongue Englishes such as colloquial Australian English, shift varieties such as Welsh English, and traditional-dialects such as Newfoundland English. Their detailed results, which repay careful examination, show amongst many other things that the low-contact traditional-dialects of English do indeed show the highest level of complexity amongst English varieties, although this does of course result in part from retention of original complexity as well as from the development of new forms of complexity that I am focusing on here.

Dahl similarly shows that the peripheral Swedish dialect of Älvdalen in Dalecarlia (Dalarna), in central Sweden, "comes out as considerably more complex than [standard] Swedish" in terms of morphology, but makes the same caveat (2009: 56).[4]

I therefore suggest that it does indeed make good sense to look for cases of spontaneous, non-additive complexification in relatively isolated low-contact nonstandardized varieties of modern European languages, such as English tradional-dialects, in comparison with their respective standard and urban varieties.

In addition, we can also look at those languages which are similarly spoken only by small groups of speakers in low-contact communities, such as Faroese and North Frisian, and

---

[4] Dahl treats the two varieties as closely related but different languages, *Swedish* and *Elfdalian*.

compare them to related languages. It is true that, as has often been pointed out to me, North Frisian and Faroese have both in fact experienced considerable contact, in that their speakers are and have for centuries been bilingual in their native languages and German/Low German/Danish. However, the relevant point here is, as we saw in Chapter 2, what *type* of contact it is: Faroese and North Frisian dialects have no significant history of having been acquired by outsiders—that is, by post-critical threshold non-native speakers. Contact in the Faroe Islands has consisted mainly of native speakers of Faroese acquiring Danish as an L2, *not* the other way round. There is no significant history of Faroese being subjected to post-critical threshold acquisition on a wide scale, and therefore no simplification. The same point can be made about North Frisian—(Low) German bilingualism. In other words, my easy cover term "isolation" may not be totally appropriate, since I am really using it to refer to absence of contact of a particular sort.

And to make myself clear on another point, I am not claiming that complexification will *inevitably* occur in low-contact varieties—a point I will discuss further in Chapter 6. Neither am I suggesting that complexification will occur *only* in low-contact varieties. The suggestion is merely that there is a tendency for complexification to be more common—probably a great deal more common—in low-contact than in high-contact varieties.

If it does turn out to be true that the most common pattern is one of complexification events occurring in traditional-dialects and "small languages", which are not paralleled on anything like the same scale by similar developments in high-contact urban, colonial, or standard varieties, then the thesis that the growth of complexity does tend to depend for its genesis largely on low-contact linguistic environments will be confirmed.

Methodology   It is important that this search for complexification events be carried out comparatively, by ranging English traditional-dialects against General English (Wells 1982), Mundart against Umgangssprache, Faroese against Swedish, and so on. And we must necessarily be concerned with *diachronically demonstrable* complexification, because different levels of complexity between high-contact and low-contact varieties could be due to simplification in the high-contact varieties just as much as to complexification in low-contact varieties. By doing this work comparatively and feature-by-feature, moreover, we will also be able to avoid the pitfalls associated with attempting to develop some kind of quantitative measure for the calculation of complexity.

Using English and other Germanic languages as examples, I now go on to produce evidence in favour of the isolation-complexification hypothesis, by producing examples of dia-chronically demonstrable linguistic changes which are of the complexification type, and which have occurred in varieties spoken in communities that most closely meet the category of *low contact*. Crucially, they are also changes which have no counterpart in related high-contact urban dialects or standard varieties.

The Germanic languages lend themselves particularly well to this investigation, because in these languages we can find striking contrasts, within a limited geographical area, between sociolinguistically very different communities speaking related dialects and languages, from which we can deduce with some accuracy which complex features are retentions, corresponding to simplification in other varieties, and which are the result of actual complexification.

I will proceed by examining in turn a number of cases of the four different subtypes of complexification, as listed above—although close examination of the actual examples will show that the distinction between the four categories is not always a clear-cut one.

Complexification 1: Growth of morphological categories

Under this heading I present examples of the historical devel-opment of new morphological categories in low-contact var-ieties which are not paralleled in other related higher-contact varieties, and where there is no evidence of the new category having been acquired as a result of additive borrowing.

(1) A few traditional-dialects in a small area of the southwest of England saw the development of a new and fascinating marking of the difference between transitive and intransitive

infinitives. Transitive infinitives were unmarked, while in-transitive infinitives in these dialects were marked by the word-final morpheme *-y*, e.g. *to hit* vs. *to runny*. So in Dorset we find (Gachelin 1991):

> *Can you zew up thease zeam?* 'Can you sew up this seam?'
> vs.
> *There idden many can sheary now.* 'There aren't many who can shear now'.

This remarkable morphological marking of intransitivity is unparalleled anywhere else in the English-speaking world—quite possibly unparalleled anywhere else at all—and is at least extremely rare. My enquiry on the *LINGTYP* list asking for examples of other languages which have morphological mark-ing for intransitive but not transitive infinitives received three answers from the linguistic typology community, none of them producing a precise parallel. The Australian Aboriginal lan-guage Warrgamay (Dixon 1981) has two sets of inflections—those that can attach to intransitive verbs and those that cannot attach to intransitive verbs—but this applies to all verb forms and not just infinitives. A similar situation applies in Ulwa, a Misumalpan language of Nicaragua.[5] The closest we can come to southwestern English distinction is in the Anywa language, a Nilo-Saharan language of Ethiopia and Sudan, where special marking does occur on intransitive infinitives, but only on those which are derived from transitives, which are then marked relative to their transitive counterparts: 'weave [tr.]' vs. 'to do weaving' (Reh 1996: 187).

My suggestion is, of course, that it is not at all a coincidence that in English this development has occurred in a traditional-dialect and not any of the mainstream varieties. In Chapter 4 below, I will consider the mechanisms by means of which this development of different infinitival forms may have taken place in English.

(2) A number of traditional-dialects in the southwest of England developed an interesting phenomenon, described by Ihalainen (1976) for East Somerset, in which there is a category distinction between habitual and punctual verb forms such as:

---

[5] Data received, with thanks, from Andrew Koontz-Garboden.

I do go there every day.
I did go there every day.
     vs.
I goes tomorrow.
I went last week.

Given that this is a distinction between two categories which is common enough in the languages of the world, this is in one sense not a particularly noteworthy development. What is highly noteworthy for the topic of this chapter, however, is that this grammatical development represents a genuine innovation in English, and one which did not occur in Standard English or in any urban varieties: the category distinction is unknown in any of the General English varieties.

(3) Traditional-dialects in the English southwest also developed the expression of a pronominal category difference between count and mass nouns (Wagner 2005), such that inanimate count nouns are pronominalized with *he* but mass nouns with *it*:

Pass the loaf—he's over there.
     vs.
I likes this bread—it be very tasty.

This too is unparalleled elsewhere in the English-speaking world, except in the tradional-dialects of Newfoundland, as Paddock describes them (1991). Here, too, we find that "cheese as a <mass> noun selects the NEUTER pronoun *it*; but a *slice of cheese selects* ... the MASCULINE *he*" (Paddock 1991: 30). However, the Newfoundland dialects in question are known to derive historically from migration from the English southwest—they have "Wessex origins", as Paddock says (1991: 29). Crucially, though, this type of system is once again unknown in any variety of General English (for a fuller discussion see Siemund 2008).

Interestingly, this development is paralleled by a similar change in the isolated Danish dialects of West Jutland, whereby non-count/mass nouns are neuter and all other nouns are common gender. Haugen (1976: 61) says—inaccurately in view of the southwest of England development—that this area has developed an entirely idiosyncratic system unparalleled anywhere else in

Germanic. The extent to which this system is unusual can be seen
from the fact that Haugen (1976: 288) actually uses an exclam-
ation mark when he points out that not only is the noun *melk*
'milk' neuter but *barn* 'child' is common, which is the reverse of
the situation in all other varieties of Scandinavian.

(4) Certain North Frisian dialects have developed a distinction between two different definite articles (Ebert 1971;
Ebert and Keenan 1973; Walker 1990: 14–15). In the Mooring
dialect of the Bökingharde area the two sets of forms are:

masc.	*di*	*e*
fem.	*jü*	*e*
neut.	*dåt*	*et*
pl.	*da*	*e*

The usage of the two forms is grammatically and semantically
complex (see Markey 1981: 228), but typically the -*e*/-*et* forms
are proximal and/or refer to a unique referent, as in *e moune*
'the moon', *e wjard* 'the truth', whereas the *di/jü/dåt/da* forms
are distal and/or are context-bound and apply to definite but
non-unique referents. For example, 'I have spoken to the
village-mayor' can be rendered in two ways:

(a) *ik hääw ma e bürgermäister snååked*
(b) *ik hääw ma di bürgermäister snååked*
     'I have with the mayor spoken'

In (a) the reference is to the mayor of one's own village, whereas
in (b) it is to the mayor of some other village. Similarly, in the
Fering dialect (the dialect of the island of Feer/Föhr), as Ebert
(1984) points out, a question posed by some non-native-speaking
outsider in a particular village along the lines of:

Huar wenet di bürgermäister? 'Where does the mayor live?'

would solicit the answer:

Hün bürgermäister mänst dü? 'Which mayor do you mean?'

A question seeking information about the local mayor should
rather employ the article *e*.

This distinction is clearly an innovation and, to say the least,
has no parallel in any of the standard forms of other Germanic

languages. In Chapter 4 below, I consider by what means this phenomenon might have developed.

(5) In the Toten dialect of Norwegian (Faarlund 2000), complexification has occurred in the demonstrative system. A system of demonstrative pronouns and adjectives has developed which is not found in either of the standard forms of Norwegian and, crucially, was not found in Old Norse either. A three-way distinction has evolved, as follows.

(a) There are, first, a group of proximal demonstratives corresponding to *this* in English and to *denne/dette/desse* (masc.-fem. sg./neut. sg./pl.) in Nynorsk and *denne/dette/disse* in Bokmål. In Toten these are *denni/detti/dessi*.

(b) Then we find the second Toten group: *danna/datta/dassa*. These distal demonstratives refer "to something which is visible in the conversational situation, and which the speaker … can point to" (Faarlund, 2000: 54, my translation):

> *Danna boka (somm ligg dær) har je itte lesi.*
> 'That book (which is-lying there) have I not read.'
>
> *Veit du åkke somm bor i datta husi dær?*
> 'Know you who that lives in that house there?'
>
> *Dassa såkka (somm ligg bortpå stola) er reine.*
> 'Those socks (which are-lying over-there-on chair-the) are clean.'

(c) The third series—*denn/ dæ/ dei*—"is used for something which is not visible to the interlocutors, but has recently been mentioned in the conversation" (Faarlund 2000: 54, my translation):

> *Denn boka (somm du næmnde) har je itte lesi.*
> 'That book (which you mentioned) have I not read.'
>
> *Veit du åkke somm bor i dæ huse (somm vi nettopp tala om)?*
> 'Know you who lives in that house (which we just were-speaking about)?'
>
> *Dei såkka (somm du spør ætter) ær møkkete.*
> 'Those socks (which you are-asking about) are dirty.'

A similar development has occurred in other Norwegian dialects, as well as in Faroese. There is, again, nothing unusual about a three-way deictic system, something which is found very widely in the languages of the world; but the fact is that this can be shown to be an innovation, and one that has occurred in relatively remote, rural varieties.

(6) The rural English dialect of the county of Norfolk has innovated a new verbal category which is not found in Standard English. The non-negative present tense of the verb *to be* is identical to the Standard English paradigm: *I am, he/she/it is, we/you/they are.* However, there is also a distinct presentative form of the verb which has *be* for all persons (Trudgill 2003):

> *Here I be!*
> *Ah, here you be!*
> *Where's Bill?—look, there he be.*

Presentatives are common enough in the world's languages—French *voici* and *voilà* are well-known examples—but the development of a distinct verbal paradigm with this particular function in this English dialect is a striking example of a complexification unknown in Standard English.

(7) Old Norse had a distinct singular imperative form, but none for the plural. One of its modern descendants, however, Faroese, has developed a singular–plural distinction for the imperative, something which is unknown in any other Nordic language:

> *Far til hús!*   Go home! (sg.)
> *Farið til hús!*   Go home! (pl.)

As Thráinsson et al. (2004: 67) write

there was no distinctive imperative plural form in Old Norse (nor is there one in Modern Icelandic), where the 2pl. indicative had this role. In Faroese, on the other hand there is a distinction between the default finite forms and the imperative forms, both in the singular and the plural

"We have here," Thráinsson et al. continue "an *innovation* in Modern Faroese" [my italics].

(8) Thráinsson et al. (2004: 92) also point out that "Germanic languages typically do not have a plural form of the indefinite article". Faroese, however, has innovated such a form. It is used with nouns that only occur in the plural, or to indicate "a pair of" something. The singular forms are as follows:

	m.	f.	n.
nom.	*ein*	*ein*	*eitt*
acc.	*ein*	*eina*	*eitt*
dat.	*einum*	*eini/einum*	*einari*

The plural forms are:

	m.	f.	n.
nom.	*einir*	*einar*	*eini*
acc.	*einar*	*einar*	*eini*
dat.	*einum*	*einum*	*einum*

Thráinsson et al. cite examples such as:

Eg keypti einar skógvar	'I bought a pair of shoes'
Eg keypti einar buksur	'I bought a pair of trousers'
Eg keypti eini hús	'I bought a home'

In the last example, the neuter noun *hús* is in the accusative plural. The singular form of the same noun, *eitt hús*, would mean 'a building'. Once again, we find an innovation in Faroese which has not occurred in any of its larger Nordic relatives, or indeed in any other Germanic language.

Complexification 2: Increase in syntagmatic redundancy

It is interesting to note that the examples I have located under this heading are of two different types. Example 9 is a case of a particular discourse strategy whereby speakers choose to optionally repeat information more frequently in some dialects than others. Examples 10 to 15, on the other hand, represent examples of grammatical agreement. It is possible or even probable that the latter type derive diachronically from earlier stages which resembled the former type—it is typical, of course, of grammaticalization that optional features become categorical (see Chapter 4).

(9) The empirical and theoretical work of Berthele (2006), which is based on field recordings of discourse in dialects of Swiss German (as well as French and Romansch), is especially helpful on the topic of redundancy development because it provides some quantitative data. One of the phenomena which Berthele has focused on is the use of complex, redundant pleonastic constructions involving prepositions and adverbials with motion and posture verbs, in which information is given twice. Swiss German examples from his recordings (Berthele 2006) include examples such as:

und iez tuet er ufe baumstamm uufchläddere (p. 183)
and now does he up-a tree-trunk up-climb
'and now he climbs up a tree trunk'

de hirsch hed ne da übernes bord abbegrüärt ine täich ine (p. 184)
the stag has him then over-a bank down-thrown into-a pond into
'the stag then threw him over a bank down into a pond'

ischer dri usse gsprunge übernes nesseli usse (p. 184)
is-he in-there out jumped over-a nettle out
'he jumped out into there over a nettle'

Of particular value is Berthele's (2004: 101) discussion of the data from the Swiss German valley dialect of Muotathal. The Muotathal

is a place with a high degree of linguistic and cultural idiosyncrasy. The population is characterised by relatively dense, close-knit and multiplex social networks, which can easily be inferred from the small set of last names borne by a large portion of the native population.

And the valley has "relatively traditional language-ecology conditions" with "low levels of migration, higher education, and valley-external ties" (p. 102).

According to Berthele, Swiss German dialects as a whole tend to show greater syntagmatic redundancy in both stative and dynamic spatial expressions than Standard German, which is of course interesting for our thesis. But it is clear from his data that this is much truer of Muotathal than of the other dialects he investigated: the rural dialect of the Wallis/Valais, the rural Sensler dialect of Canton Freiburg, the urban dialect of Berne, and Standard German. The percentage of verb phrases with redundant direction marking in the different Swiss dialects he investigated is as follows:

Wallis   12%
Berne   15%
Sensler   17%
Muotathal   23%

Speakers of the high-contact Standard German in Berthele's sample, on the other hand, use fewer than half the number of redundant expressions of those used by Muotathal speakers: 11% (Berthele 2006: 188).This is consistent with the suggestion that it is in small, dense, close-knit societies that redundancy is most likely to increase.

   (10) In the English traditional-dialect of Norfolk, a form of double tense marking or 'past tense infinitives' can be found which is absent from Standard English. For example:

Have the fox left?
No that ain't, do Bailey would've let them went.
'No it hasn't, or Bailey would've let them [the hounds] go.'
(Trudgill 1995)

The form *do* is functioning here as a conjunction with the meaning of "or, otherwise" (for the origins of this feature, see Chapter 5). But my focus here is of course on the fact that the marking of the past tense on *went*, in what in other varieties of English would be a non-finite verb form, makes for an additional element of redundancy.

   (11) De Vogelaer (2004: 190) notes that subject doubling occurs in a number of Belgian Dutch dialects. For example, the sentence

Ze hebbe-en zieder drie kinderen.
they have they three children
'They have three children.'

contains three person markers: the *-en* third person plural marker on the verb plus two forms of the subject, the clitic pronominal form *ze*, and the pronoun *zieder*.

More remarkably, in East Flemish dialects (De Vogelaer 2004: 191), subject tripling actually occurs in the first person plural. A verb can take a preverbal pronoun and two post-verbal pronouns. The three pronominal forms are *wij* 'we', *we* 'we' [weak form], and *me* 'we' [clitic form]. De Vogelaer cites as an example:

> *We zulle-me wij dat doen.*
> we shall-we we that do
> 'We shall do that.'

The signalling of the subject by three different instances of forms of the first person plural pronoun provides an excellent example of redundancy of the repetition-of-information type.

(12) Another rather extraordinary instance of redundancy development in Germanic also comes from the work of De Vogelaer on Flemish. According to De Vogelaer (2005: 35), certain Flemish dialects have developed a highly unusual system of person agreement on the words corresponding to English *yes* and *no*, referred to by him as "answer particles".

> *Zullen we gaan? Jom.* 'Shall we go? Yes [1pl.].'
> *Heb je dat gedaan? Jok.* 'Have you done it? Yes [1sg.].'
> *Is het warm vandaag? Jot.* Is it warm today? Yes [3sg.].'

This person-marking is obligatory—all instances of *jo* have to be marked for person, with *jot* being the default form unless a clear plural or first or second person subject is involved. It is, I suggest, not a coincidence that this interesting "rarissimum" has developed where it has, and not in Standard Dutch.

(13) Dialects of Bavarian German (Bayer 1984) have developed person agreement marking on complementizers—another true "rarissimum" (De Vogelaer and van der Auwera 2010). For example, second person singular marking occurs on *ob* 'whether' in agreement with the pronoun *du* 'you-sg.' and *kumm-st* 'come-2nd sg.' in:

> *... obst du noch Minga kummst*
> whether you (sg.) to Munich come
> '... whether you are coming to Munich.'

Second person plural marking also occurs on *ob*, with the suffix *-ts* being repeated on the verb, in:

... *obts ihr noch Minga kummts*
... whether you (pl.) to Munich come
'... whether you are coming to Munich.'

The same phenomenon occurs in certain dialects of Dutch/ Flemish (Van Haeringen 1939; Haegemann 1992; Corbett 1991: 113; Weiss 2005). This is also a highly interesting development; and I examine some difficulties in accounting for how it and similar phenomena might have developed in the following chapter.

Complexification 3: Increase in morphological opacity

Braunmüller (1984) has argued that morphological opacity is a typical characteristic of "small languages", such as Faroese. The most relevant aspect of opacity for our current discussion is the one which is referred to by Kusters (2003: 21) in his *transparency principle*—as we saw earlier—as a demand "that the relation between form and meaning is as transparent as possible". The highest level of transparency or analyticity is when "every single meaning is expressed in a separate form". Kusters cites the loss of allomorphy in Arabic as an obvious simplification under this heading. Correspondingly, growth in allomorphy, obviously, represents a clear case of loss of morphological transparency, and thus an increase in complexity. The examples in this section are all cases of increases in allomorphy: a lower degree of correspondence between a grammatical category and its expression (see Haiman 1980; Bauer 2001: 59).

(14) The first example of increase in allomorphy comes from an English dialect and, crucially, has not been paralleled in high-contact varieties of the language. This concerns the third person singular neuter pronoun. In nearly all English dialects, including Standard English, *it* is both the subjective and the objective form. In certain rural dialects in East Anglia (Norfolk, Suffolk, north Cambridgeshire), however, a complication has developed. In subject position the neuter singular pronoun is not *it* but *that*. This is particularly clear in the case of the "weather pronoun" where no possibility exists that we are dealing with the homophonous demonstrative:

That's raining.
That's cold in here.

But there is no doubt that it also operates in genuine prono-
minalization:

I see the cat—that was on the wall.

However, in object position the pronoun takes the form *it*:

The cat?—I just see it on the wall.

The allomorphy is apparent in examples such as:

I don't like it when that's raining.
I don't want it—that's no good.

This is not only an increase in allomorphy, it is also an extremely unusual development in the Indo-European languages
generally, where there is normally no formal case distinction
between nominative and accusative in neuter nominals.

This allomorphic distinction is not mentioned in the post-
humously published Forby (1830), who states that he is de-
scribing the Norfolk dialect as it was spoken in the period 1780
to 1800—he himself uses subject *it* in his illustrative examples.
And I have found no cases in the 15th and 16th-century letters
written by the Norfolk family, the Pastons. The distinction is
probably therefore a relatively recent instance of complexifica-
tion-development.

(15) In the traditional-dialect of East Somerset (Ihalainen
1991) and elsewhere in southwestern England (Wagner 2005),
a pronominal allomorphy more complex than that found in
other dialects of English has developed in the third person
singular masculine. The subject form of the pronoun is the
expected *he*:

He's older than what I be.

The object form is *'n* /ən ∼ n̩/, which generally functions just
like *him* in other dialects:

I looked up to un and said 'What's say?'

However, there is an additional form of the subject pronoun
which Ihalainen refers to as a question clitic, and which occurs

obligatorily in tag questions. It is not immediately obvious that this form derives from *he, him* or *'n*. Ihalainen writes it as *her* or *er,* but it is phonologically /əɽ ~ ɽ/:

He do live in Latcham, don' er?

This type of pronominal allomorphy is of course not unknown in the world's languages. The point is, however, that it has developed here out of an earlier, simpler system, and that it was in a traditional-dialect that the development occurred.

(16) Most varieties of Frisian have two forms of the infinitive, as did Old Frisian (Bremmer 2009: 84). However, the Bökingharde dialect of North Frisian (Walker and Wilts 2001: 295–6) has developed an even richer allomorphy, with three different infinitival forms.

(a) Forms with the suffix *-e* occur after modal and auxiliary verbs: *hi wal bål kaame* 'he will soon come'. In some cases, this form of the infinitive shows even greater opacity by being irregular and having palatalization in place of the *-e* suffix: *düünj* cf. *douen* 'to do, give', *schiinj* cf. *schaien* 'to happen'.

(b) Forms ending in *-en* occur when the infinitive stands alone, after the preposition *tu* 'to', and after certain verbs such as *bliwe* 'to stay', *hiire* 'to hear': *douen än fouen hiire tuhuupe* 'giving and receiving belong together'.

(c) Forms with a zero ending occur after the conjunction *än* 'and': *dåt as ai lacht än snååk tjüsch* 'it is not easy to speak German'. The corresponding form of the verb 'to do' is *dou*.

Complexification 4: Irregularization

Here I discuss two cases of irregularization. The first is quite clearly due to sound changes which, as is usually the case, were themselves quite regular. The second is rather different: some of the irregularizations are examples of regular verbs fitting into established strong verb patterns, but others of them are somewhat mysterious.

(17) Older Faroese had a complex system of noun declension, including numerous irregular paradigms such as that for *dagur* 'day':

	sg.	pl.
nom.	[dagur]	[dagar]
acc.	[dag]	[dagar]
gen.	[dagås]	[daga]
dat.	[degi]	[døgum]

This was a system which was relatively complex in post-threshold learnability terms. There were seven different forms to learn, and there was a low level of morphological transparency.

However, crucially for our hypothesis, the complexity of the nominal system of Modern Faroese is now even greater than that of the earlier language. The contemporary declension for this same noun is (Braunmüller 2001: 73):

	sg.	pl.
nom.	[dɛavʊr]	[dɛːar]
acc.	[dɛa]	[dɛːar]
gen.	[daǧs]	[dɛːa]
dat.	[deːji]	[døːvʊn]

The complexity—the irregularity—of this paradigm is colossal; and the development also represents a large increase in degree of allomorphy. As Braunmüller says, only the consonantal onset remains constant throughout the paradigm.

Braunmüller cites similar cases in a number of other Modern Faroese noun subclasses also:

	skógvur 'shoe' (masc.)		*kugv* 'cow' (fem.)	
	sg.	pl.	sg.	pl.
nom.	[skɛgvʊr]	[skɛgvar]	[kɪgv]	[kʊir]
acc.	[skɛgv]	[skɛgvar]	[kɪgv]	[kʊir]
gen.	[skɔus]	[skegva]	[kɪgvar]	[kɪgva]
dat.	[skɛgvi]	[skɔun]	[kɪgv]	[kʉun]

So not only is the amount of morphological opacity here considerable but historical linguistic studies also show that it has actually *increased through time*. It is apparent that modern Faroese has in some respects become more irregular than Old

Norse/Mediaeval Faroese, or indeed than Icelandic. High-contact continental Scandinavian, on the other hand, has lost complexity rather than adding it. The corresponding noun *dag* in Standard Norwegian Bokmål, for instance, has only two forms: *dag* (sg.), *dager* (pl.).

I look further at this Faroese development in the following chapter.

(18) Grammatical change may lead to greater irregularity as well as regularity, and it is therefore worth wondering whether irregularization may be more common in traditional-dialects than in General English varieties. In the traditional-dialect of the county of Norfolk, for example, we find a number of irregular preterites which occur in cases where Standard English has regular forms. These include (Forby 1830; Trudgill 2003):

hoe	*hew*	*save*	*seft*
mow	*mew*	*shriek*	*shruck*
owe	*ewe*/ʉ:/	*wave*	*weft*
row	*rew*	*wrap*	*wrop*
sew /sou/	*sew* /sʉ:/ (as of stitches)		
show	*shew*		
slow	*slew* ('he slew down a bit')		
snow	*snew*		
sow	*sew* /sʉ:/ (as of seed)		
thow (thaw)	*thew*		

A few of these verbs had strong or irregular preterites on their first attested appearance in Old English or Middle English. This is true of *mow* and *row*, while *sew* had both strong and weak forms in Old English. In these cases, then, regularization has taken place in Standard English and in the General English nonstandard dialects, while the traditional Norfolk dialect has preserved the original irregularity. The other irregular forms, however, are not historical. *Show,* for example, was a weak verb in Old English, with the preterite *sceawed*, as was *thaw*; and the other verbs were also regular from their earliest appearance. The only exception is *owe*, which goes back to Old English *aȝan*, with the early OE preterite *ahte*, which later gave rise to *ought*, and was superseded as preterite by regular *awede > owed*. So the Norfolk forms *ewe, hew, sew* (of *sew*), *shew, snew, thew, shruck,*

seft, weft, wrop are all innovations which involved irregularisa-
tion. The changes to *ewe, hew, sew, shew, sew, slew, thew* are
obviously the result of analogy with the *blow* class, but the
origins of *shruck, seft, weft,* and *wrop* are less clear.

In sharp contrast to this, colonial American Standard English has regularized verbs which still remain irregular in the
Standard English of England, including:

burn	*burned*
dream	*dreamed*
learn	*learned*
light	*lighted*
spell	*spelled*

Anderwald (2009) shows that the history of *burnt* as opposed
to *burned* (etc.) in English is a good deal more complex than
just this; but the fact remains that in Modern English the
regular forms are less common in England than the USA.

It is often said, as a kind of counterexample, that some forms
of American English, including Standard American English,
have replaced the regular preterite of *dive,* namely *dived,* with
an irregular preterite *dove*—clearly by analogy with the class of
irregular verbs such as *ride/rode.* However, this is not a case of
the development of irregularity in Standard English. According
to the OED, *dove* is also a form which occurs in dialectal
British English, and, more importantly, the verb was a strong
verb in Old English, with the past participle *dofen.*

Summary

In the above list, I have been able to supply 18 examples of
complexifying changes which have occurred in North Frisian,
Faroese, and relatively isolated dialects of English, German,
Dutch, and Norwegian. And for each case, it has been important to stress that no corresponding development has taken
place in any of the standard, urban, or colonial varieties of
any of the Germanic languages. In each case, moreover, it is
well attested that what I have exemplified is an innovative
complexification rather than a conservative absence of simplification. Between them, the changes that I have discussed
also represent examples of all of the four different types of

complexification: irregularization; increase in opacity; increase in syntagmatic redundancy; and addition of morphological categories.

Conclusion

I have attempted to demonstrate here that there is a good case to be made for the argument that spontaneous (as opposed to additive) complexification will develop on a large scale mainly in low-contact communities, where "low contact" refers in particular to an absence of a history of large-scale acquisition by non-native adult speakers. Note, however, that such communities simply provide a background against which complexity *can* develop. They provide conditions which permit but do not necessarily and inexorably produce complexity. We cannot say that complexification will inevitably occur under such conditions—languages spoken in low-contact communities will certainly be found which demonstrate no great complexity.

It is also worth considering the point that spontaneous and additive complexification are not necessarily mutually exclusive. A high degree of complexity is rather likely to develop in languages which have experienced large amounts of both the spontaneous *and* additive complexification type. It will be recalled that the important factor about "isolation" was not that it necessarily implied *total* isolation but rather that it implied, as in the case of Frisian, an absence of any significant history of the language having been acquired by adult non-native speakers. There are many asymmetrical contact situations in which a minority language will be isolated and "low contact" in this sense, and have therefore perhaps produced spontaneous complexification—as well as preserving prior-existing complexity—but may also, as a result of generations of contact with another majority language or languages, have experienced additive borrowing as well.

For example, as described by Kruspe (2004), the aboriginal Semelai of Malaya have "little contact with neighbouring ethnic groups" (2004: 18), but their neighbours are all speakers of (Austronesian) Malay dialects, Austronesian having arrived in the Malayan peninsula only relatively recently—between 2,000 and 1,000 years ago. Semelai is a Southern Aslian language with about 4,000 speakers. The Aslian languages are members of the Mon-Khmer family of Austroasiatic—the "oldest phylum present in mainland Southeast Asia" (Kruspe 2004: xvi). The language has two types of morphological system: a complex concatenative system of prefixes, suffixes, and circumfixes which has been acquired through contact with Malay (additive complexification); and a complex, endogenous non-concatenative system of prefixes and infixes (spontaneous complexification).

I have argued above for the legitimacy of this sociolinguistic-typological insight about spontaneous complexification with examples from morphological data, but there is some indication that it may well be valid for phonology as well (see Trudgill 2004c; and Chapter 5). My argumentation, moreover, has relied on material from Germanic languages only. These languages do provide a very suitable laboratory for this type of investigation, as we noted above. But comparisons within other language families would obviously be highly desirable.

4

Mechanisms of complexification

In the previous chapter I presented evidence to suggest that there might be a link between type of community and the spontaneous development of linguistic complexification. It is, however, one thing to produce data to indicate that this might be the case, and another matter altogether to explain *why*, if there is such a link, this should be so.

Let us now therefore examine, in turn and briefly, the four different types of complexification, as defined and illustrated in Chapter 3, and see how this kind of development might work in a little more detail. What follows will not be an in-depth account of the linguistic mechanisms and processes which lead to complexity-development. I will not ask *exactly which* but rather *what sorts of* mechanisms might in principle be involved in particular types of complexity-development. I will do this in order to be able to ask what sorts of different sociolinguistic conditions might be of relevance in permitting or encouraging the operation of such mechanisms. While we will be looking at only one or two examples of each of the four different types of complexification, the mechanisms that appear to be involved in their development will hopefully give us some indication of what social conditions might favour the operation of such mechanisms generally.

Increase in opacity

We begin with increase in opacity. This type of increase can of course take a number of forms, but let us consider initially just one kind. We saw earlier that low morphological transparency is typical of fusional languages such as Faroese, as opposed to agglutinating and isolating languages (Dixon 2010a: 226ff.).

This point can be illustrated using well-known phenomena from archetypical exemplars of the three morphological types—isolating Vietnamese, agglutinating Turkish, and fusional Latin:

	'from a man'	'from men'
Vietnamese:	*tu nguoi*	*tu nguoi*
	from man	from man
Turkish:	*adam-dan*	*adam-lar-dan*
	man-abl.	man-pl.-abl.
Latin:	*homine*	*hominibus*
	man + abl. + sg.	man + abl. + pl.

A comparison of paradigms shows that the forms of *adam* 'man' in Turkish are totally transparent:

	sg.	pl.
nom.	*adam*	*adam-lar*
acc.	*adam-i*	*adam-lar-i*
gen.	*adam-in*	*adam-lar-in*
dat.	*adam-a*	*adam-la-ra*
loc.	*adam-da*	*adam-lar-da*
abl.	*adam-dan*	*adam-lar-dan*

In Latin, on the other hand, segmentability is low, as was pointed out in Chapter 2:

	sg.	pl.
nom.	*homo*	*homines*
acc.	*hominem*	*homines*
gen.	*hominis*	*hominum*
dat.	*homini*	*hominibus*
abl.	*homine*	*hominibus*

The genitive plural of *homo* is *hominum*, but it is not possible to separate out distinct genitive and plural morphemes.

It is in fusional languages such as Latin that Kusters's (2003) *transparency principle*—the demand that the relation between form and meaning should be as transparent as possible—is most heavily violated. Any linguistic change, therefore, which leads a language in the direction of the development of a more fusional character will have as a consequence increased opacity, and therefore complexification. And indeed one does not necessarily have to accept in full the validity of the concept of the morphological cycle (Hodge 1970), in which languages are said to move from an isolating type to agglutinating to fusional and back to isolating again, to agree that agglutinating languages can indeed become less agglutinating and more fusional over time.

As an example of this kind of change, we can take the following forms from Finnish, a well-known agglutinating language, in comparison to the same paradigms from the closely related but less agglutinating Finnic language Estonian:

	Finnish		Estonian	
	'leg'	'flag'	'leg'	'flag'
nom.sg.	*jalka*	*lippu*	*jalg*	*lipp*
gen.sg.	*jala-n*	*lipu-n*	*jala*	*lipu*
part.sg.	*jalka-a*	*lippu-a*	*jalga*	*lippu*
part.pl.	*jalko-j-a*	*lippu-j-a*	*jalgu*	*lippe*

The Finnish word-forms are readily segmentable because of the agglutinating structure. It can easily be seen that *-j-* is the plural morpheme, *-n-* the genitive, and *-a* the partitive. The stem remains constant throughout the paradigm, moreover, except for the small amount of allomorphy provided by the alternation in the genitive singular between *k* and Ø in *jalka*, and *pp* and *p* in *lippu*. Crucially, these alternations are entirely predictable. The Estonian paradigms, on the other hand, are much less transparent. The forms are not readily segmentable— the separate partitive and plural morphemes in Finnish have been fused in Estonian, for instance; and the alternations—for instance, between partitive plural *-u* and *-e*—are unpredictable.

It is known that the Estonian forms are more innovative than the Finnish, and that they developed out of originally more agglutinating forms similar to those of Finnish. We can see then that Estonian has experienced changes which have not occurred in Finnish, and that these changes have had the complexifying effect of obscuring an originally more transparent morphological structure. When we come to consider what processes might have been implicated in this development, it is clear that the changes involved were phonological in origin: all original word-final segments, for instance, have been lost in Estonian.

If it is the case that fusional inflections develop out of the (originally phonological) fusing of earlier, more analytic agglutinating structures, as in Estonian—"fusional structures depend diachronically upon agglutinating ones" (Dahl 2004: 184); and if it is the case, as has been argued, that agglutinating morphology may in turn in some cases develop out of clitics, which have in turn developed out of independent lexemes through grammaticalization processes, then Comrie (1980) has given us some indication of how this might happen. He illustrates, from the Finnic languages, a typical path of development: noun > postposition > clitic > suffix > case ending. In the Balto-Finnic of the first millennium BC (Campbell 1997b), the form *kanssa* was an independent noun meaning 'people'. In modern Finnish it has become a comitative postposition:

hyvä-n poja-n kanssa   'good-GEN boy-GEN with'

Note that its independent lexical status is demonstrated in the fact that there is no vowel harmony in constructions with *kanssa*. In the related language Vepsian, on the other hand, a further stage of development has occurred, and the corresponding form *ka* has become a bound comitative suffix:

lahse-ka 'with the child'   *lehmä-kä* 'with the cow'

The bound status of the form is indicated by the vowel harmony alternation between *ka* and *kä*.

In the Finnic language Karelian, on the other hand, the comitative form *kela* has become more than just a bound suffix: here there is not only vowel harmony but also agreement within the noun phrase (see below on the development of agreement):

kolme-n-kela lapše-n-kela   'with three children'
tütö-n-kelä   'with the girl'

The final stage in the development of fusional forms, where segmentability is lost, can be seen in the example already given above where Estonian *lippe* has lost the segmentability of Finnish *lippu-j-a*.

These few examples just hint at the sorts of developments that are required for the development of fusion and inflection; but what interests the sociolinguistic typologist is what kind of social matrix is most likely to accompany and produce this kind of opacity-producing development. In what kind of social conditions are we most likely to see the development of highly fusional, inflecting languages like, say Proto-Indo European, or Latin, or Polish, perhaps out of an earlier more analytic, agglutinating ancestor of Proto-Indo-European?

In fact, it is easy to see, when it comes to considering what kind of sociolinguistic conditions are necessary here, that relatively long periods of time will be required for these grammaticalization processes to run their course (see Chapter 6 on Dahl's (2004) introduction of the notion of the "mature phenomenon"). As Lichtenberk (1991) points out, grammaticalization is *gradual*. There can be no guarantee that other forms of opacity-development, such as increases in allomorphy, can be regarded in exactly the same way. But from the sociolinguistic-typological perspective, we can suggest that processes which lead to an increase in fusional structures are such that they must be allowed to run for a long time, uninterrupted by periods of significant adult language contact, in order to result in the type of outcome we are discussing.

Of the two sociolinguistic parameters we have so far mentioned in this book, *contact vs. isolation* and *stability vs. instability*, both would seem to be crucial. High levels of contact would lead to more, not less, transparent forms; and only stable situations will permit the uninterrupted development of mature, inflectional morphology in a language over the long periods of time required. At least this particular form of opacity-development, then, is more likely to develop in relatively stable, low-contact communities.

Irregularization

Let us now turn to irregularization and ask how exactly this, too, comes into being linguistically.

The answer to this question, as far as certain forms of irregularization are concerned, is already well known from the historical linguistics literature. One of the examples we used in Chapter 3 to illustrate increase in irregularity and opacity came from Faroese. For ease of exposition I repeat the data here. Older Faroese had irregular nominal paradigms such as *dagur* 'day':

	sg.	pl.
nom.	[dagur]	[dagar]
acc.	[dag]	[dagar]
gen.	[dagås]	[daga]
dat.	[degi]	[døgum]

The complexity of the modern nominal system is now even greater:

	sg.	pl.
nom.	[dɛavʊr]	[dɛːar]
acc.	[dɛa]	[dɛːar]
gen.	[daǧs]	[dɛːa]
dat.	[deːji]	[døːvʊn]

We saw that Braunmüller pointed out that only the consonantal onset remains constant throughout the paradigm.

If we now wish to investigate the kind of mechanisms involved in producing this type of complexity-development, it is apparent that the increase in morphological opacity and irregularity in Faroese is due, once again, to phonology—to sound change. It is of course a historical-linguistic commonplace that regular sound changes can lead to grammatical irregularity (see Hock 2003: 450 on Sturtevant's Paradox); but from the point of view of sociolinguistic typology we can now expand this point somewhat further by considering the actual nature of the particular sound changes involved here in Faroese.

Most linguists would probably agree that the sound changes which have occurred in continental Scandinavian in recent centuries have been rather more natural and expected, and rather less complex, than many of those which have occurred in Faroese. For example, the vowel shift undergone by Swedish and Norwegian such that /ɑː/ >/ɔː/> /oː/ > /uː/ > /ʉː/ > /yː/ strikes no linguist as being at all strange, especially after Labov's work on vocalic chain shifts (1994). And the lenition of intervocalic voiceless stops in Danish (and in some varieties of Norwegian, Swedish, and Icelandic) is also a very common type of change:

p > b > β > w   Norw. /pi:pə/ vs. Dan. /pi:wə/
t > d > ð > ð̥   Norw. /ga:tə/ vs. Dan. /gɛ:ð̥ə/
k > g > ɣ > j   Norw. /ka:kə/ vs. Dan. /kɛ:jə/

This lenition is a change which has been repeated with high frequency in the world's language families, witness for example Latin -*atum*, Italian -*ato*, Spanish -*ado* > [-aðo] > [ao].

On the other hand, the Faroese sound changes implicated in the development of irregularity and opacity in the above paradigms are intuitively felt by many historical linguists to be rather unusual. And I would suggest that such intuitions are important and valid—when Bailey (1982) writes of languages with "incredible" consonant clusters, this is a legitimate observation (see further Chapter 5). The Faroese changes involved in this increase in morphological opacity include:

(1) the well-known "Verschärfung" or 'sharpening', whereby rather startling changes occurred which led to correspondences between modern Danish and modern Faroese such as:

Danish Faroese
/ku:/   /kigv/   'cow'
/ny:/   /nudʒ/   'new'

Sandøy (2005: 1867) explains that this development occurred during the 18th century. In diphthongs where [i] or [u] was the second element in contexts before an immediately following vowel, these second elements became respectively a palatal affricate and a "velar cluster". Thus *oyin* 'the island' became *oyggin* [ɔjj:ɪn], and *bʊa* [bʉu:a] 'live' became *bʊgva* [bɪgva]. Then, by analogy, "many words transferred the sharpened form to the final position in the other forms of the word, cf. *oyggj* 'island'. We can understand up to a point how this happened, but there is perhaps still something slightly mysterious about vowels becoming consonants in the case of [i] > [ɟj] and [u] > [gv].

Note also that this change is not totally dissimilar to the change often known as Holtzmann's Law, whereby a stop was introduced into geminate j and w clusters in Gothic and in Old Norse, giving ON *tryggva*, cf. OHG *triuwa*, 'troth'; ON *tveggia*, cf. OHG *zweiio* 'of two' (Scardigli 2002: 557). The sociolinguistic typologist cannot help but note, of course, that this change took place at a time when the ancient Germanic languages would also have been spoken only by relatively small groups of speakers.

(2) Diphthongizations also took place in Faroese in the period 1350–1550 (Haugen 1976: 256) which gave rise to forms such as /luyk/ from earlier /liːk/ 'like'. Note that some of these diphthongizations led to mergers:

iː > ui	uː > yu
yː > ui	øː > øe
æː > æɑ	oː > ou
eː > æɑ	åː > åɑ

(3) ð was lost, and g was lost intervocalically and finally, by about 1600. This gave rise to many new instances of vowel–vowel hiatus. Subsequently a new "intrusive glide" developed in many such cases of hiatus, with the identity of the glide depending on the quality of the two vowels in contact:

maður > [mɛaːvʊɹ] 'man'
blair > [blɔaːjɪɹ] 'blue' (pl. masc.)
skógur > [skouːwʊɹ] 'forest'.

Again, the development of the intrusive consonants /j/, /w/, and especially /v/, is not as expected as the earlier loss of /ð/ and /g/.

It is possible to argue, then, that not only is the increased morphological complexity of Faroese due to sound change, as is so often the case, but perhaps more especially that in this case, at least, it is also due to the fact that at least some of these sound changes can be classified as "unusual" (see more on "unusual" sound changes in Chapter 5).

Furthermore, it is very encouraging for a sociolinguistic-typological study of the social matrices in which irregularization and opacity-development occur to note that Henning Andersen (1988) has also proposed a serious sociolinguistic correlate of the development of marked as opposed to unmarked sound changes (see further Chapter 5). Andersen points to unusual sound changes in dialects which "are located in peripheral dialect areas, away from major avenues of interdialectal communication", and his hypothesis is that "there is a connection between the limited socio-spatial function of a dialect, its relative closeness, and its ability to sustain *exorbitant phonetic developments*" (1988: 70; [my italics]).

It may indeed be the case, then, that isolated communities are more likely to produce changes that could be labelled, in Henning Andersen's (1988: 70) careful words, "slightly unusual". Andersen argues that socially and geographically peripheral speech communities are more prone to develop phonologies with elaborate phonetic norms and the proliferation of low-level pronunciation rules: "dialects that serve predominantly local functions are more prone to elaborate phonetic detail rules than dialects with a wider sphere of use".

Notice that while we are clearly dealing here with the relevance of our first social parameter *contact vs. isolation*, we now also seem to be focusing as well on an additional parameter, so far not overtly discussed in this book. In an important paper, Braunmüller (1984) has argued that morphological opacity is a typical characteristic of *small languages*. Hymes, too, says that "the surface structures of languages spoken in small cheek-by-jowl communities so often are markedly complex, and the surface structures of languages spoken over wider areas less so" (1974: 50). Thurston, too, has argued (e.g. 1989—and see also Chapter 2) that there is a lower degree of variation in small traditional communities characterized by *esoterogeny*—that is, they are not acquired by non-native speakers—and that this promotes the development of morphological irregularity. And indeed there is further evidence in the literature—see for example Haudricourt (1961)—that community size may be linguistically important. There is a statistical, if inconclusive, discussion of the relevance of this parameter in Wichmann et al. (2008). More helpfully, in a detailed statistical paper which takes Trudgill (2004c) as one of its starting points, Sinnemäki (2009: 139) concludes that "by and large, the present paper indicates that language complexity is not necessarily independent of sociolinguistic properties such as speech community size".

Certainly, a number of the communities we pointed to in previous chapters as being isolated and stable, and therefore demonstrating slow rates of change and maintenance of complexity, also have languages that have always been spoken by relatively small groups. For example, there are today approximately only 45,000 Faroese and 225,000 Icelandic speakers, as opposed to 5 million Norwegians, 6 million Danes, and 8 million Swedes. Sandøy (2001: 127), moreover, writes that the population of the Faroes from the Middle Ages until almost 1800 was only about 5,000, divided into 40 or 50 settlements, giving about 100–125 people per settlement; and in mediaeval times, the population of each Icelandic settlement averaged only 7–10 people.

I therefore now add to this study of the relationship between social and linguistic typology a third, apparently relevant social parameter, namely *small vs. large community size* (in terms of numbers of speakers).

Nettle suggests a statistical explanation for this parameter. He points out that, for example, object-initial constituent order is exceedingly rare in the world's languages. Indeed, it was unknown to academic linguistics generally until the 1970s, when Desmond Derbyshire, with the crucial encouragement of Geoff Pullum, published a short but exceedingly important paper on OVS order in the Amazonian language Hixkaryana in the widely read *Linguistic Inquiry* (Derbyshire 1977). Nettle points out that all the languages which have this feature are spoken by small or very small numbers of speakers: the median number is 750, compared to 5,000 for the world's languages as a whole. He suggests that non-optimal orders are "more likely to be found in small communities than in large ones, since these would be more vulnerable to drift away from optimal states" (1999: 139). In population genetics, Nettle says, the effects of random change are known to be greater when the population is small, for statistical reasons. "This is because the probability of a slightly deleterious variant becoming fixed in a population is inversely related to the population size. The smaller the community, the greater the stochastic chance of changes in gene frequency" (Nettle 1999: 139). Nettle then hypothesizes that the same might be true of linguistic communities and linguistic features.

If we wonder what might be "non-optimal" about OVS and OSV order, it is relevant that Givón (1984: §7.3) argues that SOV is in some sense the basic order—and indeed the earliest pattern to be found in human language—and is favoured by factors to do with the role of the position of agent/topic and goal/object in the origins of human communication; he also argues that diachronic development to SVO, VSO, or VOS, where this has occurred, has been favoured for reasons of a discourse-pragmatic nature (1984: §7.11). OVS and OSV, how-ever, are not favoured in either way.[1] (We can perhaps also extend this statistical account of Nettle's to other "non-optimal", "less usual", or "exorbitant" linguistic features.)

The three different social parameters that have now been established so far—contact, stability, and size—can very readily be linked. Although our discussion of simplification in Chapter 3 focused on contact vs. isolation, my proposal now is that in fact simplification is most likely to be found in communities which are characterized not only by high levels of contact but by a particular *complex* of all three of these social parameters.[2] Linguistic simplification, I suggest, is most likely to be found in communities which demonstrate *high contact* (of the post-critical threshold type), *social instability*, and *large size*. Cor-respondingly, therefore, spontaneous complexification is most likely to emerge in communities characterized by *low contact, social stability*, and *small size*.

But why should this be so? The answer, I propose, lies in the seminal work of James and Lesley Milroy (and work following on from theirs—see for example Ross 1997). A key social distinction adumbrated in Milroy and Milroy (1985) and J. Milroy (1992b) is between communities with dense, multi-plex social networks—in layman's terms, communities where it is common for everybody to know everybody else, and where your neighbour and your second cousin and your workmate may be one and the same person—and communities with loose networks, where the reverse is the case. Zabrocki (1963), too,

---

[1] Dixon's (2010b: 75) caveat should be noted here: many languages do not have a fixed constituent order, and even for languages which do the matter is "of only marginal interest for basic linguistic theory".

[2] It is important to stress this point because certain commentators on my earlier work have focused on one or other of these factors to the exclusion of the other two—see Chapter 6.

distinguishes between tight and loose communicative communities. How tight a communicative community is, he says, depends on the speed and frequency of the communication between its members.

From the work of the Milroys, notably in Belfast, it can be concluded that dense networks lead to strong social ties, which then lead to closer maintenance of community norms—in language as in other forms of behaviour. On the other hand, loose networks lead to weaker social ties and so to a relative lack of maintenance of community norms. The Milroys argue, surely correctly, that "linguistic change is slow to the extent that the relevant populations are well established and bound by strong ties, whereas it is rapid to the extent that weak ties exist in populations" (1985: 375; see also L. Milroy 2000).

Dense social networks are most likely to be found in small, stable communities with few external contacts and a high degree of social cohesion. As Croft (2000: 192) points out, "a close-knit network is of necessity small in size: it is difficult for everyone to know and talk to everyone else in a large society". Loose social networks are more liable to develop in larger, unstable communities which have relatively many external contacts and a relative lack of social cohesion. Linguistic change is liable, other things being equal, to be faster in larger than in smaller communities;[3] and instability is also associated with faster rates of change, as we saw in Chapter 1.

We can now see that the role of instability is due to the weakening of social network ties in situations of social breakdown and chaos. Raumolin-Brunberg, for example, in her discussion of the rapid changes in English we discussed in Chapter 2, specifically claims that the period during and after the English Civil War "must have witnessed a considerable increase in weak ties" and actually gives chapter and verse from the content of her data: "many of the letters in the *CEEC* [*Corpus of Early English Correspondence*] in fact testify to the splitting up of families and broken neighbourhood ties". In her work on the loss of multiple negation in English, Nevalainen (1998: 281) also ascribes a role to social networks: "a Milroyan type of weak-ties

---

[3] Taking size as their only criterion, however, and without looking at networks, Wichmann et al. (2008) find no evidence for or against this hypothesis.

network structure could well have been the means of spreading the loss of multiple negation". This is based on research also involving data from the *Corpus of Early English Correspondence* using texts from the period 1417 to 1681.

This insight into the social-network causes of differential *speeds* of change, as discussed in Chapter 1, can now also be extended to differences between *types* of change. Given that there is a strong tendency for relative density of social networks to correlate with community size, we can note the comment made by Grace (1990: 126), who writes:

A language exists in the people who speak it, but people do not live very long, and the language goes on much longer. This continuity is achieved by the recruitment of new speakers, but it is not a perfect continuity. Children (or adults) learning a language learn it from people who already speak it, but these teachers exercise considerably less than total control over the learning process.

We must accept that no 'teachers' exercise total control, but this perspective does also suggest that, because of differences in social network structure, there is a possibility that in smaller communities the 'teachers' have more control than in larger societies. Because of this, small tightly-knit communities are better able to encourage the preservation of norms and the continued adherence to norms from one generation to another, *however complex they may be*; and the absence of external contacts and social instability will also strengthen a community's ability to maintain its own linguistic complexity.

If this is so, then it is not unreasonable to suppose that these same societal factors may also assist in the *production* of complexification. In small, isolated, stable communities, linguistic change will be slower. But when it *does* occur, there is a greater chance that it will be of the complexification type—the other side of the coin from high contact and loose networks leading to rapid change and simplification. Small isolated communities are more able, because of their network structures, to push through, enforce, and sustain linguistic changes which would have a much smaller chance of success in larger, more fluid communities—namely changes of a relatively marked, complex type. Indeed, it may even be that, as Nettle

(1999: 138) says, "if a group consists of just a few hundred people, the idiosyncrasies of one very influential individual can spread through it very easily".

So not only is there less simplification in low-contact situations, there is indeed also more complexification, as argued in the previous chapter. That is, it may well be that *innovations* of a complexification type occur with roughly equal frequency in all types of community, but that it is simply the case that these innovations are likely, perhaps much more likely, to succeed and become established linguistic *changes*, i.e. innovations which are accepted and become permanent, in small isolated communities. For opacity, for example, we can say that innovations which render forms less transparent may well develop in all types of community, but they are much more likely to be successful ultimately in communities with tight social networks. And we can see why it is in larger language communities that irregular verbs are more likely to become regular, while the reverse may occur in smaller communities—irregularization is just less likely to succeed in larger societies.

This opens up the possibility of applying the above general account of the social correlates of complexification to particular cases. Regular sound change can lead to grammatical irregularity, but the more "exorbitant" the sound change, the greater the irregularity is likely to be. The sort of remarkable irregularization found in Faroese is the result of the kind of "exorbitant phonetic development" that is more likely to occur in small isolated communities because it is in such communities, as I just argued, that social network structures make for greater likelihood of complex changes being pushed through, enforced, and sustained from generation to generation.

Maybe other forms of irregularization such as Norfolk dialect *wrapped* > *wrop* will not be so susceptible to the same kind of analysis, but it does now seem that we have found an additional, fourth social parameter to add to our list of factors that may be implicated in producing different types of linguistic structure, namely *dense vs. loose social networks*.

Growth of morphological categories

If we now turn to the spontaneous growth of morphological categories, we saw in the previous chapter that there seemed to be a greater likelihood of this type of complexification, too, occurring in certain types of community. But what mechanisms can be involved in this kind of development? And what social contexts would favour the operation of such mechanisms, and how would they do so?

If we turn to the examples I used in Chapter 3, we can see that the same kind of mechanisms were at work in a number of the cases discussed there. One of these was the development, as an innovation in southwest of England dialects, of the distinctive marking of intransitive as opposed to transitive infinitives: intransitives take *-y*, transitives are unmarked: *he can't swimmy* vs. *he can't hit it*.

How this situation came about diachronically seems to be reasonably clear. Once again, phonological change was crucially implicated in what eventually became a grammatical development. The intransitive *-y* ending is considered to be a relic of the Middle English infinitive ending *-en*, later [-ə] or presumably, in the southwestern dialects in question, [-ɪ] (Ihalainen 1991). Originally, all infinitives would have carried this vowel. Later, as is well known, the final unstressed vowel was eventually lost in most dialects. Presumably, while this loss was occurring, there was a period of variability of the type that normally accompanies change, with alternation between older forms and newer forms with and without the final vowel, respectively. A useful hypothesis would be, however, that during this period the vowel was originally lost less often in utterance-final position than when another word, e.g. an object noun, followed.

Support for this interpretation can be gained from observations of similar developments in Scandinavian dialects. Torp (2003: 249) shows how in certain of the Swedish dialects of Bohuslän, the unstressed final vowels of infinitives preceding a direct object have been subject to reduction to [-ə], while in certain other contexts, such as before an adverbial phrase, the original unreduced vowel *-a* is retained:

Ve feck järe de vi kunne
we got to-do that we could
'We had to do what we could'

vs.

Va feck du jära där på Strândräng?
what got you to-do there at S.
'What did you have to do there at S.?'

Similarly, Torp also cites Christiansen (1948: 191), who shows that in the Norwegian dialect of Vefsn a similar process has gone even further: infinitive endings alternate between -Ø and -*a* depending on sentential context, just as I am supposing happened in the English southwest:

Han sku kåm ijæn 'He should come back'
vs.
Kanj du kåmmä? 'Can you come?'

We can then suppose that it was at this kind of variability stage, in the southwestern English dialects in question, that the difference between forms with and without the vocalic ending eventually became reinterpreted in such a way that a difference without a distinction became a difference with a distinction. The difference, which was originally phonologically conditioned and variable, came to be reinterpreted as grammatico-semantic—transitive vs. intransitive—and categorical. Crucially, it was the frequent presence (vs. absence) of following object nouns which led to this transitive (vs. intransitive) reinterpretation of forms without -*y*.

This is a form of reanalysis (Harris and Campbell 1995: 30) or *exaptation* (Lass 1990; 1997): formerly meaningless differences end up being employed to make meaningful distinctions. Exaptation, as Lass (1997: 318) says, can lead "to the development of new grammatical categories", and he further argues (1997: 319) that exaptation is "conceptual invention" and "what was once a predictable alternation ... can be ... reanalysed as a new primary categorical marker"—which is precisely what has happened here.

A similar argument can be made for the development of the distinction between the two different sets of definite articles in

North Frisian. It will be recalled from Chapter 3 that in the Mooring dialect the two sets of forms are:

masc.	*di*	*e*
fem.	*jü*	*e*
neut.	*dåt*	*et*
pl.	*da*	*e*

and that the *-e/-et* forms are proximal and/or refer to a unique referent, such as *e moune* 'the moon', while the *di/jü/dåt/da* forms are distal and/or are context-bound and apply to definite but non-unique referents.

The forms in the left-hand column descend directly from the nominative definite article forms of Old Frisian: *thi, thiu, thet, tha* (Bremmer 2009: 54). As Hoekstra (2001: 777) indicates, the forms in the right-hand column are in origin "weak variants" of the forms in the left-hand column, i.e. they were originally phonologically reduced forms which occurred in unstressed environments. So in origin they were simply phonologically conditioned and therefore predictable variants, as they still are in many dialects. However, in the Mooring and other innovating dialects, the two types of variant have been reanalysed as having distinct semantic-grammatical functions, and refunctionalized as applying to non-unique (etc.) vs. unique (etc.) referents (Löfstedt 1968). Of course, "have been reanalysed" does not really answer the question as to why the exaptation took the form that it did—why the variants have been reanalysed in this particular way: strong forms = distal, weak forms = proximal. But we can perhaps hazard a guess that it might have had to do with the more demonstrative-type function of the stonger unreduced, perhaps more frequently stressed, variants.

Given that this type of diachronic exaptational refunctionalization of variants is common enough in linguistic change generally, the question then is: why might reanalysis, leading to morphological-category development, be more likely to occur in some social matrices than others?[4] The answer would appear

---

[4] I do not intend to suggest that reanalysis is necessarily the only mechanism leading to new morphological categories, although I currently have no suggestions as to what the other mechanisms might be.

to be that this is the type of change which naturally takes place when a language is not in contact with other languages— changes which Bailey (1982) refers to as *connatural*. We can suppose that it is more common in low-contact, smaller, stable communities because it requires some generations of uninterrupted native-speaker development for completion. As Croft (2000: 193) puts it, "linguistic isolation allows for processes of change to evolve to an elaborate degree that would otherwise be curtailed by levelling or simplification in a larger, more loose-knit society".[5]

Exaptation of this type, however, will be less common in high-contact communities because it makes for greater L2 difficulty.

Increase in syntagmatic redundancy

Finally, let us now turn to the fourth type of complexification— the tendency for syntagmatic redundancy, or repetition of information, to become more common in what we can now describe as being smaller, more isolated, low-contact communities with dense social networks.

This, it has to be said, is less obviously explicable. Indeed, it might have seemed more logical if it were the other way round. In small tightly-knit communities where there is a higher degree of shared knowledge and information, one would have thought that less repetition would be necessary, not more. The clue, however, may lie in the word "necessary". Linguistic change is not teleological (Lass 1990; 1997: 340ff.); changes are never "necessary"—they just happen. And the development of agreement, the most common form of syntagmatic redundancy, does seem to be an extraordinarily common process in linguistic change. According to Corbett (2006: 1), agreement is "a widespread and varied phenomenon".

Part of this problem of agreement-development being less obviously explicable than other changes may have to do with the fact that, as Corbett says, the functions of agreement are by no means totally clear, and "agreement often appears to

---

[5] For more on the social matrices that favour the growth of morphological categories, see Chapter 6.

involve a lot of effort for a questionable payoff" (2006: 274). Acuña-Fariña (2009: 390) also writes that "maybe the greatest puzzle about agreement systems lies in their apparent arbitrariness and uselessness". And so it is hardly surprising that pidgins, creoles, and other high-contact language varieties tend to manage without it, and that adult language contact tends to reduce it.

In this chapter we are trying to produce insights into the social settings which favour complexification by considering some of the linguistic mechanisms involved in its production. We therefore need to consider how agreement develops. There is actually a considerable consensus in the literature about the nature of the development of at least certain types of agreement. Lehmann (1988: 59), for example, argues that "the most important and most regular diachronic source of agreement is pronominal anaphora (including cataphora). More precisely, agreement markers usually stem from pronouns". Corbett (2006: 264) agrees, saying that "it has long been accepted that pronouns provide a major source of agreement morphology, progressing from full pronouns, to clitics, to inflections along a well-established grammaticalisation path", with the result that referential pronouns become agreement markers. Number and gender agreement arise specifically from the grammaticalization of third person pronouns, which get cliticized and then become affixes. From original structures where there was, say, a cliticized subject pronoun as well as an overt subject, the grammaticalization process produces a situation where the overt subject now agrees with the verb by means of the newly grammaticalized marker.

Where the development of agreement markers out of pronouns is relatively recent, there may be clear evidence that this is what has happened. In Manambu, a Ndu language of Papua New Guinea with about 2,500 speakers investigated by Aikhenvald (2008b: 51), there is phonotactic evidence for this hypothesis. In monosyllabic monomorphemic words, "if C_1 and C_2 have the same place of articulation, the coda (C_2) cannot be more voiced than the onset (C_1). That is, words like **pab* and **tad* are not well-formed". However, this constraint is not operative when the final consonant is an agreement marker, thus *ta:d* 'he stands', which is bimorphemic and where the -*d* is the third person masculine singular marker, is well formed. Aikhenvald argues (p.c.) that words which contain a morphological boundary behave differently from monomorphemic words because agreement markers such as -*d* are derived from independent pronouns. It was not so long ago since *ta:d* was actually two words, she suggests, so

a synchronic violation of the constraint on distribution of voiced and voiceless consonants within a monosyllabic word of CVC structure can be used as a piece of evidence in favour of the origin of agreement markers from independent pronouns.

Indeed, the pronominal origins of agreement markers can be seen not only in cases of verb agreement but also in some instances of the remarkable phenomenon of complementizer agreement that was noted in Chapter 3. Haegeman (1992), for instance, gives Flemish examples such as:

K'peinzen dan-k   ik morgen   goan
I think   that-1sg.   I tomorrow go
'I think I'll go tomorrow'

where it is clear that the -*k* postposed to the conjunction *dan* is historically derived from the pronoun *ik* 'I'.

Not all cases of agreement-development, however, involve pronouns. Aikhenvald argues that different types of agreement develop in different ways diachronically. She concurs that verbal agreement "usually arises from an anaphorically-used independent pronoun which is subsequently cliticised to the verb; it then becomes incorporated as an agreement marker. The mechanism is basically pragmatic, and it involves reanalysis and grammaticalisation of independent members of a closed class" (2000: 392).

But the development of gender agreement within a noun phrase can be the result of two different mechanisms, as proposed by Heine and Reh (1984: 230–1). In the first, the path for creating gender agreement does indeed once again include pronouns: it "involves the pragmatic use of third person pronouns as a kind of 'afterthought' to specify additional information" (Aikhenvald 2000: 393). In the second, however, "agreement may arise if demonstratives develop into subordination markers, e.g. relative clause markers, as the result of their grammaticalisation" (2000: 392). She cites an example from the work of Heine and Reh (1984: 231) from the Nilotic language Maasai as follows:

in-kíshú na-á-apshana na-á-ibor
PL-cattle REL-PL-seven REL-PL-be.white
'seven white cows'

The key mechanism in all these cases, then, seems to be some form of grammaticalization, although there are many aspects of developments of this type which are not fully understood. The extent to which grammaticalization is the result of pragmatic and cognitive (Heine et al. 1991), discourse (e.g. Comrie 1980), morphological, syntactic (see Li 1975), or phonological (e.g. Comrie 1980) processes is an important and unresolved question, although factors of all these types would appear to be involved. And Joseph (2001, 2004) has argued that grammaticalization is not really a "process" as such at all. Rather,

most of what is observed and labelled as such under this rubric is best taken as a result of independently needed and recognised processes of language change, namely (phonetically driven) sound change, (morphologically and conceptually driven) analogy, semantic change (especially metaphor), reanalysis, and borrowing, and not as a separate process in and of itself. (Joseph 2009: 199)

Fischer (2009) agrees about grammaticalization: "as a process, it is an analyst's generalization, a convenient summary but not something that has actually 'happened'" (2009: 18). (For a critique of these views, see Wischer 2006.) Dahl (2004) argues that phonological change plays a crucial role in grammaticalization: "I see changes in structure as typically driven by phonological changes". And Harris and Campbell (1995: 67) agree that grammatical reanalysis can be triggered by phonological change: they show, for example, that in some Nuclear Micronesian languages such as Ponapean (Pohnpeian), noun incorporation has developed in certain constructions as a result of the phonological erosion of verb forms. (See more on the importance of phonology in Chapter 5).

To return to the genesis of agreement, however, it turns out that there are many other more perplexing cases where grammaticalization does not seem to be involved at all. For example, the Bavarian examples of complementizer agreement cited in Chapter 3 do not fit into this scenario. In forms such as:

... obst du noch Minga kummst
whether you-sg. to Munich come
'... whether you are coming to Munich.'

the agreement marker *-st* on *ob* 'whether' is clearly not the result of the grammaticalization of a pronoun—it is simply a repetition of the person marker that originally appeared only on the verb *kumm-st*. So how and why does this repetition develop? Why would a verbal person-marker end up attached to something which is not a verb?

The same question can be asked of the scenario outlined by Marchese (1988). She examines the development of agreement systems via noun class markers in the Kru languages of Liberia and Ivory Coast, and suggests that the trajectory is: subject pronoun > definite marker > (noun) class marker, with the class marker "eventually collapsing into the stem" (1988: 339). Beginning with original proto-Kru topic-comment structures such as

li ɛ kʊ mɔ
spear it is over-there
'The spear, it's over there'

Marchese hypothesises that the subject pronoun then undergoes cliticization and reanalysis as a definite marker on the noun. For example, in Godié the outcome is:

li-ɛ kʊ mɔ
spear-DEF is over-there
'The spear is over there"

But how exactly does this definite marker turn into a noun class marker—where does the actual *agreement* come from? The degree to which agreement-development is such a poorly understood phenomenon is nicely illustrated by Marchese's account of how this happened: "once the reanalysis had taken place in this position, the definite suffix would eventually make its way onto other NPs in the clause" (1988: 339). Yes, but how and why do such markers "eventually make their way" onto further elements, something which has to happen if agreement is going to develop? Similarly, why did Karelian speakers start saying *kolme-n-kela lapše-n-kela* 'with three children'?

Some mechanisms that may lie behind these developments have been proposed. For the very rare Bavarian, and similar, complementizer agreement cases, De Vogelaer and van der Auwera, (2010) argue for "analogical extension". And De Vogelaer (2010) describes 'pathways' via which such extensions occur, again appealing to analogy. But do we understand why and how this "extension" would happen? And what exactly is "analogical" about it? If we are to claim that person markers are added to complementizers by analogy with person markers on verbs, we have to be clear that this is surely not analogy as it is usually understood, since this normally involves proportional relations.

Andersen similarly suggests that agreement-development of this type stems from what he calls *expression doubling*—"expression doubling is presumably the typical source of concord and agreement" (2008: 26).[6] But is this actually an explanation? Why are expressions "doubled" in this way? What exactly happens?

Similarly, Dahl writes of the development of gender agreement in Indo-European languages that one of the major problems is how to explain "how gender markers come to be obligatory parts of e.g. adjectives and verbs" (2004: 199). The standard theory, he says, and as we saw above, is that gender markers derive from pronouns. "Then one has to assume a stage where there is obligatory 'redundant' or doubled use of these pronouns" (2004: 199). But what he does not say is why and how this doubling happens.

The answer seems to be that experts in the field do not yet fully understand what happens. Corbett's book (2006) on *Agreement* consists of 284 pages of text, only five of which are actually devoted to origins. As Corbett states, "agreement remains deeply puzzling" (2006: 1).

Perhaps we can content ourselves for the time being with noting that human languages are "like that". And, happily, it is

---

[6] Comrie (p.c. 2009) has similarly suggested that apposition might be involved.

rather clear why languages should be "like that". Aikhenvald
has hit the nail on the head when she points to "pragmatic
use" and to the fact that "the mechanism is basically pragmatic". As she explains it, a prerequisite to the emergence of
some forms of grammatical agreement is likely to be a repetition technique, whose function is "to clarify what is being
talked about" (p.c. 2009). Redundancy, in the form of "expression doubling", develops because redundancy is very helpful to
human speakers in actual, real-life discourse. We have already
noted in Chapter 3 the optional repetition that occurs to
different extents in various Swiss German dialects (Berthele
2006), as in

> *und iez tuet er ufe baumstamm uufchläddere* (p. 183)
> and now does he up-a tree-trunk up-climb
> 'and now he climbs up a tree trunk'

And I already suggested there that this helpful discourse strategy could be a stepping stone towards obligatory, grammatical
repetition.

In the examples cited in Chapter 3 from Berthele (2006), the
repetition illustrated in Swiss German cases such as:

> *de hirsch hed ne da übernes bord abbegrüärt ine täich ine*
> (p. 184)
> the stag has him then over-a bank down-thrown into-a
> pond into
> 'the stag then threw him over a bank down into a pond'

is simply a discourse phenomenon, where the speaker apparently has some choice in the matter. On the other hand, the
Flemish examples of person agreement on answer particle
cited from De Vogelaer (2005), such as

> *Zullen we gaan? Jom.* 'Shall we go? Yes [1pl.]'

represent a later stage of agreement-development (with the -*m*
derived diachronically from the clitic form of the first person
plural pronoun *me*) where the person marking has become
compulsory.

Taking all this into account, the widespread occurrence of
agreement in the languages of the world implies that, if linguistic change proceeds without the large-scale involvement of

adult non-native speakers in contact situations, agreement is rather likely to develop over time even in constructions where there was none before. And if repetition—redundancy, expression doubling—for the purpose of "clarifying what is being talked about" occurs frequently enough in discourse, then it may become grammatical and thus compulsory. But, it seems, it will only do that if, as it were, it is given enough time to do so. That is, agreement, too, can be considered to be a *mature phenomenon* (see Chapter 6).

Agreement-development is once again, then, the type of change described by Bailey (1982) as *connatural*—the sort of change which takes place when languages are not in contact with other languages. We can suppose that this type of development is less common in large fluid high-contact communities because, as we said above, repetition of information means that there is more for non-native speakers to learn—it makes for L2 difficulty/outsider complexity. And it is more common in smaller, stable communities because complexity-development of this kind needs many generations uninterrupted by contact to come to fruition.

In Chapter 6 there will be a further discussion of the implications for sociolinguistic typology of these complexity-producing mechanisms.

5

Contact and isolation in phonology

We have now established a number of interconnected social factors which can be argued to have consequences for linguistic structure, notably complexity. It will be recalled that, as outlined in Chapter 4, these factors are: linguistic contact vs. isolation (with "isolation" as defined in Chapter 3), social stability vs. instability, small vs. large community size, and dense vs. loose social networks. In this chapter, I examine the possibility that these, and maybe other, factors might also have certain consequences for phonology. The question is whether sociolinguistic-typological generalizations can be made for this linguistic level as well. It is, I would suggest, not prima facie nearly so obvious that this can be the case as it is for morphology and morphosyntax.

Contact and simplification in phonology

In Chapter 3, I proposed that insights into the distribution of certain linguistic features over the world's languages could be gained by noting that:

- short-term adult language contact tends to lead to simplification
- long-term language contact tends to lead to additive complexification
- isolation tends to lead to spontaneous complexification.

This proposal was made on the basis of mostly morphological data, but in Chapter 4 we did note that phonological factors are crucially involved in the production of linguistic complexity, and it seems legitimate to ask whether the proposal can be extended to aspects of phonology too.

As far as short-term language contact involving adult speakers is concerned, there is in fact considerable evidence to suggest that this can indeed lead to simplification in phonology—although of course in this case simplification has to an extent to be defined rather differently. For those most extreme outcomes of language contact, pidgin languages, Sebba (1997: 47) says that they normally have "relatively simple" phonological systems. Features which we can regard as instances of simplification include the fact that "typically pidgins avoid phonologically marked sounds", and that they tend to favour CVCV phonotactics. Labov (1990) adds that pidgins typically have little stylistic variation at the phonological level, and little allophonic variation.

The most obviously quantifiable aspect of this simplification, however, is the fact that pidgins generally have smaller phoneme inventories than their lexifiers. And the picture is broadly similar as far as creoles are concerned. The English-lexifier pidgin/creole Bislama, as spoken in Vanuatu, is typical in its mesolectal form in having fewer consonants—18—than its lexifier, lacking a number of (relatively marked) articulations found in most varieties of mainstream English: it has no /θ ð z ʃ ʒ dʒ/. Different basilectal varieties lack even more of the consonants of English, notably /v/. (Bislama also has phonotactics which "can be described in general as being somewhat simplified with respect to the consonant-cluster possibilities that we find in English" (Crowley 2004: 686), so that *stamp* is /stam/ and *box* is /bokis/.)

The same is true of vowel systems. Bislama has a 5-vowel system, compared to the 20 or so of most varieties of English English (Crowley 2004). And Holm (1988) shows that the English-based creoles of the Caribbean have all merged a number of the vowels that are distinct in the English of England. At the most extreme end, he reports that Sranan has a 5-vowel system, like Bislama. Basilectal St Kitts Creole (Cooper 1979), on the other hand, has 13 vowels, having merged the vowels of the lexical sets of NURSE and STRUT, TRAP and LOT, NEAR and SQUARE, GOAT and FORCE, START and NORTH, and PRICE and CHOICE.

There is one particular problem to consider with pidgins and creoles, however, in that it can always be argued that the relatively simple phonological inventories and other features that they demonstrate are the result, not of contact-induced simplification as such, but of interference. For Bislama, for example, it could be said that the segmental phonological system is the result of contact between English and indigenous Austronesian languages which themselves have rather small systems.

It is therefore helpful that insights about contact and phonological simplification also emerge from work on dialect contact (Trudgill 1986). Labov has maintained (1994) that in dialect contact situations, mergers tend to spread at the expense of contrasts. Obviously, other things being equal, mergers lead to smaller inventories. Just one example out of many of contact-induced simplification is provided by the new mixed urban dialect of Norwegian spoken in Høyanger, which has lost the affricate /ʝʝ/ which is found in all the surrounding dialects (Omdal 1977). Even more interesting, while a majority of Norwegian varieties have four indigenous diphthongs, and while the original local dialects in the area have five, the modern koinéized Høyanger dialect has only three (Trudgill 1986: 105):

ORIGINAL DIALECT	MODERN HØYANGER	GENERAL NORWEGIAN
/ei/		/ei/
/ai/	/ai/	/ai/[1]
/øy/		/øy/
/oy/	/oy/	
/æu/	/æu/	/æu/

This also tallies with observations by other writers. For instance, Jakobson (1929: 82) suggests that the geographically more widely used varieties of a language, particularly prestige varieties (which, I would argue, tend to be the most heavily koinéized), tend to have simpler phonological systems than dialects with a more restricted function: "dialects which serve as vehicles of communication in large areas and gravitate

---

[1] /ai/ actually has a rather marginal status in General Norwegian.

towards the role of koiné tend to develop simpler systems than dialects which serve purely local purposes".

Additive complexification in phonology

We also saw in Chapter 3 that long-term contact involving childhood bilingualism leads to complexification via additive borrowing. Can this also be demonstrated for phoneme inventories? It would certainly seem to be likely that, if stable, long-term contact situations involving childhood bilingualism can lead to additive complexification, then large phoneme inventories might be favoured by such situations because the long-term presence of many neighbouring languages would mean that segment-types can readily be borrowed from one language to another, thus leading to increased inventories.

Happily, this does indeed seem to be the case. Rivierre (1994), for example, supplies a range of phonological examples of what he refers to as contact-induced phonological complexification in the Austronesian languages of New Caledonia. These include the acquisition of voiceless aspirated consonants in Koné-area languages from Polynesian and other sources. And the process can certainly also be seen to have been at work in the case of certain Polynesian languages themselves. Hajek (2004: 349) observes that "there is no doubt that language contact through close proximity with non-Polynesian languages has led to phoneme borrowing, through intensive and longstanding childhood bilingualism". Some Polynesian Outlier languages which came into contact with phonologically more complex languages, as in parts of Melanesia, have added consonants: Proto-Polynesian had an inventory of only 13 consonants (Clark 1976; Krupa 1982), while West Uvean, an Outlier, has 26 (Clark 1994).

As with morphological categories, additive borrowing is also very obviously apparent in the phenomenon of the Sprachbund, or linguistic area. From the Caucasian Sprachbund, Haudricourt (1961) cites the extinct Caucasian language Ubykh, mentioned in Chapter 2, which had a very large phoneme inventory including (at least) 78 consonants. Velaric ingressive consonants ("clicks") are found in the languages of southern Africa regardless of genetic affiliation. And, similarly, nearly all the languages of the South Asian sub-continent, of whatever language family, have retroflex consonants.

It is usually clear in cases such as these that Sprachbund-type effects have developed as a result of additive borrowing. For example, it is obvious that those Bantu languages of southern Africa which possess clicks have acquired them as the result of contact with Khoisan: all Khoisan languages have clicks, and the vast majority of Bantu languages do not. The addition of a whole new manner of articulation—a new and unusual airstream mechanism in fact, and thus a whole new series of consonantal articulations, to Bantu languages such as Zulu, Xhosa, Swazi, Ndebele, Sesotho, and Tsonga represents an additional degree of contact-induced linguistic complexity.

Mithun (1999: 317) also describes a small Sprachbund in Northern California in the region of Clear Lake, about 100 miles north of San Francisco. Here members of four different language families are in contact: Lake Miwok (Utian),[2] Wintuan, Pomoan, and Wappo. Wappo is an isolate, but the crucial point is that the Clear Lake members of the other three families differ significantly from other members of the same family spoken in different areas. Lake Miwok, for example, "differs strikingly in its phonological inventory from its relatives". Miwok languages generally have only one series of stops, but Lake Miwok is considerably more complex, having added aspirated, voiced, and ejective stop series, as well as four additional affricates, plus /r/ and /ɬ/. Importantly, 30% of the lexical items having these articulations can be shown to be loans from neighbouring languages.

But there is perhaps more to be said about this. It is also relevant, I suggest, that the clicks of Khoisan and southern African Bantu are articulatorily complex, and very rare indeed in the world's languages. Phonological systems having clicks can be said to have a degree of complexity which systems without them do not have: they are inherently more complex than systems without clicks.

Similarly, front rounded vowels of the type /y/, /ʏ/, /ø/, /œ/ are found in a remarkably contiguous area of northwestern Europe which stretches from northern Norway to the Alps,

---

[2] This is a different language from the Southern Sierra Miwok discussed by Nichols (1992).

and from western Ukraine to the Atlantic. Languages which have at least one such vowel include Norwegian, Swedish, Danish, Finnish, Estonian, Dutch, Frisian, German, Hungarian, Breton, French, and Occitan. On the northern fringes of the area, South Sami has /ø/; and on the southern fringes, front rounded vowels are found in northwestern Italian varieties, certain Romansch dialects, and northern Basque varieties spoken in France—but not in other varieties of these languages. Specifically, the area with front rounded vowels excludes all the other Sami languages, Spanish, Catalan, all the other Basque dialects, the Baltic and Slavic languages, Rumanian, other Romansch dialects, and most of Italian.[3]

Front rounded vowels are rare, occurring in only about 9% of the world's languages, according to the data presented in Maddieson (1984: 248–51). Vowels of this type are perceptually complex and are sometimes regarded by phonologists, like clicks, as marked articulation types (though see Haspelmath 1996), being not only rare but mastered late by children during first language acquisition, and highly susceptible to loss during linguistic change.[4] Thus, to find them in a single geographical area, and in so many European languages which are in many cases unrelated or not closely related, suggests that this is not a coincidence. The supposition has to be that this areal phenomenon is at least in part the result of the (spatial) diffusion of this feature from one language to another. This is most obviously so in the case of the front rounded vowels of Breton and the relevant varieties of Basque, whose speakers are all bilingual in French; and of South Sami, whose speakers are generally bilingual in Swedish or Norwegian—and of course diffusion from one language to another cannot occur without contact between speakers of those languages.

There would seem, then, to be an easy parallel between morphology/morphosyntax and phonology: adult language contact leads to a reduction in phoneme inventory size, and long-term co-territorial contact leads to an increase in inventory size. As we shall now see, however, there may be other factors involved in producing such changes in size.

---

[3] Outside this area, front rounded vowels also occur in Turkish, and Albanian also has /y/.
[4] Languages which have lost front rounded vowels in historical times include English, Icelandic, and Greek.

Spontaneous complexification in phonology

I suggested in Chapters 3 and 4 that small isolated communities are more able, because of their network structures, not only to maintain but also to *produce* complexity. Is there any evidence that this might be true of phonology?

There does appear to be some data to support this point of view in terms of phoneme inventories. One group of languages which is known to have very large phoneme inventories are the San languages of southern Africa: on one analysis, !Xu has 95 consonants (Maddieson 1984). It seems unlikely that we can explain this as being due to a high degree of contact and thus additive complexification, especially since very many of the consonants are clicks which, although they have been borrowed from San into a few southern African Bantu languages, as we just discussed, are otherwise unknown in the area outside the Khoisan grouping. It would therefore seem to be a typical example of complexification in isolation, and indeed a typical example of a mature phenomenon (see Chapter 6) in that it can be supposed that the accrual of larger and larger numbers of consonantal articulations will have taken many generations to complete.

However, this cannot at all be the full story of developments occurring in isolation, since there are a number of isolated languages in the world which have very small inventories, considerably smaller indeed than most pidgins. Consider the East Polynesian languages. Proto-Polynesian had a small inventory of 13 consonants (Clark 1976; Krupa 1982):

m   n   ŋ
p   t   k   ʔ
f   s   h
v
     l
     r

After eastward expansion into the Pacific had carried Polynesian peoples from the Tonga/Samoa area into ever more remote areas of the Ocean, this number was reduced to ten consonants in Proto-Eastern Polynesian as a result of the loss of /h/ and /ʔ/, and the merger of /r/ with /l/. This was already a very minimal consonant system (bearing in mind too that there were only five vowels). But then, rather remarkably, as further migration progressed to the extreme northern edge of the Polynesian triangle, Hawai'ian experienced the reduction of its consonant system even further to eight, by merging /f/ and /s/ as /h/, and merging /ŋ/ with /n/ (see Sutton 1994). In addition to this, /k/ became /ʔ/ and /t/ changed to /k/:

```
m   n
p       k   ʔ
            h
v
    l
```

The Rurutu language of the Austral Islands (Tubuai), situated on the extreme southern fringes of French Polynesia, also developed an extremely attenuated consonant system in which the glottal stop had three different historical sources:

```
m   n
p   t   ʔ
f
v
    r
```

Similar reductions—though only as far as 9-consonant inventories—can be found in a number of other remote Polynesian languages (Clark 1976: 20; Krupa 1982: 26; Trudgill 2004c). In contrast, the English-lexifier pidgin, Papua New Guinea Tok Pisin, has 15 or 16 consonants.

These reductions are a puzzling development, given the claim I made above about the possibility of small inventories being a typical result of contact-induced simplification. These Polynesian languages, after all, can be supposed to have been isolated, low-contact varieties. However, I do have a perhaps somewhat surprising suggestion about a possible role for a sociolinguistic-typological explanation here (see also Trudgill 2004c). This is that when attenuation of consonant systems develops to this very extreme extent, it actually represents, not a simplification but a genuine complexification—of the type we have come to associate with isolated, small, stable, tightly-social networked languages.

My reasoning is as follows. According to Maddieson (1984), Hawai'ian, with five vowels and eight consonants and CVCV phonotactics, has only 162 possible syllables. As a comparison, the total number of possible monosyllables in English approaches 6,000,000, according to Harley (2006).

My suggestion is that possessing only a small number of available syllables—and therefore a relatively small amount of redundancy—may, other things being equal, lead to greater communicative and/or cognitive difficulty because of a lack of contrastive possibilities. I suggest that while this lack of contrastive possibilities is entirely unproblematical for native speakers, languages such as Hawai'ian will cause difficulties for non-natives. Languages with very small phoneme inventories cause problems of *memory load* for foreign learners—they are L2 difficult.[5] The problem lies in the relative lack of distinctiveness between one vocabulary item and another, due to the necessarily high proportion of usage of possible syllables: Harlow (2001) says of North Island Maori that a very high proportion of all possible words consisting of two morae actually occur.

The difficulty is one of *confusability*. Consider the case of Maori, which has five vowels and ten consonants. Two-vowel sequences are also permitted within syllables, giving V, VV, CV, CVV as possibilities. Given that a high proportion of possible words of two morae actually occur, nevertheless if we turn to three-syllable words, mathematics indicates that the proportion of possible such words which actually occur in Maori will be quite low. However, I submit that the proportion is *much* higher than it would be if the phoneme inventory were larger. I suggest that learning and remembering, as an adult, which of the following 45 three-syllable words is which, is no easy task:

pakoke	'random'
pakoki	'distorted'
pakoko	'dried up'
pakakuu	'grating sound'
pakake	'minke whale'

---

[5] There is some anecdotal evidence for this—tourists complain of not being able to remember and distinguish one Honolulu street-name from another.

pakake	'seaweed'
pakeke	'adult'
pakikau	'garment'
pakuku	'glide'
pakakau	'fodder'
pakakee	'bitumen'
paakaakaa	'scorched'
paakaka	'hem in, surround'
paakeke	'follow on'
paakoki	'trigonometry'
paakaka	'trap'
paakeka	'exhausted land'
paakiki	'inquisitive'
paakoukou	'shoulder blade'
paikaka	'home-brew beer'
piikoikoi	'masturbate'
piikaokao	'cockerel'
piikookoo	*phormium tenax*
piikoko	'hungry'
pokake	'presumptuous'
pookaakaa	'stormy'
pookeka	'cape'
pookeka	'perplexed'
pookeka	'chant'
pookeke	'small'
pookaku	'mistaken'
pookiikii	'confused'
poukoki	'stilts'
pukoko	'lichen'
pukukai	'greedy'
pukoko	'lichen'
puukaakaa	'burning fiercely'
puukaki	'source of river'
puukeko	'swamp hen'
puukiki	'stunted'
puukaka	'femur, ulna'
puukakii	'boil, swellings on neck'
puukaka	'straight'
puukeke	'determined'
puukoki	'self-sown potato'

Some of the above are homonyms, which presumably does not help recall. (As Dixon says, the degree of homonymy in a language "depends, in part, on the number of distinct word forms which the phonology of the language permits" (2010a: 290).) And, while it is true that some of these Maori forms are compounds, and that a number of the words are rare, my suggestion is that any adult would find learning and remembering this list difficult. This is because, according to Lively et al. (1994: 274), there are *neighbourhood effects* (also called *lexical similarity effects*), which have to do with what other words a given word has to be differentiated from (Luce and Pisoni 1998). "Neighbours" are words that differ from a given target word by only one phoneme (see also Luce 1986; Goldinger et al. 1989). Lively et al. show that words are identified less accurately if they come from "dense neighbourhoods" than if they are from "sparse neighbourhoods" (1994: 275). Therefore, if we can generalize from recognition to memory, my point is made—and it does seem clear that we can generalize in this way, since recognition obviously depends on memory. I suggest, then, that there is a sense in which very small systems of vowels and consonants can produce L2 complexity.

As far as the changes which led to these very small systems are concerned, we can say that a number of our societal factors may have been implicated. Initial small *community size* (the number of people who could arrive on a relatively small number of relatively small boats) would have led, in remote Polynesia, to very tight *social networks*. Crucially, however, in a *stable* community with few external *contacts* this would have produced large amounts of *communally shared information*. A large fund of communally shared knowledge would have made for a situation in which communication with a relatively low level of phonological redundancy would have been relatively tolerable.

Bernstein, in his work in the 1970s, made the crucial and interesting observation that people who spend most of their lives in relatively small social circles, who are part of relatively tight social networks, and who are used to communicating mainly with people with whom they share considerable amounts of background information, will tend to talk in what he (1971) called "restricted code". This term implies, amongst other more controversial things, that they would take shared information for granted, even, perhaps, when this was not appropriate. On the other hand, those who moved in wider social circles and were more used to communicating with people they did not know well would be more likely to talk in "elaborated code", a term which implies the surely accurate observation that they would be more likely to supply background information to those without it.

Sasha Aikhenvald, an extremely experienced fieldworker, has a similar insight. She writes (p.c.) that small tightly-knit communities tend to employ discourse which is very elliptical, "which is understandable, since in a small language community—say, one or two villages—people usually know what is being talked about. I observed this in Tariana, the Arawak language I am working on". She also points out that large classifier systems are found in many small group languages, and that such classifiers are a powerful deictic device permitting elision in situations with much shared background information. She reports that she spent four days in a canoe with Tariana Indians, and speakers hardly used any full nouns, all the work being done through classifiers.[6]

It is interesting to suppose that this insight concerning background information could be extended to phonology. Just as less information, generally, needs to be imparted in small non-fluid communities with large amounts of shared background information than in larger, more fluid ones, less phonological information is also necessary for successful communication in these small communities. In smaller communities with relatively large amounts of shared information, the listener more often than in other communities may already have a good idea of what is going to be said, and less redundancy is required.

This leads me to suggest the addition of a new, albeit related, fifth social parameter to our list of those which are pertinent to sociolinguistic typology: *large vs. small amounts of communally shared information*. In the case of phoneme inventories, I do

---

[6] In her work on syntax, Martowicz (2010) has also shown that the smaller a community a language is spoken in, the fewer devices (such as temporal and causal conjunctions) it is likely to have for explicitly marking the nature of connectivity between clauses.

not intend to imply that a large amount of communally shared information will necessarily lead to small phoneme inventories—of course it will not; it is simply the case that it *permits* this kind of development.

Perhaps, then, we have arrived at a certain amount of sociolinguistic-typological insight here. However, even if we have actually done this, it is still difficult to see that any significant predictive generalizations can be made. Not only are we dealing with tendencies and probabilities, as always in this sort of work, but, as we have seen, small inventories may be associated *either* with adult contact, as in pidgins, *or* with isolation, small community size, and shared information. Perhaps it is significant, though, that spontaneous complexification of the Polynesian exceedingly-small-inventory type involves a reduction of inventory size beyond anything found in most pidgins.

Similarly, large inventories may be associated *either* with additive borrowing in high contact Sprachbund-type areas, *or* with spontaneous complexification—a proliferation of articulation types—in low contact situations as with !Xu.

Something can be said, however, about time-scales. The simplification that accompanies pidginization can be assumed to take place relatively rapidly, in the space of a generation perhaps, as is typical of adult-language contact. On the other hand, the expansion of inventories as a result of long-term contact will, obviously, only occur in the long term—and this may be very long-term indeed: recall that Mithun (2007) discusses a Californian Sprachbund in terms of thousands of years of development. And we can also suppose that the complexification-in-isolation production of very large inventories, as with !Xu, will also be the end-product of very many generations of change, uninterrupted by contact.

As far as the complexification that is associated with extremely small systems is concerned, we also have some indications about the chronology of this development. The consonant system of the parent Austronesian branch of Polynesian, Proto-Oceanic, which consisted of 23 items, was reduced in its daughter language Proto Central Pacific to 21, and then in Proto-Polynesian to 13, as we saw above. Central Eastern Polynesian (the parent of Marquesan, Tahitian,

Hawai'ian, and Maori) then reduced this to ten, and Hawai'ian to eight.

Proto-Oceanic is thought to have been spoken in the Bismarck Archipelago of Papua New Guinea; and the reduction of inventories accompanied the move of Austronesian peoples in the direction of Fiji, and then further and further via Tonga and Samoa into the remote, open Pacific (Pawley 1996a, 1999; Pawley and Ross 1993; Kirch and Green 2001). An approximate date for Proto Oceanic is 1500 BC (Pawley 2009: 517), and although there are conflicting accounts, the Polynesian settlement of Hawai'i was perhaps around AD 800 (Kirch and Green 2001). Even if the new reduced consonantal system developed very quickly in Hawai'i, this still gives us a time depth of 2,500 years or so. So all types of complexification in phoneme inventory size—borrowed and spontaneous—appear to be long-term processes. Only contact-induced reduction in inventories happens rapidly.

Spontaneous complexification: Sound change

Measuring phoneme inventory size is a straightforward quantitative task. I now move on, however, to more qualitative and therefore perhaps more controversial evaluations of phonological complexity. I begin by returning to an issue we already touched on in Chapter 4, namely sound change.

In earlier chapters we compared the two Scandinavian languages Norwegian and Faroese, noting that Faroese is both a much more isolated language than Norwegian and is also characterized by a great deal more morphological complexity. As far as phonology is concerned, most linguists would probably also agree, as we noted in Chapter 4, that the sound changes which have occurred in Norwegian in recent centuries have been rather more "natural" and expected, and rather less complex, than many of those which have occurred in Faroese. Obviously one has to be careful about this kind of judgement, but as Blust (2005: 226) says, most historical linguists have expectations "about types of change that are likely to occur".

It is clear that experts on Faroese are often perplexed by the complexities of the phonological developments in this language. Arnason (1980: 81) writes that "to give a simple and reliable

picture of the history of Faroese vocalism is difficult, partly
because the development seems to have been so complicated";
while Küspert says that "the development of vowels in stressed
syllables from Old Norse to modern Faroese is clearly a complex
and opaque one" (1988: 197, my translation). And we have
already noted the possibility that languages spoken in isolated
communities such as Faroese may be more likely to produce
sound changes that could be labelled, as Andersen says (1988),
"slightly unusual": a good example would be /i:/ > /ui/.

Crowley (1987: 48), in a section of his book called "Abnor-
mal Sound Changes", warns that apparently unusual changes
can usually be accounted for in terms of a series of intermediate changes which are all actually perfectly normal in themselves. Blust (2005: 226) similarly issues a reminder that
sometimes changes that appear to be inexplicable may be due
to "accumulations of sound changes" which "can produce
telescoping, whereby a reflex appears to involve a phonetically
unmotivated sound change, but is actually the product of
successive natural changes". (The term 'telescoping' was first
used by Lass (1997: 223), who makes the same point convincingly and at some length—see also Orr 1999.) Blust cites an
example from Rotuman, a language related to Fijian, where /f/
is a reflex of Proto-Oceanic /t/. This apparently bizarre change,
however, is much more comprehensible when we note that it
occurred via an intermediate stage: /t/ > /θ/ > /f/.

Crucially, however, Blust then cites a number of genuinely
"bizarre" changes in Austronesian languages where telescoping is not available as an explanation, and which appear not to
have any obvious linguistic motivation. For example, Proto-
Manus had a prenasalized alveolar trill /ⁿdr/. In Drehet, one
of the languages spoken on the Admiralty Island of Manus
in Papua New Guinea, this consonant has—extraordinarily—
become an aspirated voiceless velar plosive /kʰ/ (2005: 226).

Andersen (1988) also gives an extended example of a sound
change which would seem to fall into the category of "unusual": an "unprovoked fortition" which strikes many historical linguists as odd. This is a—significantly—historically
unconnected series of developments of parasitic velar consonants out of high or mid vowels, in several isolated areas of
Europe. This has occurred in dialects of a number of languages,

including Romansch, Provençal, Danish, German, and Flemish—changes which are absent from metropolitan varieties and less isolated varieties of the same languages. The Danish dialects Andersen cites are spoken in out-of-the-way places including "the extreme western, most isolated parts of Funen and Jutland" (1988: 70). Examples include *bi* [bik] 'bee'; *missil* [misigl] 'missile', *hel* [hekl] 'whole' (Nissen 1945; Nielsen 1947; Søndergård 1970).

The same development is discussed in some detail for Romansch by Haiman (1988), who refers to it as "the peculiar diphthongisation known as Verschärfung 'sharpening' whereby inherited [i] becomes [ik] or [ɛk]"—note the adjective "peculiar". He gives examples such as /durmɛkr/ 'to sleep', cf. /durmɛr/ and /dykr/ 'hard', cf. /dyr/. According to Andersen, the dialect of Bergün on the River Albula has forms such as /ʃkregver/ 'to write', cf. /ʃkrever/; /krekʃta/ 'ridge', cf. /kreʃta/; /voks/ 'you (pl.)', cf. /vos/.

In western Europe, these unprovoked fortitions do seem to be confined to small communities in geographically remote and/or peripheral areas. In Romansch, for instance, parasitic consonants occur in three separate and non-contiguous dialects—suggesting independent development—in the upper reaches of three separate river basins, namely the Inn, the Albula, and the Oberhalbstein branch of the Rhine.

Outside Europe, Mortensen describes a similar development in Tibeto-Burman languages as "surprising" and "maladaptive" (ms. a); and he also describes this kind of development as "both formally and functionally aberrant" (ms. b). The Tibeto-Burman languages in question are also spoken in relatively small, isolated communities. For example, the Huishu language of Manipur, India, is spoken by a speech community which consists of fewer than 1,000 people living in a single village which was historically very insular and was in a perpetual state of conflict with neighbouring villages. Mortensen says (p.c.) of the languages he knows which have this feature that "none are spoken primarily by urban populations".

The point of view that unusual sound changes are relatively more likely to occur in isolation than in contact is also supported by Johnston (1997: 448), who writes of Insular Scots, i.e. the dialects of Orkney and Shetland, that it is plain, however, that the 'weird' varieties, the ones that go their own way the most, come from the most tight-knit communities, perhaps consisting of only one social network. According to local lore (Brian Smith, p.c.), the Whalsay [Shetland] dialect was shaped by the speech habits of a single family, to whom everyone on the island is related. While such explanations usually can be dismissed as smacking of myth, it may be true in the particular case of such tiny island communities.

We may recall here Nettle's point cited earlier that "if a group consists of just a few hundred people, the idiosyncrasies of one very influential individual can spread through it very easily" (1999: 138).

Spontaneous complexification: Vowel systems

Unusual and complex sound changes such as the above do not necessarily lead to unusual and/or complex sound systems, of course. For instance, the Drehet change from /ⁿdr/ to /kʰ/ is surely a simplification in some sense. But I now want to discuss the way in which changes, "peculiar" or not, may lead to complex or marked or "weird" systems. It might be possible to argue that related dialects or languages which have different demographies, and different histories of contact and isolation, might be shown to have systems of different degrees of "aberrance".

In this section I therefore want to examine the extent to which Johnston's adjective "weird" might legitimately be used of phonological systems as a whole, and the extent to which, if so, there might be sociolinguistic-typological insights into the distribution of such systems over linguistic varieties.

Having focused earlier on consonantal systems of different sizes, I now want to have a look at vowel systems of different types. An elementary and totally obvious fact about vocalic systems is that the whole point of a vowel is to be different from other vowels. Linguistic common sense would therefore dictate that, other things being equal, vowels should be as distinct from one another as possible. We would thus expect to find that, in any given language, vowels are distributed relatively evenly across vowel space. Linguists would be very surprised indeed if, in a language with three vowels, those vowels were /i/, /ɪ/ and /ɨ/.[7]

A number of things follow from this principle of distinctiveness. One is that a change in the phonetic quality of a particular vowel may lead, through chain shifts, to changes in the quality of other vowels in order to retain maximum distinctiveness, as outlined by Martinet in his study of the economy of phonological changes (1955; 1962), and as was subsequently illustrated in further detail by many others scholars, notably Labov (1994). The English Great Vowel Shift is a very well-known example. Another consequence is that languages with fewer vowels are able to permit greater variation in the realization of those vowels, allophonic or otherwise, than languages which have a larger number.

In the last three decades, this linguistic common sense has been given empirical and theoretical confirmation. First, following on from early work on vowel systems by Trubetzkoy (1939), scholars carrying out research in linguistic typology have illustrated, by a comparison of large numbers of languages, that the assumption of the even distribution of vowels across vowel space is basically correct (Crothers 1978; Disner 1984). Crother's survey shows that the most frequent vowel patterns in the world's languages are those where vowels are maximally different from one another, and that "the arrangement of vowel qualities is determined to a large extent simply by the number of vowels; for a given number of vowel qualities, only one or two arrangements occur with any frequency in the world's languages" (Crothers 1978: 100).

Secondly, theoretical refinement has come from work in acoustic phonetics. Liljencrants and Lindblom's (1972) Vowel Dispersion Theory claims that a number of typological trends in the phonetic structure of vowel inventories can be explained on the basis of the assumption that the phonetic realization of vowel categories is indeed "maximally dispersed in the available auditory space". It is this principle of maximum

---

[7] Vowels can, of course, differ from one another in various other ways, such as length, movement (diphthongization) and nasalization, but I concentrate solely on quality here as I have not developed any suggestions about languages, such as the Germanic languages, which have vowel systems with front rounded vowels, diphthongs, and distinctive vowel length, with possible interactions between different subsystems.

dispersion which means that if a language has three vowels, they are extremely likely to be /i/, /a/, and /u/; that if a language has five vowels, like Standard Modern Greek, they are extremely likely to be /i/, /e/, /a/, /o/, and /u/; that if a language has seven vowels they will be /i/, /e/ /ɛ/, /a/, /ɔ/, /o/, /u/; and so on. The suggestion is that the maximal dispersion of vowels in phonological space leads to maximal contrast and thus to maximal efficiency of communication: "distinctive sounds of a language tend to be positioned in phonetic space so as to maximise perceptual contrast" (Johnson 2000: 1)

In two papers, Schwartz et al. (1997a; 1997b) make refinements to the original theory without, however, changing its fundamental basis. They examine the vowel systems of the 317 languages in the UCLA Phonological Segment Inventory Database (UPSID), and show that 265 of these languages have systems of nine vowels or fewer. Of the 14 languages which have 3-vowel systems, 100% have /i, a, u/. Of the 100 languages which have five vowels, 97% have /i, e, a, o, u/. And of the 41 languages which have seven vowels, 23 (56%) have /i, e, ɛ, a, ɔ, o, u/. An additional 110 languages have 4-, 6-, 7-, 8-, or 9-vowel systems which are totally symmetrical. In total, of the 265 languages, 200, i.e. at least 75% would appear to support the maximal dispersion hypothesis in that their vowel systems are symmetrical.

Vowel dispersion theory, then, is based on an understanding on the part of linguists which derives from our widespread knowledge of the world's languages, as well as from more recent empirical and experimental research. As Butcher (1994: 32) says, the theory "is fairly widely accepted". In the context of the present book, however, there is an interesting Dixonian "why"-question here which remains unanswered. Given that, as Schwartz et al. (1997a; 1997b) have shown, a majority of languages seem to fit in with the maximal dispersion theory, why are there some languages, as Schwartz et al. have also shown, that do not? Why do some varieties have asymmetrical systems (see below), and others not? And why is it those varieties and not others?

The material I have presented in this book so far suggests that there may be a sociolinguistic-typological answer. We can begin to explore this answer by noting that the total legitimacy of the maximal dispersion theory has been queried by a number of writers. For example, Butcher (1994) has analysed the vowel formant patterns of a number of indigenous Australian languages which have small vowel systems, including Arrernte, Warlpiri, and Burarra. These languages have two, three, and five contrastive vowels respectively. Butcher finds that rather than actually illustrating maximum dispersion relative to size of vowel inventory, the acoustic vowel spaces of these languages tend to be "compact" compared to languages with large vowel inventories like English or Swedish—they are symmetrical but do not make use of the entirety of vowel space. Butcher suggests that they therefore illustrate the principle of *sufficient dispersion*, as opposed to maximum dispersion. The claim is that, at least in some languages with small vowel systems, articulatory economy counterbalances the perceptual demands for a contrast. This thesis has subsequently been strengthened by e.g. Fletcher and Butcher (2003) for three further languages of northern Australia: Kayardild, Dalabon, and Mayali; and by Fletcher et al. (2007) for northern Australian Kunwinjku.

Another series of challenges to the theory of maximal dispersion is provided by languages which have "holes" in their vowel systems. For example, Maddieson (1984) describes Gilyak, a language isolate spoken in outer Manchuria, as being "defective" in having no vowels at all in the vicinity of /e/. Additional striking evidence is provided by Jackson (2003), who has described Pima, an Uto-Aztecan language spoken in Arizona. This language, like other closely related languages in the area, also has a "missing vowel" with, as it were, a hole in the system: the vowels are /i, a, o, u, ɯ/, with nothing in the vicinity of /e/. Jackson (2003) writes that while

simple theories of vowel dispersion (e.g. Liljencrants and Lindblom 1972) explain the cross-linguistic tendencies of vowel inventories by predicting a set of vowels which is maximally dispersed in the available formant space, such models do not predict languages with relatively uneven distributions or unfilled perimeters of the vowel space; the fact that such languages exist shows that other considerations besides maximal distinctiveness are responsible for the distribution of vowels. More complex theories of vowel dispersion (Lindblom and Maddieson 1988; Schwartz et al. 1997b) respond to this by including both dispersing forces (such as maintaining maximal distinction) and attracting forces (such as articulatory simplicity or auditory salience).

However, he continues: "although such theories allow for multiple vowel systems with the same number of vowels—which simpler theories did not do—large unfilled areas of vowel space are still predicted to be relatively rare".

From a sociolinguistic-typological perspective, we can now see that it may well be relevant that the maximal dispersion theory was initially developed by linguists working on the vowel systems of standard varieties of large European languages. Such varieties, as mentioned earlier, tend to be the outcome of situations characterized by a large degree of dialect contact and dialect mixture. Maybe then, since dialect mixture has been shown to have certain regularizing linguistic consequences, concentration on such varieties may have produced a skewed and somewhat sociolinguistically naïve picture.

It may not be immediately obvious that acoustic phonetic work can benefit from being more sociolinguistically sensitive; but perhaps, too, it is not a coincidence that some of the scholars such as Butcher, Fletcher, and Jackson who have queried and modified the original dispersion theory are people who have been working on small, nonstandardized, low-contact indigenous languages spoken in remote communities in Australia and the USA. Again we are dealing with tendencies and probabilities, but I suggest that we are most likely to find the principle of *maximum dispersion* at maximum operation in varieties which are the outcome of contact and which are spoken in larger communities with relatively loose social network structures; and the principal of *sufficient dispersion* in smaller, low-contact, and tightly networked communities.

The probability is that one of the real stories here is the balance insightfully outlined by Butcher between articulatory economy—of the sort represented by the usage of smaller areas of vowel space—and the perceptual demands for a contrast. These two principles are obviously in conflict. Dressler (1984: 31) says that phonological processes "serve the communicative function of language by serving their proper functions: pronounceability and perceptibility", but that "the goals of better perception and better articulation often conflict with each other".

Indeed, efficient communication generally is said to result from achieving an equilibrium between the needs of the speaker and the needs of the listener. The speaker wants to communicate quickly or at least with little effort, while the listener needs enough information to process the message accurately. Martinet (1962) argued that in spoken communication, a dynamic equilibrium exists between the needs of the speaker to speak quickly and easily, on the one hand, and the needs of the listener to comprehend what is being said, on the other. This was, of course not a totally new insight. More than a hundred years ago, Gabelentz (1901: 256) made a similar point, contrasting the drives to *Bequemlichkeit* and *Deutlichkeit* in language—the twin but conflicting drives towards 'ease' and 'clarity'. And the same point has been much repeated in different ways: "the demands of the articulatory system tend to produce phonetic reduction of words, and massive coarticulation of segments, but one's pragmatic desire to be understood favours maximal elaboration and clarity of the speech signal" (Nettle 1999: 19). There is clear agreement that, while the speaker wants to communicate with little effort, the listener needs enough information to process the message accurately.

However, sociolinguistic typology suggests that there may be more to it than just that (Trudgill 1996a): I suggest that in some sociolinguistic contexts the equilibrium may be skewed in favour of *Bequemlichkeit*, in others in favour of *Deutlichkeit*. Flemming (2004: 232) points out that

most phonetically-driven or functionalist theories of phonology propose that two of the fundamental forces shaping phonology are the need to minimize effort on the part of the speaker and the need to minimize the likelihood of confusion on the part of the listener.

But I have proposed (1996a) that in some social contexts, the need to avoid the "likelihood of confusion on the part of the listener" is going to be greater than in others. As Nettle says, "we know that speakers will under-articulate tokens *to the extent that the communicative situation allows them to*" (1999: 142; [my italics]).

In small communities with tight social networks and large amounts of shared information, such as the remote Polynesian communities, the "likelihood of confusion" will be relatively low. The equilibrium therefore swings in favour of the speaker, who can get away with less articulatory effort without thereby increasing the risk of not being comprehended. The drive to maximize distinctiveness in vowel systems will therefore similarly be reduced in small, stable communities, particularly if these are relatively isolated, with relatively few external contacts. Because of large amounts of knowledge shared among speakers who are in communication with one another frequently, less information is required from speakers at all linguistic and discourse levels, including acoustic information about which vowel is which.

On the other hand, in contexts where speakers and listeners do not know each other well and do not have a large body of shared information, the equilibrium must swing in favour of the listener. This will be particularly so in cases where native speakers of different languages and dialects are involved. Here, the equilibrium will be disturbed, and the conflict complicated, by the needs of non-natives. This is because the needs of non-native learner-listeners are in some important respects very different from those of native language/dialect speakers.

There is a considerable body of work which demonstrates this for foreign language comprehension, but the same will apply, if to a lesser degree, to dialect comprehension also. Weber and Cutler (2004: 1) say:

Listening in one's native language is effortless; but listening to a second language can be distressingly hard work. Unfamiliar words, unknown idioms, and hitherto unencountered accents can at any moment present new challenges. Speech can seem unnervingly fast, because procedures for segmenting speech of the native language into words fail to work with the second language. The experience of being tired out by simply listening, for instance to a lecture or a theatre, is one that many second-language listeners have undergone.

Greater difficulties in comprehension are experienced by non-native listeners, because they typically require more information than natives. We have considerable experimental evidence to show that non-natives do much worse than natives in comprehension in less than ideal conditions (see for example

Florentine 1985; Nabelek and Donahue 1984). Meador et al. (2000) write that "research has shown that non-native speakers are less 'tolerant' of masking noise than are native speakers when faced with the need to comprehend connected speech materials". Phonological information is also relatively more important for non-natives than for natives. According to Dalton and Seidlhofer (1994: 26), because of non-natives' relative lack of background knowledge, contextual information is much less available to them: "Just how much implicit knowledge feeds into our communication with others becomes evident as soon as we enter a different dialect area. ..."

We can conclude that perceptual demands will be favoured in high contact situations involving large fluid communities and small amounts of shared information. In such high-contact situations, therefore, the maximal distinctiveness of vowels is more important, and the likelihood of the principle of maximal dispersion being adhered to is greater.

Fast speech

In view of these observations about the dynamic equilibrium, one further aspect of the sociolinguistic typology of phonology might be worth investigating. It has not been very usual in linguistics to discuss, at least in print, whether some languages or dialects employ more fast speech phenomena than others, but it is at least possible that this is so. Fast-speech phenomena make things easier for the native speaker: the same message can be got across more quickly and with less articulatory effort—with more ease. However, crucially, they also make life much more difficult for the non-native listener by reducing the amount of phonetic information available for processing. This is because, as we saw above, the needs of non-native learner-listeners are in some important respects very different from those of native-language speakers. The less proficient one is in a language, the more difficult it is to understand a message where "the natural redundancy of language is reduced" (Gaies et al. 1977).

This is a matter of common observation. For instance, in the *Guardian Weekly* of 8th January 2004, Mike Allan writes in his 'Letter from Rio':

My Portuguese is fairly good after three years in Rio, but I still find it difficult to hear when there is a lot of background noise. Here, for example, where a diesel engine is revving anxiously and a group of perplexed bus riders are all asking questions simultaneously. *The message gets through to them*, however. [my italics]

Paradoxically enough, fast speech phenomena, especially insofar as they are variety-specific rather than universal, can also make things more difficult for the non-native *speaker*, because they constitute an extra set of rules to learn and remember—and to remember to implement while speaking. English speakers often observe of, say, highly-educated Swedes that "they speak English better than we do". This most often means that the Swedes in question do not use many fast speech processes, and this is obviously because, quite simply, they are unable to do so. Consider a low-level phonetic rule (Trudgill 1974) of the lower working-class English of the city of Norwich (the capital of the English county of Norfolk) which converts /nð/ to /l/:

[nᴧ ə ɪʔ bdæ̃ lɛ læi̯ʔlɪi]   No, I in't been down there lately

The rule:

/Vn/##/ð/ → /V/##/l/

gives [dæ̃ lɛ] as a realization of *down there*. This is not obviously motivated by universal or natural factors—it is variety-specific. Such rules constitute extra material for the adult learner in contact situations to acquire, remember, and implement. It is therefore quite possible that low-contact varieties are likely to demonstrate more fast speech phenomena than high-contact varieties because these phenomena cause problems for outsiders both as listeners *and* as speakers. Insofar as these processes may become generalized (see below) to slower forms of speech through linguistic change, then we would also expect this to occur more often in low-contact than in high-contact varieties.

Anecdotal evidence supports the view that some, often non-standard, varieties are harder to learn to understand than others—for precisely, I would suggest, this sort of reason. We can suppose that Bernstein's insight concerning background information can be extended to fast speech. Just as less information, generally, needs to be imparted in small non-fluid communities with large amounts of shared background information than in larger, more fluid ones, I would repeat the argument made above that less phonetic information, in particular, is also necessary for successful communication in these small communities. Fast-speech processes obviously reduce the amount of phonetic information available. As I have already argued, in smaller communities with relatively large amounts of shared information, the dynamic equilibrium might be weighted somewhat in favour of the needs of the speaker, since the listener more often than in other communities may already have a good idea of what is going to be said, and fast speech phenomena might therefore be more common.

Dressler and Wodak (1982), on the subject of the dynamic equilibrium, have further argued that formal speech situations are typically those where the needs of the speaker are subordinated to the needs of the hearer, while in casual situations the balance is tipped in the other direction. I would suggest (and Dressler p.c. kindly agrees) that it is very probable that some societies and some social groups are more characterized by the occurrence of formal situations than others. If this is true, then we can suppose that the balance between the needs of the speaker and hearer will not necessarily be constant between one society and another. The balance may be swayed in one direction or another by the extent to which a society favours or disfavours formal situations; and fast speech phenomena are more likely to be prevalent in communities which do not favour formal situations.

In support of this thesis, I showed (Trudgill 1974) that the speech of the Norwich lower working class, a relatively close-knit social group, was characterized by more phonetic reduction processes—one of them illustrated above—than upper working-class speech. The Norwich research revealed examples of extreme phonological reduction in lower working-class speech which were simply not found amongst other social groups.

As with "restricted code", social network structure is also involved. Fast-speech phenomena are not only less likely to occur in high-contact situations; they are also more likely to occur in small tightly-knit, perhaps isolated, communities which have large amounts of shared information in common and where individual personalities are known to all, than in larger communities, or those with looser network ties where more phonetic information may be required. How tightly-knit a community is in network terms may therefore have an influence on the phonetics of its language or dialect.

George Grace (p.c.) has also suggested that there might be different kinds of fast speech for different purposes and with different motivations. One motive might simply be to make comprehension difficult for third parties in order to preserve the privacy of the message. Another motive might also be to make comprehension difficult for overhearers, or for the addressee him/herself with the purpose of conveying to them that they're outsiders ("if you can't understand this, that says something about you, and maybe what was said isn't any of your business"). Still another motive is deprecatory (of the message or even oneself) ("I feel apologetic about consuming even this amount of your time with this unworthy message"). The first two of these motivations might be expected to be more associated with small tightly-knit communities.

If we can now extend this discussion to linguistic change, one of the things which may happen to fast speech phenomena in linguistic change is that they may become institutionalized, i.e. they become slow speech phenomena as well (pace Hock (1991: 49), who claims that "by and large, fast speech phenomena do not seem to have any lasting effect on linguistic change"). Browman and Goldstein (1991), for instance, suggest from the perspective of Articulatory Phonology that speakers tend, as they speak faster, to reduce the magnitude and/or duration of each articulatory gesture, and/or increase the overlap of gestures; and that these adjustments in articulation may lead to more permanent sound changes. Dressler (1984: 34) similarly says, "a typical scenario of diachronic change consists in the generalisation of assimilatory processes which are first limited to casual speech into more and more formal speech situations until they become obligatory processes". The community size and social network factors will therefore be relevant. That is, the institutionalization of fast speech phenomena into slow speech phenomena will be more typical of small tightly-knit communities where everybody knows everybody else and where there is a large fund of shared information—and where there are fewer formal situations.

It is not impossible, for example, that the enormously greater degree of phonetic erosion that has taken place in French as opposed to, say, Italian can at least partly be explained in this way. It might perhaps be that the contrast between Latin *homo* > Italian /uomo/, > French *on* /ɔ̃/; Latin *augustum* > Italian /agosto/, > French *août* /u/; Latin *unum* > Italian /uno/, > French *un* /œ̃/ (see Chapter 1) can be ascribed partly to the degree to which French had no formal role, under a Germanic-speaking Frankish aristocracy, until relatively late in its development.

Also, if it is true too that non-native speakers have active and receptive problems with fast speech processes, then we would expect this institutionalization of fast speech phenomena to occur less often in high-contact situations in which languages and dialects are employed by speakers for whom they do not represent a mother tongue. This expectation is certainly confirmed at least by pidgins, which as we saw earlier have very few stylistic differences in phonology, especially in their early stages (Labov 1990; Mühlhäusler 1986). The institutionalization of fast speech phenomena is less likely to occur in high-contact varieties, including high-prestige standard koinés.

This may well have some really rather far-reaching consequences for spontaneous linguistic complexification. We saw in Chapter 4 that phonology appears to play a vital role in many complexity-producing mechanisms; and that Dahl, Campbell, and others have ascribed an important role to phonology in the initiation of processes resulting in grammaticalization.[8] I suggest that this may have much to do with fast speech phenomena; amongst the processes outlined by Joseph as constituting grammaticalization, phonological reduction associated with fast speech phenomena is crucial.

I have also argued elsewhere that, to the extent that fast speech phenomena are implicated in grammaticalization, then they may well be more influential in producing grammaticalization in some communities than others (Trudgill 1995):

---

[8] In an important argument, Carstairs-McCarthy (2010) argues that phonology, including fast speech assimilation processes, played a crucial role in the evolutionary development of morphology in the first place.

grammaticalization may therefore be a more frequent result of linguistic changes in those communities which favour fast speech phenomena than in those which do not. My speculation, then, is that grammaticalization outcomes which are due ultimately to phonological reduction and deletion may be more common in small, tightly-knit communities with relatively few outside contacts, i.e. the same sorts of communities which particularly favour fast speech phenomena.

In Trudgill (1995) I suggested that such reduction and eventual loss of phonetic material might lie behind the development of the large, perhaps unusually large, numbers of new conjunctions in the traditional-dialect of Norfolk. These include (with examples taken from local dialect literature):

1. *yet = nor*
   There weren't no laburnum, yet no lilac.
   'There wasn't any laburnum, or any lilac.'

2. *more = neither*
   Aunt Agatha she say "You don't know the difference."
   Granfar say "More don't you."
   'Aunt Agatha says "You don't know the difference."
   Grandfather says "Neither do you".'

3. *time = while*
   Go you and have a good wash and a change, time I get tea ready.
   'Go and have a good wash and a change while I get tea ready.'

4. *do = otherwise*
   You better go to bed now, do you'll be tired in the morning.
   'You'd better go to bed now, or you'll be tired in the morning.'

I suggest that, for instance, the development shown in example 2, in which *more* can be seen to have become a conjunct, came from an original structure of the form *and no more don't you*. This took place as a result of the reduction of *and no more* to *more* through the gradual phonetic erosion of material via a sequence such as:

[ən nuː mɔ > ən nə mɔ > n̩nə mɔː > n̩n̩ mɔː > nmɔː > mɔː]

And the use of *do* as a conjunction, as in example 4 (see also Chapter 3), came from original forms such as 'You'd better not stay up late, [because if you] do you'll be tired in the morning', followed by subsequent reduction of the phonetic material associated with *because if you*. This eventually led to the grammaticalization of *do* as a conjunction, which then permitted its extension to opposite polarity contexts where *don't* would originally have been expected rather than *do*.

The establishment of *more* and *do* as new conjunctions presupposes a number of processes of grammatical and semantic reanalysis. But I suggest that the initial impetus for the linguistic changes which occurred in the Norfolk dialect was surely, as suggested by Campbell and by Dahl, phonological. Bybee et al. (1994) argue in favour of the Parallel Reduction Hypothesis, which suggests that, in grammaticalization, semantic reduction and phonetic reduction go hand in hand—"semantic reduction is paralleled by phonetic reduction" (1994: 19). There may, they say, be a causal relationship between the two. In the case of the development of the new conjunctions in the Norfolk dialect, I suggest that the evidence is in favour of the impetus for grammaticalization beginning with the phonetics and only subsequently spreading to semantics.

Conclusion

We have seen, then, that there is some evidence that the two different types of language contact may have the same or similar consequences for phonology as for morphology; and that spontaneous complexification in social isolation also occurs in the case of phonology. As far as spontaneous complexification is concerned, we have noted that it can take the form of the development of very large or very small inventories, unusual sound changes, and non-maximally dispersed vowel systems. We have also noted that fast speech processes may be differentially distributed, and therefore differentially involved in producing linguistic changes leading to grammaticalization, in different types of community. We return to a discussion of the role of grammaticalization in the following chapter.

6

Mature phenomena and societies of intimates

We have seen that linguistic complexification is most likely to occur in communities with certain social characteristics. The most favourable environment of all for complexity-development is in communities with the following constellation of societal features:

- low amounts of adult language contact
- high social stability
- small size
- dense social networks
- large amounts of communally-shared information.

It should be stressed once again that I am not suggesting that this constellation of features *necessarily* leads to complexification; rather, it is simply the case that these features represent something like a precondition for complexity-development.

It should also be stressed that these social factors are not bipolar dyads but rather admit of very considerable degrees of more or less.

Equally, it is also necessary to stress the role of the *interaction* of the different social factors. If we look at just the three of the five societal factors, *size*, *network* and *contact*, and if we assume that the combination of large community size and tight social networks is unlikely, their interaction still produces six possible combinations, ignoring for the moment the major issue of "how large is large":

	1	2	3	4	5	6
size	**small**	small	small	small	large	**large**
network	**tight**	tight	loose	loose	loose	**loose**
contact	**low**	high	low	high	low	**high**

In my work I have often used the label 'small' as a kind of shorthand for 'small, tightly-knit, isolated', and 'large' as shorthand for 'large, loosely-knit, high contact'; and I have often focused on the two most polar opposites as represented by categories 1 and 6. However, it has always been clear to me that it is important in principle to deal with all of the societal factors in combination, even if I have sometimes been guilty of not always clarifying that.

It is therefore interesting to note what happened when the editor of *Linguistic Typology* kindly invited commentators to critique my paper on phoneme inventories (Trudgill 2004c— and see Chapter 5), in which I also employed these five social factors: most of the commentators focused in their discussions on only one of them.

Bakker, for example, (2004) focused only on contact; and Pericliev's (2004) response was entitled "There is no correlation between the size of a community speaking a language and the size of the phonological inventory of that language". Elsewhere, an important paper by Hay and Bauer (2007), "Phoneme inventory size and population size", which comments on the same paper, also concentrated only on size. (Wichmann et al. (2008) is another paper which deals simply with size.)

I understand that there are practical reasons for this kind of narrow focusing by scholars. Typologists tend to use databases that can tell us nothing about *networks*. And in order to learn about the extent and nature of *contact* in individual cases, detailed historical and anthropological work, of the sort Rice (2004) reports on for Athabaskan in her helpful comments, is required. Databases can also usually tell us little or nothing about *stability* and *shared information*. Statistical typologists need something to count, and straightforward measures of population size lend themselves to this in a way the other factors do not.

It is, however, vital to consider the different social factors in combination if at all possible because, as Rice (2004) very clearly illustrates, other types of combination than 1 and 6 can very readily be found (see Sinnemäki 2009: 128). The Athabaskan communities Rice cites, for example, are typically *small* in size but *high* in contact, and would therefore probably fall into category 2 above. In fact, if we look hard enough, we will probably be able to find representatives of all six possible combinations. We can certainly find examples of category 3—small, isolated, low-contact communities with *loose* network structures. Rural Newfoundland, as outlined by Paddock (1975), and West Falkland, as discussed in Trudgill (1986) and Sudbury (2000), are both cases where focusing in the LePageian sense (LePage and Tabouret-Keller 1985) has not taken place and where dialects differ from hamlet to hamlet or family to family because of loose social network structures. An example of category 4 might be the minority Vlach-speaking "language islands" (Berend and Mattheier 1994) of the southern Balkans, including Greece (Winnifrith 1987). And a case of category 5 might be 18th-century Japanese. We can expect categories 2, 3, 4, and 5 to be, in some as yet to be investigated way, intermediate between categories 1 and 6, though this is simply speculation at this stage, in terms of spontaneous complexification.

Mature phenomena

In Chapter 4, I carried out only a relatively cursory examination of the complex linguistic processes which are, or might be, involved in spontaneous complexification. But it was clear, I hope, that the relevance of these five societal features stems from the fact that, linguistically, complexification at the morphological and morpho-syntactic levels arises as a result of linguistic processes such as fusion, reanalysis, and refunctionalization, plus a complex of processes leading to grammaticalization, and with an important role at many points for phonology. And it was also clear, I hope, that these were processes which involve linguistic changes of a type which are likely to require considerable periods of time in order to develop undisturbed and go to completion—something which it seems is most likely to be the case in communities characterized by stability, low contact, and tight networks.

We saw, for example, that agreement-development is the sort of connatural change which naturally takes place when a language is not in contact with other languages; and that it needs many generations uninterrupted by adult language contact to come to fruition. Like other such features, however, it can be lost very rapidly—in a single generation, if a high-contact situation suddenly develops.

In stating that complexifying linguistic changes require long periods of time to go to completion, we are saying that the outcomes of these changes are linguistic forms which can be described, in a label introduced but not fully defined earlier in this book, as *mature phenomena,* in Dahl's (2004) striking and insightful term. Mature linguistic phenomena are, according to Dahl, linguistic features which imply a lengthy period of historical development—they "presuppose a non-trivial pre-history" (2004: 2). For example, Dahl singles out syntactic agreement as "belonging to the later stages of maturation processes" (2004: 197). We made a suggestion in Chapter 5, too, that the very large and very small phoneme inventories of certain isolated languages such as !Xu and Hawai'ian could also represent (admittedly rather different) examples of phenomena which take a very long time to develop. According to Dahl, "linguistic phenomena have life cycles in the sense that they pass through a number of successive stages, during which they 'mature', that is, *acquire properties that would not otherwise be possible*" (2004: 2; [my italics]).

My sociolinguistic-typological point of view is of course that in large, high-contact, unstable communities with loose social networks, such lengthy periods are less likely to be available. Mature phenomena are also very vulnerable to being lost if high-contact situations develop, as already mentioned: according to Dahl (2004: 207), mature phenomena "are highly prone to being filtered out in suboptimal language acquisition", and "there is a significant overlap" between mature phenomena and "those linguistic features which are most recalcitrant in second language learning" (2004: 286).

Dahl lists several linguistic features as examples of mature phenomena, and I will now discuss two of these in some detail, and consider their implications for sociolinguistic typology.

Fusional languages

Events we have discussed so far in this book as representing complexification include the development of morphological categories, and the growth of opacity, agreement and irregularity. I argued in Chapter 4 that these are all the result of long-term development; and Dahl confirms that examples of features falling under these headings are for him indeed mature phenomena.

Dahl states that "reviewing the candidates for inclusion in the class of mature linguistic phenomena, we find that the most obvious one is inflectional morphology" (2004: 111). He also focuses on the role of fusion in producing mature phenomena, and points out that phonological change is crucial in the development of fusional opacity: "structural condensation would depend on phonological condensation—the fusion of two words into one is conditioned by their having been phonologically integrated" (2004: 179). He also cites irregularity as a mature phenomenon: "lexical idiosyncrasy" (p. 112) occurs when a rule applies to lexical items in an unpredictable way—and irregularity includes also the presence of different inflectional classes. Highly fusional languages, then, are the supreme example of the outcome of linguistic complexification, as well as the supreme demonstration of the nature of mature phenomena.

The extent to which mature phenomena are linguistic features which imply a lengthy period of historical development can be gauged from the timing of morphological-typological changes that lead to the development of inflecting/fusional languages. As mentioned earlier, we do not necessarily have to accept the theory of the *morphological cycle* (Hodge 1970; Bynon 1977: 265; Dixon 1997) in its entirety to gain insights from it, but the theory suggests that languages change in such a way that they, as it were, move around a typological circle from isolating to agglutinating, from agglutinating to fusional, and eventually back to isolating again. If, following Dixon (1997), we present this circle graphically with purely isolating languages like Classical Chinese at, say, 4 o'clock, agglutinating at 8, and fusional at 12, we can say that modern Indo-European languages represent a movement from Proto-Indo-European at an approximately 12 o'clock position towards a more isolating type at 2 o'clock or, in the more advanced cases, 3 o'clock. Dixon (1997: 42) goes on to suggest that

Present-day agglutinative languages may have had an ancestor of more isolating profile, with what were distinct words having developed into grammatical affixes (e.g. postpositions into cases). The Dravidian family is roughly of this type, and here one can successfully recover a good deal of the proto-language.

According to Dixon, Proto-Finno-Ugric was perhaps at about 9 o'clock, while the modern languages in the family have moved to 10 or 11 o'clock, with Estonian clearly having moved further than Finnish, as we noted in Chapter 4. Now, if Proto-Finnic was at 9 o'clock and modern Finnish is, say, at 11 o'clock, then we can obtain a chronological estimate of how long this kind of change takes. Proto-Finno-Ugric dates back to about 4000 BC (Campbell 1997b), i.e. 6,000 years ago. Even if modern Finnish has been at 11 o'clock for as long as 1,000 years, this would mean it took 5,000 years to "travel" from 9 to 11, and arithmetic therefore indicates that for a language to transform from fully isolating to fully fusional (i.e. from 4 o'clock to 12) would, if the same trajectory speed was maintained, take 20,000 years. I claim absolutely no reality at all for this figure. I merely observe that it suggests that the development of at least certain mature phenomena requires very long periods of time indeed. A discussion of centuries-long periods, even if they are nothing like as long as 20 centuries, makes it clear that mature phenomena depend for their development on lengthy periods with relatively little interruption or "punctuation" (Dixon 1997) of the type that results from significant periods of social instability and/or adult language contact.

What implications does this have from a sociolinguistic-typological perspective? Consider the following. Faarlund (2005: 1149) writes, in connection with simplification, of "the well-known drift from a synthetic to an analytic type". This drift is indeed well known, and was pointed out for English and the Romance languages by Schlegel (1846). But I think we can also note a tendency amongst linguists for us to regard this kind of development as "normal". This is because we are so familiar with changes of this type in the histories of many of the Indo-European languages, as well as the Semitic languages, that it is very easy to think of simplification as simply "what happens". In comparing English with Old English, German with Old High German (Faarlund 2001), French with Latin (Wanner 2001), Bulgarian with Old Slavonic, we expect to find features such as reduction in overt case-marking; reduction in conjugations, declensions, and inflections; loss of the dual number; increase in periphrastic verb forms; and so on. As I argued long ago (Trudgill 1983), we may even have been tempted to regard it as a kind diachronic universal. Lass says that "there is apparently a traditional intuition of evolutionary direction ... we prefer morphological complexity to decrease" (1997: 253), which might suggest that we could establish a uniformitarian directional principal, namely that complexity gives way to simplicity. But, says Lass, this traditional intuition is not in fact well supported by the evidence.

My point, indeed, is that simplification is actually not normal. If it were normal, all languages in the world would by now have been highly regular and maximally transparent. I suggest that it is actually complexification that is, in an important sense, more normal. If languages are "left alone", the natural tendency is for them to accrue more and more complexity, as a result of connatural changes (Bailey 1982), not to simplify.

A decline in complexity

Things, however, are changing. As Bailey's terms *connatural* and *abnatural* imply, what is normal in isolation is not normal in contact. So even if linguistic complexification has been more normal for most of human history, this is no longer so true. If simplification is, in Bailey's terms, abnatural—"abnatural developments occur as a result of contact with other systems" (Bailey 1982: 10)[1]—then it is "normal" in certain sociolinguistic settings for simplification to occur, and those settings are becoming more and more common.

It is no doubt true that "the human brain can only tolerate a limited degree of complexity in a grammar" (Dixon 2010a: 13). But, as I argued earlier, some languages are more complex than

---

[1] However, as we saw in Chapter 2, contact has to be a particular type for simplification to occur.

others (Sampson et al. 2009): we saw that there is no evidence of the validity of the "negative correlation hypothesis", which supposes that if one component of language is simplified, then another must be elaborated in compensation (Shosted 2006). And the current diachronic trend is now in the direction of an increasingly higher proportion of languages which are increasingly less complex (always bearing in mind that I am making no claims about syntax). In other words, the fact that some linguists hold the view that simplification is "normal", even if historically unjustified, is becoming increasingly understandable.

As an illustration of this diachronic trend, a number of the English traditional-dialect features illustrating complexification listed in Chapter 4 have already disappeared, or are in the process of disappearing (see e.g. Gachelin 1991). And certain fusional European languages can currently be observed to be becoming less inflectional. For example, Faarlund (2000: 97) says of the Toten dialect of Norwegian:

The dative case has survived better in most dialects, but it too is in retreat. In Toten it is still in use amongst the older generation, but amongst younger people it is mainly found only in the southeast of the area [my translation].[2]

Braunmüller (2001: 74) reports a number of ongoing developments in Faroese which also point in the direction of simplification:

There is a certain tendency for the reduction of both stem and suffix allomorphy, at least with a number of feminine forms. There is a possibility that sooner or later a new structural type will develop, producing regular plural forms. Already, such forms do occur today. [my translation][3]

He cites some examples, including the regularization of the singular–plural alternations discussed in Chapter 4 such as *kígv—kúír* to *kígv—kígvir*. He then states (2001: 74):

---

[2] In the original Norwegian: Dativ har holdt seg bedre i de fleste dialekter, men også den er altså i tilbakegang. På Toten er den fremdeles i bruk hos den eldre generasjon. Blant yngre folk finnes den særlig i de sørøstlige deler av bygda (f.eks. i Totenvika).

[3] In the original Danish: Der findes en vis tendens til at reducere både stamme- og suffiks-allomorfi, i hvert fald ved en del af feminina-formene. Der er en chance for, at der før eller senere opstår en ny type, som vil føre til regelmæssige pluralisformer. Disse former kan forekomme allerede i dag.

The current tendency for developments in the direction of greater regularity represents an example of a gradual transition from a highly flexional to a more agglutinating linguistic type in modern Faroese as a whole. This linguistic-typological change can be seen in all flexional word classes. [my translation][4]

For example, the genitive has more or less been eliminated from the spoken Faroese language and is being replaced by prepositional constructions. This loss of the genitive, Braunmüller points out (2001: 75), also reduces opacity since it leads to the disappearance of those inflected forms which diverge most strongly from the nominative forms.

Grammatical gender

A second feature cited by Dahl as being a very typical example of a mature phenomenon is grammatical gender. Note that I am discussing *gender* here in the traditional sense of "small systems of nouns classes as in French or German (where adjectives and demonstratives agree with the head noun)" (Dixon 2002: 452) (grammatical gender); and semantically-based natural (sex-based) gender, as in English. That is, I am not principally concerned in this discussion with large, often semantically-based systems, or with phonologically determined systems like that of the Arapesh language of Papua New Guinea (Fortune 1942; Foley 1986; Aronoff 1994), which are frequently referred to as *noun classes*; but rather systems based on "a small system of noun classes, which includes a sex-based contrast" (Dixon 2010a: 156).

Dahl says that "grammatical gender systems generally presuppose rather long evolutionary chains and are in this sense among the more clearly mature elements of language" (2004: 112); and "gender, inflectional morphology and syntactic agreement make up an interesting cluster" of mature phenomena (2004: 197). He adds that "gender systems undoubtedly belong to the most mature phenomena in language" (2004: 199); and Corbett, too, writes of "the Indo European gender

[4] In the original Danish: Denne aktuelle udviklingstendens i retning af mere regularitet står eksemplarisk for en graduel overgang fra den højtreflekterende til en mere agglutinerende sprogtype i moderne færøsk i det hele taget. Denne sprogtypologiske forandring kan nemlig konstateres ved alle ordklasser med fleksion.

system whose origins lie so far back that much work [on their origins] has been largely speculative" (1999: 168). The sort of consequences that stem from the very long-term maturation of linguistic phenomena can be seen most clearly in these arbitrary Indo-European-type gender systems—systems which are not mainly and obviously semantically (or phonologically) based (Corbett 2005).

The way in which natural and grammatical gender are marked in the world's languages varies considerably, and this therefore provides a convenient site for testing our insights about the social matrices involved in the development of different linguistic phenomena.

One obvious way of marking gender is through pronouns. Greenberg showed (1966) that there are hierarchies and implicational universals in the expression of natural gender in pronoun systems. Some languages, like Hungarian and Finnish, have no gender marking on pronouns at all. Others, like English, have gender only in the third person singular. Still others, such as French, have it also in the third person plural— but there are no languages which express gender in the third person plural but not in the singular. A smaller number of languages also mark gender in the second person, where there may also be complications involving T and V pronouns: Polish, for example, has gender marking for the second person V quasi-pronouns *pan/pani* (which are actually third person forms equivalent to 'Mr' and 'Mrs' in origin) but not for T pronouns; Spanish has gender marking only in the second-person plural T pronoun but not for the V pronoun, and not at all in the singular. Yet other languages may have gender marking in the first person. Some have this feature only in the first person plural, such as Spanish *nosotros* vs. *nosotras*. Others have it also in the first person singular (see below). Here again there are implicational universals: if gender is marked in the first person it will also be marked in the second or third, but not necessarily vice versa (Greenberg 1966: 96).

Gender marking can also be effected through articles and adjectival agreement in the noun phrase, as in French. And it can be effected through finite verb forms, as in past tense and conditional verb forms in some Slavic languages: Russian, Ukrainian, and Belorussian have gender marking in these verb forms in the singular; Polish has it in both the singular and the plural; and modern forms of Kashubian (Stone 1993) also have it for both numbers.

From the point of view of sociolinguistic typology, however, the important question concerns not so much the way in which grammatical gender is marked but its function—which turns out to be rather obscure. (The function of natural gender is a good deal less puzzling—it is not surprising that human languages have gender marking for human beings, since the distinction between male and female is the most fundamental one there is between human beings, and it is therefore often important to know if a man or a woman is being talked about. But even this type of marking has its mysteries, as we shall see below.)

If we ask "What exactly is grammatical gender for?", it is very interesting to observe that, of the 323 pages of text in Corbett's enormously erudite book *Gender* (1991), 321 are devoted to the origins, nature and workings of gender systems, and only two to the function of grammatical gender: it would seem that it is not entirely clear to Corbett what its function is. As Hickey (2000) says: "grammatical gender ... is largely semantically redundant". Of the grammatical categories listed in Chapter 2 of this book—number, case, tense, aspect, voice, mood, person, and gender—some are more frequently found than others. *Person*, as I said there, occurs in all the languages of the world, but the other categories vary in their frequency of occurrence. They may also therefore be assumed to be of different statuses or degrees of importance, and their functions are also apparently less or more obvious. Clearly, languages can function perfectly well without grammatical gender (Trudgill 1999b)—it is a feature which has, to employ Dahl's very helpful term that we met already in Chapter 2, *cross-linguistic dispensability* (2004: 54). So, as Corbett asks of those languages which do have them, "why do languages have gender systems?"

As far as noun-class languages are concerned, Aikhenvald (1998) gives one illustrative example of a possible function: in languages in which noun-class assignment is semantically based, this can have a minor semantic function. In languages like Manambu (East Sepik Province, Papua New Guinea), assignment of noun-class to nonhuman animates is such that large animals belong to the masculine gender, and smaller animals belong to the feminine gender. For inanimates, it is based on their size and shape, so that long and/or large objects are treated as masculine, and small and/or round ones as feminine. However, there are a number of cases in which the same noun can be either masculine or feminine, depending on an object's size or other characteristics. Thus *val* 'canoe' is masculine if big, but feminine if small.

But what of grammatical gender systems of the Indo-European or Afro-Asiatic type? The function of this type of gender which has been most commonly cited is that grammatical gender systems help with disambiguation and reference tracking, as do natural gender-marking and noun-class systems. For noun class languages, Foley and Van Valin (1984) do give extensive evidence showing the importance of classes in languages in which they function "as the dominant system of discourse cohesion" (1984: 326). Dixon too (2002: 459) says that "one clear function is anaphoric reference". And Heath (1975) in fact argues that there is an inverse relationship between the number of verbal means—such as switch-reference, passive and anti-passive—for reference tracking in a particular language and the number of nominal classes, the point being that the more you have of the one, the less you need of the other.

But can this also truly be said to be a function of actual gender systems? Lyons (1977: 288) writes that "it is clearly the pronominal function of gender which is of primary importance in communication". Thus, for example, the by-now famous German sentence (Zubin and Köpcke, 1981) *Der Krug fiel in die Schale, aber er zerbrach nicht* is not ambiguous (as the corresponding English translation *The jug fell into the bowl but it didn't break* would be) because the two nouns are of different genders. And Fodor (1959: 206) makes the related point that gender concord assists with parsing in languages with free word order, particularly in literary genres, as in the classical Latin of Ovid: *lurida terribiles miscent aconita novercae* ('frightful stepmothers mix ghastly wolfbane', where *lurida* agrees with *aconita* 'wolfbane' and *terribiles* with *novercae* 'stepmothers'). In actual fact, there does not have to be anything literary about this: Dixon (2010a: 233–4) reports that Dyirbal generally has "almost unlimited ordering of words", and that the random ordering of clause elements always gives results which are grammatically acceptable to native speakers. He cites the clause:

bayi waɲal ba-ɲu-l yara-ɲu bulgan-u ba-ŋgu-n jugimbir-u bura-n
'The woman saw the big man's boomerang'

bayi	THERE + ABS + MASC
waɲal	boomerang + ABS
ba-ɲu-l	THERE-GEN-MASC + ABS
yara-ɲu	man-GEN + ABS
bulgan-u	big-GEN + ABS
ba-ŋgu-n	THERE-ERG-FEM
jugimbir-u	woman-ERG
bura-n	see-PAST

According to Dixon, this clause could just as well appear as:

bayi yaraɲu jugumbiru buran waɲal baŋgun baɲul bulganu

or any other ordering of the elements.

But we can see that in Dyirbal it is by no means only noun classification that does the job of reference tracking: the ergative and absolutive marking are vital; and it is only by chance that the two human referents happen to be respectively male and female.

So surely the reference tracking role of gender can only be seriously important in languages with systems where there are many more classes than the three which German has (or the two of French, or the four of Dyirbal). Foley and Van Valin do convincingly demonstrate (1984: 326) the very important reference tracking role noun classes play in the New Guinea language Yimas which, however, has about 16 different classes; and they say that even reference tracking of this type only works if "there is only one noun from each class in a discourse" (1984: 324).

In any case, one cannot help wondering whether this reference-tracking function in gender languages is, as it were, "worth it". After all, it is not an enormous effort to say, in

English, *The jug fell into the bowl but the jug didn't break*. In what sense does the (one has to assume) occasional German sentence such as the above "justify" the wealth of morphological complexity demonstrated by the German gender system, particularly in view of the fact that the disambiguation only works anyway if the two nouns involved just happen to be of different genders?

Further problems with this interpretation of the function of grammatical gender can also be noted:

(1) Gender marking can in some cases lead to tracking failure and ambiguity: in German, *Katze* 'cat' is feminine and *Hund* 'dog' is masculine, so that in a household with a male cat and a female dog, conflict between natural and grammatical gender can lead to considerable pronominal confusion.

(2) There is also the important point made by Croft (1994: 162) that "people talk about people more than about anything else" and that, therefore, reference tracking is most important for human referents—which is precisely where we find natural as opposed to grammatical gender.

(3) We also have to consider the perplexing fact, pointed out by Fodor (1959), that languages with gender often do not employ it in an efficient, functional way. He notes that, for example, German distinguishes between male and female horses lexically (*Hengst* vs. *Stute*) rather than by means of grammatical gender; and that the French for a female elephant is not *une éléphant* or *une éléphante* but *un éléphant femelle*, just as it is *nóstényelefánt* (literally 'female elephant') in Hungarian, a language without gender.

A further possible, psycholinguistic role for noun classification has to do with processing, as has been suggested by Paul Fletcher (p.c.). Given that most adults know several thousand nouns, and given that the time available for the recognition of a word can be measured in milliseconds, listeners need all the help that they can get in finding the right item in the lexical store. Anything which might cut down the range of possibilities for identification of an upcoming noun might be functional in this sense (see also Grosjean et al. 1994). And Dahl (2004: 202) also has a suggestion based on perception. He hypothesizes that grammatical gender "is essentially an error-checking mechanism. We know that a masculine article has to go with a masculine noun, if we perceive any other combination we know something has gone wrong." Once again, however, these perceptual gains seem likely to be of serious benefit only in languages which have large numbers of noun classes or very extensive classifier systems.

To return now to natural gender, even this, as mentioned above, is not without its enigmas. Natural gender marking in the third person may very often tell us something that we did not already know, as well as, sometimes, help with reference tracking. But what of natural gender marking in the second and first persons? This, like grammatical gender generally, most often tells us very little indeed that we do not already know. It is very unlikely to help us with reference tracking: all of Foley and Van Valin's crucial examples involve the importance of gender as a reference tracking device in the third person. There can by definition be no reference tracking problems in the case of the first person singular, and such problems are also very unlikely to occur very often in the first person plural or in the second person.

It is possible that some disambiguation may occur from time to time with second person pronouns. For example, a question such as *How are you* [sg.]? addressed to one person in the presence of another might be ambiguous as to the addressee unless one is male and one female and the language in question distinguishes between male and female second person pronouns (or, in pro-drop languages, verb forms). The same may also be true with first person plural pronouns—making it precisely clear, sometimes, who "we" are if there are different groups of people involved that are distinguished by sex.

But what can possibly be the function of gender distinctions in the first person singular? This form of gender marking is particularly puzzling. It is true that there is the secondary function that written narratives in languages which have such marking reveal the sex of the narrator in a way which is not possible in other languages. But except in the written language—and the masculine/feminine first person distinctions we see in some of the world's languages cannot be assumed to have arisen as a result of the advent of writing (or crackly telephone lines)—this form of gender marking gives us no "information" as such at all. It is quite normal to be able to tell whether a speaker is male or female—we do not, most usually, need distinct pronouns or other forms of grammatical marking to tell us this.

The gender of *self-reference* is really, then, an especially remarkable phenomenon (see Trudgill 1999). Nevertheless, the languages of the world show a number of different possibilities for its grammatical expression:

(1) As a feature which is very obviously cross-linguistically dispensable and "verbose", it may not occur at all—as in English and Hungarian. This appears to be linked to the fact that such languages do not have grammatical gender.

(2) It may occur through the use of adjectival gender marking, as in French *je suis heureuse* vs. *je suis heureux* 'I am happy'. In European languages this appears to occur only in languages which also have grammatical gender, although of course it is not inevitable in such languages—witness many languages including, for example, German, where it does not occur except, as Theo Vennemann (p.c) has pointed out to me, in appositional de-adjectival nominal predicates such as *Ich unglückliche(r)!* 'poor me!' f.(m.). In many Slavic and Romance languages, verbal past participles also behave like adjectives as far as gender marking is concerned. (Interestingly, this gives rise in Portuguese to gender marking in the word for 'thank you': *obrigado* vs. *obrigada*.)

(3) It may occur through the use of distinct gender-marked verb forms in the first person singular, as in Polish past tense and conditional verb forms. This also appears to be true, at least in Europe, only of languages which also have grammatical gender.

(4) It may occur through the use of distinct gender-marked first person singular pronouns, as in the southern African Khoekhoe language !Ora (see below). From New Guinea, Laycock (1965: 133) reports that Ngala has the forms /wn/ 'I (m.)' and /ɲən/ 'I (f.)'.

But clearly no new knowledge is communicated to us if:

(a) a Ngala man says /wn/ while a Ngala woman says /ɲən/; nor

> (b) an Italian man says *sono stanco* while an Italian woman says *sono stanca* 'I am tired'; nor
> (c) a Polish man says *przyjechałem* while a Polish woman says *przyjechałam* 'I arrived'.

We can conclude the following from the evidence cited above. Grammatical gender is obviously a relatively marginal grammatical category, as its absence from very many languages makes clear—Dahl (2004: 198) quotes Corbett as suggesting that 56% of the world's languages do not have grammatical gender *or* noun-class systems. Its failure to reappear in creoles after it has been lost through pidginization also suggests the same thing—Haitian Creole lacks the gender marking of French, for example.

It is true that natural gender marking in the third person may have a number of functions. However, grammatical gender marking in languages such as European languages which have only two or three genders seems to be almost totally non-functional. As Hickey (2000) says, grammatical gender is a category which is "not guided by semantic needs"; if it was, why would we find languages such as Modern Danish and (Standard) Swedish which do not distinguish between masculine and feminine grammatical gender at all but simply between neuter and "common" gender (historical masculine and feminine combined)? Similarly, natural gender marking in the second and first persons—particularly the first person singular—has little or no function.

The only way we can explain these non-functional or marginally functional phenomena is historically. We know that languages drag along with them a certain amount of "unnecessary" historical baggage. This is most obvious in the case of grammatical irregularities which all languages appear to be able to tolerate up to a point. If the plural of *foot* in English is *feet* rather than **foots*, native learners can cope with this, and linguists can explain why it is so on historical grounds.

But from a sociolinguistic-typological perspective, we have to note that some languages have much more of this afunctional historical baggage than others. For example, the presence of cognitive irritants such as different declensions for nominal forms and different conjugations for verbal forms in inflecting languages, as discussed by Dahl, provides good evidence that languages can have large amounts of complex and non-functional differentiation which provide afunctionally large amounts of redundancy and whose presence can again only be explained satisfactorily in historical terms. As Croft (2000: 195) says, "functional considerations do not play a role"; and "elaborated 'dysfunctional' innovations" can readily be propagated in small stable communities, as I argued earlier.

As far as origins are concerned, Corbett argues that a likely source of noun-class systems is to be found in nouns themselves, and in particular in "nouns with classificatory possibilities such as 'woman', 'man', 'animal' " (Corbett, 1991: 312; see also Corbett, 1999). We then have to suppose the operation of long-term diachronic processes involving the grammaticalization of such nouns as classifiers (see also Lee 1988), which is well known to have occurred in languages such as Chinese. Classifiers can then in turn either come to be used anaphorically and turn into demonstratives—and subsequently pronouns and other gender markers—or they can be repeated within the noun phrase and give rise to gender agreement in that way (see also Harris and Campbell 1995: 341–2). Dixon (1980: 273) reports precisely this kind of development in a number of Australian languages. He writes that "some northern languages show a grammatical system of noun classes … that has probably developed out of the syntactic pattern of including generic and specific nouns within an NP" as in 'the PERSON old man speared an ANIMAL wallaby'. He then continues: "most languages of Arnhem Land and the North Kimberleys have between four and eight classes, each marked by prefix to the noun." He goes on to say that "there is evidence that the noun class prefixes developed out of generic nouns where the generic nouns were operating very much as classifiers" (see also Dixon 2002: Chapter 10).

But as far as Indo-European and Afro-Asiatic-type gender systems are concerned, things are clearly more mysterious. Dahl (2004: 199) says, with respect to the question of how non-semantic gender arises, that "the natural assumption is that animate gender(s) come to be extended to inanimates through various processes, although the full story of how a system like e.g. that of French and German arises has not yet been told". Indeed, it most certainly has not yet been told, and the "various processes" remain obscure.

Other, probably secondary, forms of gender marking can be explained historically. For instance, Slavic gender-marked verb forms derived originally from compound tenses which consisted of the verb *be* plus a past participle which, like adjectives, agreed in gender. Then developments such as that which occurred in Russian took over: "the present tense of the verb 'be' in Modern Russian [became] the null form, which has left the original participle as the only verb element present" (Corbett 1991: 126).

However, in any discussion of explanations it should be clear what manner of explanation we are talking about. Carstairs-McCarthy argues (2010: 6) that human language demonstrates "imperfections" and "bad design" as a result of the evolutionary processes that led to its development. These mature grammatical and natural gender phenomena are thus "linguistic male nipples", in the sense of Lass (1997: 13): they can be said to have come into being, over long periods of time, for a reason but with no purpose. The reason was a series of linguistic events leading to grammaticalization, as suggested by Corbett, Dixon, and Harris and Campbell—and Dahl also stresses the important role of grammaticalization in producing mature phenomena. These gender features are "invisible hand" phenomena, in the sense of Keller (1994), in that they occur for reasons which have nothing to do with the ultimate outcome. They are phenomena which, as biologists would say, have an *explanation but no function*.

Whether or not it is clear why such complexifying grammaticalization events take place, it certainly is clear that their motivation is not originally to divide nouns into agreement classes, or to aid with reference tracking or disambiguation. The possibility of reference tracking and disambiguation using gender differentiation in the third person of the type described by Foley and Van Valin is a bonus, an example of *exaptation*—the co-optation of "material that is already there, but either serving some other purpose, or serving no purpose at all" (Lass 1990: 316)—as mentioned in Chapter 4. If "useful" in language means "relating either to communication or cognition" (Carstairs-McCarthy 2010: 6), then originally useless phenomena, serving no purpose at all, can over time become useful. Croft (2000: 127) links Lass's term *exaptation* to Greenberg's *regrammaticalization* (1991: 301) and to his own *hypoanalysis*. But for our purposes, the crucial difference is that, while Croft and Greenberg both talk of reanalysis leading from one function to another, Lass is prepared to allow for the possibility of material "serving no purpose at all". Note also that this "bonus" is one which is scarcely operative in languages with few genders, or in gender marking in the second person and the first person plural; and it is not operative at all in gender marking in the first person singular.

Other minor forms of exaptation can also be seen in occasional, subsidiary functions of grammatical gender that have been identified in the literature. For example, Fodor (1959: 206) suggests that gender "lends itself to the purposes of animation, sexualisation and personification in literature" and cites a Russian folk song where a rowan tree (*r'abina* f.) is yearning for an oak tree (*dub* m.); and Holmqvist (1991) describes how, in the Spanish of Cantabria (northern Spain), gender reassignment can be used jokingly, for instance in deprecating references to young girls using the masculine gender.

We can assume that having arisen for a reason but with no serious purpose, and having developed as mature phenomena as a result of connatural changes, gender systems can subsequently, like much other "junk" in natural languages (Lass 1990: 309), survive indefinitely under certain conditions. Gender marking occurs with a very high degree of frequency indeed in those languages which have it, and so is a feature with a very high degree of *entrenchment,* in the sense of Langacker (1987: 59). It is thus very readily maintained in the speech of individuals; and because of the amazing language learning abilities of the human infant, languages readily maintain this type of complex historical baggage from one generation to another, even though it represents a complication and/ or an excess of redundancy, and even though it may have no particular or very important function.

Dahl disputes the view that "junk" is an appropriate term to use here, pointing, for example, to "the frequency of manifestations of gender systems in discourse" (2004: 200) and to the centuries-long stability of gender systems (2004: 199). My argument, as we have just seen, however, is that it is precisely this level of frequency in discourse that permits the passing on of gender from one generation to another even though it is relatively unimportant. Features of a language do not have to be important: as Carstairs-McCarthy says (1994: 784), "a characteristic of language with an obviously useful function may have byproducts which are not obviously useful at all, but which are *tolerated because they do no harm*" [my italics].

Gender marking of this afunctional type disappears only when adults start playing an influential role in language learning in contact situations of the post-critical threshold type. "As is well known," writes, Dahl (2004: 200) as quoted earlier, "second-language learners have great problems with grammatical gender, both learning to apply agreement rules and learning the gender of individual words". As we saw in Chapter 2, English and Afrikaans have lost grammatical gender altogether, and certain high-contact varieties of the mainland Scandinavian languages have reduced their gender categories from three to two through the loss of the feminine (as referred to in Hickey 2000), while other lower-contact varieties have retained the original three-gender system—reduction in gender systems is "highly correlated with the degree of external contacts" (Dahl 2004: 200).

A similar thing has happened in Dutch, where the metropolitan varieties in the north of the Netherlandic-speaking area, including Standard Dutch, have merged feminine and masculine, while dialects of the Flemish south (and neighbouring areas) have retained the three original genders (De Vogelaer 2009). For example, while Standard Dutch has the definite article forms *de* (common gender—masc./fem.) and *het* (neut.), the southern dialects have *den* (masc.), *de* (fem.), and *'t* (neut.), with corresponding adjectival agreement (Taeldeman 2005: 62):

Standard Dutch: *de dunne boer*   vs. *de dunne boerin*
Flemish: *den dunnen boer* vs. *de dunne boerin*
                 'the thin farmer'   'the thin farmer's wife'

Crucially, the effects of this merger can also be seen in the case of grammatical (as opposed to natural) gender:

Standard Dutch:	*De tafel—hij* (= 'he') *staat buiten*
Flemish:	*De tafel—ze* (= 'she') *staat buiten*
	'The table—it's standing outside'

The noun *tafel* was originally feminine in all varieties of Dutch, and is therefore pronominalized by "she" in varieties which preserve the masculine–feminine distinction. In standard Dutch, where masculine and feminine have been merged into a single common gender, all common gender nouns, regardless of historical gender status, are now pronominalized by "he"— except for animate feminines such as *vrouw* 'woman'.[5]

One sociolinguistic-typological prediction which stems from these observations is: given that "junk" begins to disappear in situations of high post-critical threshold contact, it is not unlikely that languages with large numbers of grammatical devices of little or no functionality, such as grammatical gender, will become less numerous in the decades and centuries to come. And indeed it is not entirely impossible that linguistic gender, except for natural gender in the third person, will one day disappear from the languages of the world, never to return.

Societies of intimates and their languages

To the extent that linguistic complexity is made up of mature phenomena, such as inflectional morphology and grammatical gender, an interesting if depressing possibility now opens up— a possibility which I will also explore further in the Epilogue to this book.

One of the fundamental bases of modern historical linguistics has been the *uniformitarian principle* (Labov 1972). This principle was initially developed by geologists, but its relevance to linguistics has long been recognized, and powerfully argued for by William Labov. It states that *knowledge of processes that operated in the past can be inferred by observing ongoing processes in the present*. In other words, we can suppose that language structures in the past were subject to the same constraints as language structures now in the present. For

---

[5] In the two-gender dialect of Slovenian spoken (significantly) in the bilingual area of Sele Fara in southern Austria (Priestly 1983), it is the neuter gender which has disappeared—as in the modern Romance languages—and been replaced by the masculine.

example, as Dixon has said (1997), it is likely that the reason there are no primitive languages today is that there never have been. The principle also implies that we can suppose that the mechanisms of linguistic change that we see operating around us today are the same as those which operated even in the remote past. This leads to the methodological principle of *using the present to explain the past*: we cannot seek to explain past changes in language by resorting to explanations that would not work for modern linguistic systems.

However, sociolinguistic typology shows us that there is one very important respect in which the present is not like the past at all. This has to do with the enormously rapid development of transport and communications facilities in the past 150 years—but even more importantly, it has to do with demography, and, as a consequence, social network structure. There are very many more of us human beings on the planet now than there have ever been: in the past 500 years the population of England has increased from about 4 million to about 50 million, for instance. Increasing populations and increasing mobility have led to more and more language and dialect contact, and larger and larger language communities, so that languages and dialects spoken in small, low-contact, isolated communities with tightly-knit social networks and large amounts of communally shared information are becoming less and less common.

Labov himself, in his discussion of the uniformitarian principle, warns that we must be "wary of extrapolating backward in time to neolithic preurban societies": the methodology of using the present to explain the past might be less useful the further back in time we go (Labov 1994: 23). But his use of the word "neolithic" is very thought-provoking. If we think about it, we realize that most of the linguistic past—nearly all of the history of human language—took place in pre-neolithic or neolithic societies. Human language came into existence perhaps something like 100,000 years ago (Corballis 1999; Dixon 1997). The earliest date for a post-neolithic society anywhere in the world is about 5,000 to 6,000 years ago, in the Middle East (Langer 1987), and later, sometimes very much later, everywhere else. This means that human languages were spoken in neolithic and pre-neolithic societies for something like 95% of their history.

Until the domestication of plants and animals, our ancestors were all hunter-gatherers. As such, they belonged to "societies of intimates"—that is, societies "where all *generic* information is shared" (Givón 1979: 297). As described by Givón and Young (2002), such societies contrast with "societies of strangers" (Givón 1979: 297), the larger and more complex human groups which began to develop around 10,000 BC and which most of us inhabit today (Givón 1979: 287; 1984: 249). For nearly all of human history, we lived in societies characterized, according to Givón and Young, by stability, small size (no more than 150 people), restricted territorial distribution (with a radius of no more than 20 miles), cultural uniformity, and what they call *informational homogeneity*—that is, in my terms, having large amounts of communally shared information. And these were, of course, also societies with dense social networks.[6]

It is therefore probable that widespread adult-only language contact is a mainly post-neolithic and indeed a mainly modern phenomenon, associated with the last 2,000 years.[7] Nichols (2007: 176) agrees that language contact "may well have been rare in prehistory, though it is responsible for much reduction in morphology in Europe over the last two millennia" (which is of course why some of us have been inclined to think of simplification as so normal). Given that the development of large, fluid communities is also a post-neolithic and indeed mainly modern phenomenon, then a sociolinguistic-typological perspective suggests that the dominant standard modern languages in the world today are likely to be seriously atypical of how languages have been for nearly all of human history, a point with which Wray and Grace (2007) concur.

This poses an interesting problem for linguistic typology. A great deal of attention has been paid by workers in this field to the sampling of the world's languages for typological purposes. It is acknowledged that it is important in constructing samples to avoid *areal* bias, so that languages in one part of the world are not favoured at the expense of languages elsewhere; and

---

[6] Wichmann, 2010b, discusses the characteristics of neolithic languages.

[7] This figure tallies rather well, give or take 1,000 years or so, with calculations concerning the migration rate of languages presented in Wichmann (2010a), where he demonstrates that, starting around 1000 BC, this rate began to rise very steeply.

that it is also vital to avoid *genetic* bias, so that certain language families are not overrepresented (Dryer 1989; Song 2001: 1.5.3.–4). What is suggested by the perspective I am presenting here, however, is that there is also a problem of *chronological* bias. This problem is insuperable. There is obviously no way we can make a genuine sample of all the languages that have ever existed; and if modern languages are not, as a whole and on average, typical of how languages have been for most of human existence, then a representative modern sample will not in fact be representative. It could be argued that this puts seriously into question the value of language sampling in linguistic typology at all. Dixon (2010a: 257ff.) argues against sampling in linguistic typology, not least because many of the materials currently being sampled are taken from inadequate descriptions, and because, as he argues, we should rather be devoting our efforts to improving and expanding these descriptions. But even if, in the fullness of time, that defect could be remedied, there is no likelihood that the problem of chronological bias will ever be overcome.

This perspective also indicates that we are likely in future to see fewer and fewer mature linguistic phenomena in languages. And the long-term diminution in the number of communities which are "societies of intimates" suggests that linguists should also consider which other, not necessarily so "mature" aspects of linguistic structure might also be most likely to be associated with such societies, and therefore most likely to be in danger of being lost to the world and to linguistic science.

The sort of phenomenon I am thinking about here is illustrated in Blust's account of bizarre sound changes in Austronesian languages (see Chapter 5), which includes a suggestion that "speakers may sometimes engage in a conscious, arbitrary manipulation of linguistic symbols" (2005: 264)—in other words, the only way he can think of explaining certain phonological changes is to suppose that speakers produced these sound changes deliberately—consciously and on purpose.

For those of us who feel doubtful about the possibility of linguistic change being indulged in deliberately by speakers, Blust refers us to Laycock, who describes a situation in the Uisai dialect of Buin, a Papuan language of Bougainville Island, where all masculines have become feminine and all feminines have become masculine. Laycock argues that, since "there is no accepted mechanism for linguistic change which can cause a flip-flop of this kind and magnitude", he believes—reminding us of the suggestions made by Johnston (1997) and Nettle (1995), cited earlier, about the possible role of individuals— that "at some stage in the past, some influential speaker of the Uisai dialect announced that from now on his people were not to speak like the rest of the Buin. Once the change was adopted, it would become the natural speech of the community within one or two generations" (Laycock 1982: 36). Whether or not this is true, it is certainly not the kind of development that is likely to succeed in anything other than a small, tightly-knit society of intimates.

But there are many other, rather less bizarre linguistic features which, I suggest, are likely to be lost as societies of intimates disappear. Some of these involve morphological categories which are most obviously, as Dahl says, *cross-linguistically dispensable* or superfluous (Gil 2009). I now go on to describe four candidates for membership of this category.

Cross-linguistically dispensable categories:
Dual (plus) number

Nearly all European languages have lost the dual number in the last 2,000 years or so. Some, like English, lost it long ago. Others, like Polish, lost it much more recently. Yet others still retain it.

One striking thing about this development is that this loss of "verbosity" (Dahl 2004) has gone hand in hand with demographic expansion. This is unlikely to be just a coincidence; it is noticeable that those European languages which have retained the dual number are spoken by relatively small numbers of speakers, by European standards, such as Slovenian (2.5 million or so), or by very small numbers of speakers, such as Sami. According to Haugen (1976: 303), "Tylden (1956) speculates on the gradual disappearance of the dual in Indo-European as evidence of social change from a 'primitive' face-to-face society to one of greater mobility".[8]

---

[8] It is interesting that in Icelandic, in the case of the first person plural pronoun, it is the original dual that survives rather than the plural.

Some suggestive work which gives us some insight into why this might be so has been carried out by Perkins (1980, 1995). Perkins takes, as the starting point for his research, a suggestion by Keenan (1976) that deictic systems are better developed in non-literate communities with fewer than 4,000 speakers than in larger communities. Kay (1976: 18) alludes to the social factor of *communally shared information* and says that "in small, homogeneous speech communities there is a maximum of shared background between speakers, which is the stuff on which deixis depends. As society evolves toward complexity and the speech community becomes less homogeneous, speakers share less background information, and so one would need to build more of the message into what was actually said." Givón (1979), too, observes that people in more complex cultures are more frequently required to interact with other people who they do not know.

Linguists are naturally sceptical about relating linguistic and cultural complexity. As Bickerton (1996) states,

if there were any link between cultural complexity and linguistic complexity, we would expect to find that the most complex societies had the most complex languages while simpler societies had simpler languages. ... We do not find any such thing.

Interestingly, indeed, we now have data which can be interpreted as suggesting that the relationship is the other way round: I have been arguing that certain aspects of linguistic complexity seem to be more evident in simpler than in complex societies.

Perkins's argument is that deictics identify referents by connecting them to the spatial–temporal axis of speech events. Deictics in his terms include persons, tenses, demonstratives, directionals (*here, there*), inclusive vs. exclusive, etc. The point about deictics, he argues, is that they involve the requirement that the spatio-temporal context of their use be available for the interpretation of the intended referents.

Perkins thus conjectures that deictics will be more salient in less complex than in more complex cultures. He then goes on to say that deictics are therefore more likely to appear in the central inflectional systems of the languages concerned than more peripherally in the lexis or periphrastically. This is in turn because the more frequently free deictic morphemes occur, the more likely they are to be subject to grammaticalization processes which turn them into bound morphemes through coalescence and morphologization.

Perkins investigated fifty languages and their usage of seven deictic affixes: tense, person on verb, person on nouns, spatial demonstratives on verbs, spatial demonstratives on nouns, inclusive vs. exclusive on person markers, and dual in person markers. Communities are ranged for cultural complexity from 1 (e.g. Andamanese) to 5 (e.g. Vietnamese). The measurement of cultural complexity that Perkins uses is based on the work of anthropologists such as Carneiro (1973), and is computed in terms of factors such as type of agriculture, settlement size in terms of population, craft specialization, and numbers of levels in political and social hierarchies.

Perkins shows statistically that there is a correlation between social complexity, so computed, and the presence of deictic affixes. For example, languages associated with the most complex cultures—those scoring 5—have on average 1.22 deictic affixes, while those scoring 1, the lowest, have on average 3.28. Perkins concludes that deictic affixes are lost as cultures become complex.[9]

Many linguists are likely to feel perhaps a little uncomfortable about the notion of cultural complexity. I am therefore happy, at least for the time being, to leave this issue to the anthropologists, and to point out that we probably do not need to look any further, for our own linguistic purposes, than to actual community size and shared information. What is probably crucial here is simply how many individuals are involved in a particular speech community, and how much shared information is available—to what extent, in other words, they meet the profile of a society of intimates.

In any case, it would seem to be perfectly possible that an increase in community size and loss of intimacy in the modern world could lead to an increasing loss of deictic categories, including loss of systems involving dual (trial, etc.) number, from the world's languages.

---

[9] Frei (1944) suggests that two-way demonstrative systems are typically newer than three-way systems.

Cross-linguistically dispensable categories:
Large pronominal systems

Personal pronominal systems (see Dixon 2010b: 189ff.) also seem to be related to societal type in the same kind of way. In the Prologue to this book, I noted that social factors have played a role in the development of the Korean personal pronoun system. Thai, too, has a famously complex personal pronoun system whose complexity is due to issues involving social hierarchy, power, and politeness factors (Campbell 1969).

However, some languages have highly elaborated systems whose elaboration has nothing to do with hierarchy or politeness. Aikhenvald and Dixon, in a paper on evidentials (1998: 254), suggest in a section entitled "Some Speculations" that there is a strong possibility that there can be an even greater role for social factors in personal pronoun development; they point out that the most complex pronominal systems in the world's languages "tend to be found in small-scale language communities with a classificatory kinship system" (see also Dixon 1997: 117). There does indeed appear to be a very good prima facie case for investigating this possibility. In particular, the presence of the category we have just been discussing—dual (or trial or even higher number systems)—in such small-scale language communities can help, in combination with the exclusive–inclusive distinction mentioned by Perkins, to produce very large systems indeed.

To give just a few examples, the small-group indigenous languages of Australia typically have at least 11 personal pronouns, involving first, second, and third persons; singular, dual, and plural numbers; and inclusive and exclusive 'we'. For instance, Nyamal (Dench 1994: 170) has:

		sg.	dual	pl.
1	incl.	*ngatja*	*ngalilu*	*nganjtjula*
	excl.		*ngaliya*	*nganartu*
2		*njunta*	*njumpalu*	*njurralu*
3		*palura*	*piyalu*	*thanalu*

Fijian has an even larger system because of the addition of trial number. Dixon (1988: 54) gives this system for Boumaa Fijian:

	sg.	dual	trial	pl.
1 excl.	*yau*	*'eirau*	*'eitou*	*'eimami*
incl.		*'eetaru*	*'etatou*	*'eta*
2	*i'o*	*'emudrau*	*'emudou*	*'emunuu*
3	*'ea*	*(i)rau*	*(i)ratou*	*(i)ra*

The trial number here is probably best described as "paucal", since it can also be used to refer to "a few".

In terms of size of systems, moreover, this is by no means the end of the story. Hutchisson (1986: 5) shows that Sursurunga, an Austronesian language of Papua New Guinea with about 3,000 speakers, has a 5-way number system, i.e. singular, dual, trial, quadral, and plural, and thus 19 'persons'. The system is as follows:

	sg.	dual	trial	quadral	pl.
1 excl.	*iau*	*giur*	*gimtul*	*gimhat*	*gim*
1 incl.		*gitar*	*gittul*	*githat*	*git*
2	*iáu*	*gaur*	*gamtul*	*gamhat*	*gam*
3	*-i/on/ái*	*diar*	*ditul*	*dihat*	*di'wuna*

If we now add the possibility of pronominal gender to the equation, Siewierska (2004: 111) claims that the fullest pronoun paradigm that she has ever seen is that of !Ora, which has 31 pronouns (Güldemann 2001). !Ora is a Khoekhoe language of southern African nomads which *Ethnologue* showed to have 50 speakers in 1972 and which is now extinct. This 31-pronoun system, which distinguishes between male and female in the first and second as well as third persons, which has dual number, and which contrasts exclusive and inclusive 'we', is as follows (*c.* stands for "common gender"):

	sg.	dual	pl.
1 incl. c.		*sam*	*sada*
1 incl. f.		*sasam*	*sase*
1 incl. m.		*sakham*	*satje*
1 excl. c.		*sim*	*sida*
1 excl. f.	*tita*	*sisam*	*sise*
1 excl. m.	*tire*	*sikham*	*sitje*
2 c.		*sakhaoo*	*sadu*
2 f.	*sas*	*sasaro*	*sasao*
2 m.	*sats*	*sakharo*	*sakao*

3 c.	*ll' ãi'l*	*ll' ãikha*	*ll' ãine*
3 f.	*ll' ã is*	*ll' ãisara*	*ll' ãide*
3 m.	*ll' ãib*	*ll' ãikhara*	*ll' ãiku*

This contrasts dramatically with, say, the simple 8-pronoun system of French:

je	*nous*
tu	*vous*
il	*ils*
elle	*elles*

or the 7-pronoun system of Standard English:

I	*we*
you	
he	*they*
she	
it	

and especially with the genderless and transparent 6-pronoun system of Cantonese (60 million native speakers):

ngo'h	*ngo'deih*
le'ih	*le'ihdeih*
ke'uih	*ke'uihdeih*

However, it is not entirely clear that the link here is actually solely with the existence of a classificatory kinship system, as Aikhenvald and Dixon originally suggested; nor is it clear exactly how that link would work. It is likely, however, that it has to do, as well or instead, with at least some of the five social factors that I have investigated in this book for their importance in producing sociolinguistic-typological consequences. For example, the !Ora 31-pronoun system does indeed tally with Perkins's hypothesis about deixis and small communities.

I suggest, moreover, that the development anew of such pronominal systems, in any of the languages of the modern world that are spoken in societies of strangers, is now rather unlikely. And of course, tragically, the !Ora system has now already been lost; while, according to Geraghty (1983), a number of modern varieties of Fijian are currently losing the

distinction between trial and plural in their pronominal systems (with the trial form being the one to survive).

Cross-linguistically dispensable categories:
Generationally-marked pronouns

Another very clear example of a linguistic phenomenon that
could only have developed in a society of intimates comes from
the work of Uri Tadmor (forthcoming). Tadmor is the first
linguist to have worked on Onya Darat, a West Malayo-
Polynesian (Austronesian) language which is spoken in the
interior of southwestern Indonesian Borneo. It belongs to the
Land Dayak sub-group of languages which are found in a large
area stretching from Sarawak in the north to the Ketapang area
of Indonesian Kalimantan in the south.

According to Tadmor, Onya Darat distinguishes between
singular, dual, and plural in its personal pronominal system,
and it also has an exclusive vs. inclusive distinction in the first
person dual and plural. Remarkably, however, as Tadmor
shows, the system also incorporates another highly unusual
grammatical distinction: generational affiliation.

The singular pronouns indicate the generational affiliation
of the referent(s) vis-à-vis the speaker(s) or the interlocutor(s),
with the two-way distinction of forms being between those for
members of the same or a younger generation, on the one
hand, and those for members of an older generation, on the
other. The dual and plural pronouns work differently in that
they indicate the generational relationships with the distinction of forms being between those for members of the same
generation and those for a different generation—except that
the first person dual and plural inclusive pronouns are not
marked for generation in this way. This gives a total of
$3 \times 3 \times 2 + 2 = 20$ pronouns.

As an example, the third person forms are as follows:

singular $\leq$ *iyo*
singular $>$ *idoh*
dual $=$ *doduh*
dual $\neq$ *damaaq*
plural $=$ *diyen*
plural $\neq$ *denaq*

Thus if a woman were talking about her granddaughter and great-granddaughter, she would have to say *damaaq* 'they (dual)', while if she were talking about two granddaughters she would say *doduh* 'they (dual)'.

Similarly, if two speakers of the same generation are talking, they use the pronouns *oko* 'I' and *omo* 'you (sg.)', but if they are of two different generations, the older generation will instead say *maaq* 'I' and will be addressed as *okam* 'you (sg.)' by the younger generation. On the other hand, when addressing, for example, two cousins, the pronoun *kanduh* 'you (dual)' is used, but when addressing, say, a man and his niece *kamaaq* 'you (dual)' must be employed because they are members of different generations.

Clearly, such a system can only work in a society where everybody knows everybody else: generation does not necessarily match with age—one's nephew might perfectly well be older than oneself. A speaker actually has to know the generational affiliation of everyone in the community in order to be able to use the correct pronoun. Formerly, this always worked very well, because each traditional Onya Darat village consisted of a single longhouse, with a newly established village consisting perhaps of as few as six families, an older village of maybe sixty—but "crucially all the inhabitants of the village lived in the same house and knew each other *intimately*" (Tadmor, forthcoming [my italics]).

Sadly, extensive destructive logging of the forest habitats of the Onya Darat has now more or less destroyed this traditional way of life; the longhouses are disappearing—and this perhaps unique society-of-intimates pronoun system is, as Tadmor reports, disappearing with them.

Cross-linguistically dispensable categories: Evidentials

Finally, in languages with evidential systems, as we saw in Chapter 2, there is a grammatical requirement that the source of the speaker's information should be morphologically marked (rather as all finite verbs in English must be marked for tense). Recall that the evidential system of Tariana mentioned in Chapter 2, as described by Aikhenvald (2003a: 287–323), is very highly developed. The morphological markers are fused with tense suffixes. In the recent past tense

(Aikhenvald 2004) for example, the five evidential verb suffixes are:

VISUAL: *-ka*
NONVISUAL: *-mahka*
INFERRED: *-nihka*
ASSUMED: *-sika*
REPORTED: *-pidaka*

According to Aikhenvald (2003a: 294), the VISUAL evidentials refer to events which have been seen by the speaker; the NON-VISUAL to events heard or otherwise sensed non-visually; the INFERRED category relates to "information obtained through observing direct evidence of an event or state"; the ASSUMED to "information obtained by reasoning or common sense through observing evidence of an event or state without directly experiencing it"; and REPORTED refers to second-hand or third-hand information (doing the same work that can be done in English by using the adverb *apparently*). Aikhenvald (2004: 2) gives an extended example of how this works, based on the five different Tariana translations of the English sentence *José has played football*. The equivalent in Tariana cannot be uttered without an evidential marker—this would be ungrammatical. The form *irida* means 'football', *di* is the third person singular marker, and *manika* is the verb 'to play':

> *Juse irida di-manika-ka* 'José has played football' [we saw it]
> *Juse irida di-manika-mahka* [we heard it]
> *Juse irida di-manika-nihka* [we infer it from visual evidence]
> *Juse irida di-manika-sika* [we assume this on the basis of what we already know]
> *Juse irida di-manika-pidaka* [we were told]

As Aikhenvald explains, the INFERRED marker would be used "if one sees the football is not in its usual place in the house, and José and his football boots are gone (and his sandals are left behind), with crowds coming back from the football ground". The ASSUMED marker would be used if José is not at home on a Sunday afternoon and "we know that he usually plays football on a Sunday afternoon".

The sociolinguistic-typological question here, of course, is why do some languages have evidentials and others not?—a question also asked by Aikhenvald (2004: 355). Can we, for example, provide an answer by saying that an evidential system is necessarily a mature phenomenon, dependent for its genesis on a long period of social stability and low adult-only contact?

Although much remains unknown about the origins of evidential markers, Aikhenvald (2004) outlines a large number of different origins. She shows that where they are spontaneously generated rather than borrowed, evidential markers may come from grammaticalized verbs—such as verbs of saying and seeing; spatial deictics; demonstratives; pronouns; locatives; participles; and copulas, to name only some of the sources. For example, the VISUAL marker-*ka* in Tariana may derive diachronically from the verb form *nu-ka* 'I see'; and the NONVISUAL marker -*mha* derives from the verb *hima* 'to hear, feel' (Aikhenvald 2004: 273, 286). So evidentials are clearly the result of processes that have resulted in grammaticalization. Dahl also believes that they have a non-trivial prehistory: evidential systems "are clear examples of maturation (or grammaticalization) processes leading to an increase in system complexity" (2004: 189).

It also appears to be possible, however, that they too are typical products of societies of intimates. Aikhenvald (p.c.) has indicated an answer to the question she herself has posed—of why some languages have evidentials and others do not—by pointing out that large complex systems of evidentiality—with four, five, or six specifications—are found only in small communities. Earlier, Dixon (1997: 120) had said that "detailed systems of evidentiality tend to be found only among non-industrialised people"; and he then went on to say that "this is a topic at present little understood". Aikhenvald, however, now suggests that the explanation may lie in the fact that in such communities there is pressure for everybody to be fully explicit about their source of information. In her book *Evidentiality* (2004: 60–3), she confirms that "complex evidential systems, in their vast majority, are confined to languages with smallish numbers of speakers, spoken in small, traditional societies" (Aikhenvald 2004: 355).

Aikhenvald cites a number of languages with evidential systems which have, or had, five or more contrasts. There are three languages from the Vaupés area of northwestern Amazonia which have 5-way systems: Tariana, the Arawakan language which we just mentioned above and in Chapter 2, which currently has about 100 speakers (Aikhenvald 2003a); Tuyuca, an East Tucanoan language, with about 800 speakers; and Hupda or Hup, a Maku language with about 1,500 speakers (Epps 2008). And there is one language from northern California, Wintu, a Wintun language (Mithun 1999), which has only a handful of speakers.

Aikhenvald also cites two languages which have six contrasts. They are both from the Southern Highlands of Papua New Guinea: Foe which has about 2,780 speakers, according to *Ethnologue*; and Fasu, with 1,200—they are both members of the Kutubuan family, but not closely related.

Finally, Aikhenvald lists two Pomoan languages from northern California which have, or probably have, seven contrasts. These are Kashaya and Central Pomo, which are listed in *Ethnologue* with 45 and four speakers respectively.

Aikhenvald (2004: 359) then goes on to provide an excellent explanatory insight, which reminds us of the arguments of Perkins above:

being specific in one's information source appears to correlate with the size of a community. In a small community everyone keeps an eye on everyone else, and the more precise one is in indicating how information was acquired, the less the danger of gossip, accusation, and so on. No wonder that most languages with highly complex evidential systems are spoken by small communities.

Aikhenvald also wonders, cautiously, if there are cultural correlates of large evidential systems. She supposes that some language communities may have sets of beliefs, mental attitudes, behavioural conventions, and discourse conventions "which are compatible with the independent development of evidential systems with their requirement to be as precise and as specific as possible about information source" (2004: 359). In an interesting passage which suggests that the same kind of cultural motivation for evidential-system development is unlikely these days to be found in larger, more fluid communities, Aikhenvald writes (2004: 358):

In the context of Amazonian societies, the requirement to be precise in one's information source may be related to the common belief that there is an explicit cause—most often sorcery—for everything that happens. So as not to be blamed for something that in fact they had no responsibility for, a speaker is careful always to be explicit as possible about what they have done.

It may, then, not be a coincidence that, as Aikhenvald and Dixon (1998) report, grammatical evidentiality has been independently innovated in at least six different sites in Amazonia.

In any case, there is good reason to believe that highly developed evidential systems may indeed be a linguistic feature particularly strongly associated with societies of intimates. If this is so, they are therefore also, we can assume, in danger of being lost from the world's languages. Certainly, we know that the northern California Wintu evidential system (see above) was reduced from five terms to two between the 1930s and the 1960s (Aikhenvald 2004: 300).

Conclusion

Today, as we saw in Chapter 3, most of the world's major languages are already koinés or creoloids which have relatively few complex, mature phenomena. As McWhorter (2007) has pointed out, Mandarin has much less complexity than other varieties of Chinese. Standard Modern Persian is often said to be "marvellously simple" compared to its relatives, such as Pashto. Modern Arabic dialects are much simpler, in the technical sense, than Classical Arabic (see Chapter 2). And Standard Malay/Indonesian is much less complex than its Western Malayo-Polynesian relatives. One could also point to Swahili—a typical creoloid-cum-koiné—amongst Bantu languages.

Creoles, indeed, provide us with a wealth of instructive, negative evidence for the sorts of linguistic developments that depend on low-contact dense social networks, and long periods of "equilibrium", for their genesis. Pidgin languages usually lack all morphology: there are no cases, numbers, tenses, aspects, moods, voices, persons, or genders that are morphologically marked. Person can be signalled by pronouns or nouns; case can be pragmatically deduced or, perhaps, marked by word order; location of events in or through time can be indicated if necessary through adverbs, as can modality. Interestingly, though, there is no role at all for grammatical gender, and only a very small role, except lexically, for natural gender.

However, the expansion process inherent in creolization—the "repair" of the reduction of pidginization—involves the reintroduction of some of the grammatical categories that have been lost (Muysken 2001). Creole languages typically have (optional) aspect and tense markers, such as the Sranan particles *ben* 'past' and *de* 'habitual', which are preposed to the main verb. And they typically have (optional) plural markers, such as Jamaican Creole *dem* which is postposed to nouns. But they are still totally lacking in mature linguistic phenomena. It is no surprise, of course, that they lack grammatical gender, since as we saw before this is a phenomenon which "crosscuts lexicon, morphology and syntax" and "gender, inflectional morphology and syntactic agreement make up an interesting cluster of phenomena that all belong to the later stages of maturation processes" (Dahl 2004: 197). And they have no person markers on verbs—they continue the pidgin practice of signalling person by pronouns. There is no morphological case-marking—case is marked by word order, even for pronouns: Jamaican Creole has *mi* 'I, me'; *im* 'he, him, she, her', *wi* 'we, us', *dem* 'they, them'. And mood has to be signalled lexically. In particular, creoles also typically lack evidentials, trial number, and very large pronominal systems; and they lack features such as switch-reference systems, subjunctives, postposed definite articles, noun incorporation, polysynthesis, pronoun hierarchies, and inalienable vs. alienable possession markers.

To some extent these absences may be based on areal features associated with the different languages that were in contact prior to the development of modern creoles. But the total absence from creoles of all of these features, many of which would appear to be mature phenomena and/or to involve heavy memory load or other difficulties for adult language learning, cannot be a coincidence. We might expect that creoles would eventually—and "eventually" might mean after a very long period of time indeed—develop more complex features, if the social conditions were right for connatural changes to take place—if they were "left alone". But that now seems to be increasingly unlikely.

We can therefore suppose that features such as evidentials, trial number, noun incorporation, polysynthesis, and pronoun hierarchies are relatively unlikely to be created afresh in the societies of strangers that predominate in modern conditions. And they are also relatively likely to be lost in high adult-contact situations. In other words, they might eventually disappear from the world's languages altogether. And to return to our discussion of phonology in Chapter 5, it is also relatively likely that languages with phoneme inventories which are extremely large (like Ubykh—now extinct—and the Khoisan languages—endangered), or extremely small (like Hawai'ian—endangered), may also be lost to the world, never to return.

Epilogue: On the future of linguistic complexity

Linguistic complexity developed in societies of intimates. It was in such societies that the five major complexity-producing social factors were maximally operative: small size, dense social networks, large amounts of shared information, high stability, and low contact. According to Dixon (2010a: 7), "the most complex grammatical systems ... are typically found in languages spoken by small tribal groups". It is possible, therefore, that with the gradual disappearance of societies of intimates, we will also see the disappearance of complexifying linguistic changes. And this is especially so because, as it will be remembered, there is no guarantee that linguistic complexity will necessarily develop even in such societies where they remain. The social matrices afforded by these societies provide the sociolinguistic conditions which *permit* linguistic complexity development; but they do not compel it to occur. There may well also be a trend towards a predominance of simplifying changes—as Wray and Grace put it "a language that is customarily learned and used by adult non-native speakers will come under pressure to become more learnable by the adult mind, as contrasted with the child mind" (2007: 557). In the long run, obviously, these two factors would combine to produce a significant reduction in overall worldwide linguistic complexity.

In a now very dated-sounding argument, Jespersen (1894, 1922) refers to synthetic, inflexional languages as typically "ancient", encumbered with morphological baggage; and he describes analytic languages as being streamlined and typically "modern", as if there was some inevitability about this. But maybe he was right, and maybe it is a development approaching inevitability—though not at all for the reasons that he suggested. He regarded the path from the one type to the other as representing "progress", but we can now see that, as I wrote in 1977 (Trudgill 1983: 107),[1]

it is not entirely out of the question that, although for demographic and sociolinguistic rather than straightforward linguistic reasons, our philosophical forbears were right when they pointed to a kind of evolutionary trend in linguistic change.

I have mentioned above the possibility that it may be the case that languages go through a morphological cycle (see Bynon 1977: 265) in which fusional languages lose their morphology, perhaps through phonetic erosion, and gradually become isolating, only later to acquire further morphology as phonological and other processes turn independent lexical items into clitics and then into bound morphemes. Forms with bound morphemes may then subsequently undergo fusion, and ultimately fusional languages may result once again. Now, however, if there actually is such a thing as the morphological cycle, we have to suppose that it may gradually be grinding to a halt. It is true that Chinese is currently acquiring a certain amount of morphology (Dai 1992; 1997). Crowley (1987: 165–6) also describes a certain amount of development in Tok Pisin, the English-lexifier creole of Papua New Guinea, from isolating towards agglutinating, for example in the development of prepositions into prefixes, as in *em kar bilong mi* 'that car of me' > *em kar blomi* 'that is my car'. And Li and Thompson (1976) describe the apparent ongoing development of a case system in Wappo, though we have to note that this is occurring in a very small Californian Amerindian language of precisely the type I have been discussing as being under threat. But as we look around the world's languages, there are currently rather few signs of isolating or even agglutinating languages turning into fully-fledged complex fusional languages of, say, the classical Indo-European type.

Bickerton (1981) has argued for the importance of the study of the development of creole languages by children in high-contact situations as a window into the nature of linguistic competence. I agree. But I want to suggest too, in a kind of mirror-image of his argument, that if we are keen to learn

---

[1] This point is repeated by Dahl (2004: 296).

more about the inherent nature of linguistic systems and their propensity to change in certain ways, we must focus our attention on linguistic changes of the type that occur in low-contact varieties. Even if isolated languages do have, to those of us of a European-language background, and to those of us who speak standard creoloids and koinés, amazing and unusual features, they are of interest precisely because they represent, to the clearest extent possible, the limits to which languages can go when, as Bailey (1982) says, they are "left alone".

Wohlgemuth (2010) suggests that "rarities"—very rarely occurring or even unique linguistic phenomena—are more likely to be found in languages spoken by small numbers of speakers, which are therefore more likely to be endangered. This provides us with another reason for arguing that more linguistic fieldwork should be carried out more urgently before such features—if language preservation efforts are unsuccessful—are lost to linguistic science for ever.

Some years ago I was in conversation with a very eminent, intelligent, and humane generative linguist. I asked him how he would handle, in his current theoretical model, the phenomenon of switch reference. He said something like: "I don't know. That's something you only get in exotic languages, isn't it? I don't know anything about exotic languages." Perhaps I am being unfair, but one implication could perhaps be drawn. If a phenomenon occurs only in a small far-away language which appears exotic to an academic speaker of a standard variety of a European language, it is not really worth bothering about.

In fact, as I have been suggesting in this book, these "exotic languages" with their mature phenomena are actually, especially from a diachronic perspective, not exotic at all. They are normal. They are precisely what we *should* be bothering about. This is what all human languages must have been like throughout most of the tens of thousands of years of human history on this planet. It is the creoloids and koinés and creoles that have developed in the last 2,000 years, and particularly in the last 500 years, that must be weird and unrepresentative.

The consequence of this is clear. If we are keen to learn more about the inherent nature of linguistic systems, we must urgently focus most of our attention on linguistic structures and linguistic changes of the types that occur in the ever-dwindling number of low-contact, dense social network varieties of language in the modern world. If we want to pursue any kind of linguistic typology—and more importantly, if we want to build up an accurate picture of the nature of human languages throughout human history—we had better hurry, as I argued in Trudgill (1992) and as was stated extremely eloquently by Dixon (1997), not only because most of the world's languages are in danger but also because most of those that are going to be left behind will increasingly tend to be of a single, historically atypical type.

As Orr (1999) points out, Dixon's (1972) ground-breaking study of the Australian language Dyirbal, which "revolutionised our view of ergativity" (Comrie 1978: 393), was a close-run thing: Dyirbal was a dead language before the next decade was out. As Schmalstieg (1980: 18) says, if it had not been for the timing of Dixon's fieldwork, "it seems quite possible that the Dyirbal population might have disappeared without a trace, and notions of ergativity would have remained unhampered by new facts". How much other knowledge about human language are we going to miss out on? A very large proportion of the world's isolated languages and dialects, and of languages and dialects spoken in small tightly-knit communities, may not be with us much longer. It would not be at all surprising if in a few generations' time there were no languages at all in the world with any of their typical social— and I would therefore argue—linguistic characteristics (Dixon 1997; Trudgill 1992).

We can assume that the human language faculty has remained unchanged for very many millennia indeed; but our observations in this book suggest that the sociolinguistic-typological matrices within which linguistic changes occur have changed significantly. It would therefore not be totally unreasonable to suppose that, in the future, we are increasingly unlikely ever again to see the development of highly inflectional, fusional language varieties; and it is increasingly unlikely that we will ever again witness the growth of languages with 80 consonants, or 31 personal pronouns, or seven-term evidential systems. Linguists of the future may well find themselves envying the linguists of today the opportunities we still have for the study of highly complex languages at first hand. But the possible future loss of linguistic complexity is surely for us too a matter, to say the very least, of some very considerable regret.

Bibliography

Acuña-Fariña, Juan Carlos. 2009. The linguistics and psycholinguistics of agreement: A tutorial overview. *Lingua* 119: 389–424.

Adams, Karen Lee. 1989. *Systems of numeral classification in the Mon-Khmer, Nicobarese and Aslian subfamilies of Austroasiatic.* Canberra: Pacific Linguistics.

Aikhenvald, Alexandra. 1996. Areal diffusion in northwest Amazonia: The case of Tariana. *Anthropological Linguistics* 38: 73–116.

——1998. Physical properties in a gender system: A study of Manambu. *Language and Linguistics in Melanesia* 27 (1996).

——1999. Arawak languages. In R.M.W Dixon and A.Y. Aikhenvald (eds.) *Amazonian languages.* Cambridge: Cambridge University Press, 65–106.

——2000. *Classifiers: A typology of noun categorization devices.* Oxford: Oxford University Press.

——2001. Areal diffusion, genetic inheritance and problems of subgrouping: A North Arawak case study. In R.M.W. Dixon and A. Aikhenvald (eds.) *Areal diffusion and genetic inheritance: Problems in comparative linguistics.* Oxford: Oxford University Press, 167–94.

——2002. *Language contact in Amazonia.* Oxford: Oxford University Press.

——2003a. *A grammar of Tariana, from northwest Amazonia.* Cambridge: Cambridge University Press.

——2003b. Mechanisms of change in areal diffusion: New morphology and language contact. *Journal of Linguistics* 39: 1–29.

——2004. *Evidentials.* Oxford: Oxford University Press.

——2008a. Multilingual imperatives: The elaboration of a category in northwest Amazonia. *International Journal of American Linguistics* 74: 189–225.

——2008b. *The Manambu language of East Sepik, Papua New Guinea.* Oxford: Oxford University Press.

——and R.M.W. Dixon. 1998. Evidentials and areal typology: A case study from Amazonia. *Language Sciences* 20: 241–57.

Allan, Keith, and Kate Burridge. 2006. *Forbidden words: Taboo and the censoring of language.* Cambridge: Cambridge University Press.

Allen, W.S. 1987. *Vox Graeca* (3rd edn). Cambridge: Cambridge University Press.

Andersen, Henning. 1988. Center and periphery: Adoption, diffusion, and spread. In J. Fisiak (ed.) *Historical dialectology: Regional and social.* Berlin: Mouton de Gruyter, 39–84.

——2008. Grammaticalization in a speaker-oriented theory of change. In Th. Eythórsson (ed.) *Grammatical change and linguistic theory: The Rosendal Papers.* Amsterdam: Benjamins, 11–14.

Anderson, Stephen R. 1985. Inflectional morphology. In T. Shopen (ed.) *Language typology and syntactic fieldwork,* vol. III. Cambridge: Cambridge University Press, 150–201.

——and David W. Lightfoot. 2002. *The language organ.* Cambridge: Cambridge University Press.

Andersson, Lars Gunnar. 2005. Some languages are harder than others. In L. Bauer and P. Trudgill (eds.) *Language myths.* London: Penguin, 50–7.

Anderwald, Lieselotte. 2009. *The morphology of English dialects: Verb-formation in non-standard English.* Cambridge: Cambridge University Press.

Ansaldo, Umberto, and Sebastian Nordhoff. 2009. Complexity and the age of languages. In E.O. Aboh and N. Smith (eds.) *Complex processes in new languages.* Amsterdam: Benjamins.

Anttila, Raimo. 1989. *Historical and comparative linguistics.* Amsterdam: Benjamins.

Aquilina, Joseph. 1959. *The structure of Maltese: A study in mixed grammar and vocabulary.* Valletta: Royal University of Malta.

Arnason, Kristjan. 1980. *Quantity in historical phonology.* Cambridge: Cambridge University Press.

Aronoff, Mark. 1994. *Morphology by itself: Stems and inflectional classes.* Cambridge, MA: MIT Press.

Askedal, John Ole. 2005. The typological development of the Nordic languages I: Morphology and syntax. In O. Bandle (ed.) *The Nordic languages: An international handbook of the history of the North Germanic languages,* vol. II. Berlin: de Gruyter, 1872–86.

Auer, Anita, and Victorina Gonzalez Diaz. 2005. Eighteenth-century prescriptivism in English: a re-evaluation of its effects on actual language usage. *Multilingua* 24: 317–41.

Bailey, Charles-James. 1977. Linguistic change, naturalness, mixture, and structural principles. *Papiere zur Linguistik* 16: 6–73.

——1982. *On the yin and yang nature of language.* Ann Arbor: Karoma.

Bailey, Guy, Tom Wikle, Jan Tillery, and Lori Sand (eds.). 1996. The linguistic consequences of catastrophic events: An example from the American Southwest. In J. Arnold, R. Blake, B. Davidson,

S. Schwenter, and J. Solomon (eds.) *Sociolinguistic variation: Data, theory and analysis.* Stanford: CSLI, 435–51.

Bailey, Richard W. 1996. *Nineteenth century English.* Ann Arbor: University of Michigan Press.

Bakker, Peter. 1997. *A language of our own: The genesis of Michif, the mixed Cree-French language of the Canadian Métis.* Oxford: Oxford University Press.

——2003. Pidgin inflectional morphology and its implications for creole morphology. In I. Plag (ed.) *Yearbook of Morphology 2002,* Dordrecht: Kluwer, 3–33.

——2004. Phoneme inventories, language contact, and grammatical complexity: A critique of Trudgill. *Linguistic Typology* 8: 368–75.

Bartoli, Matteo. 1945. *Saggi di linguistica spaziale.* Turin: Bona.

Bauer, Laurie. 1988. What is lenition? *Journal of Linguistics* 24: 381–92.

——2001. *Morphological productivity.* Cambridge: Cambridge University Press.

Bayer, Josef. 1984. COMP in Bavarian syntax. *Linguistic Review* 3: 209–74.

Beaken, Michael. 1996. *The making of language.* Edinburgh: Edinburgh University Press.

Bennardo, Giovanni (ed.). 2002. *Representing space in Oceania: Culture in language and mind.* Canberra: Pacific Linguistics.

Berend, Nina, and Klaus Mattheier (eds.). 1994. *Sprachinselforschung.* Frankfurt: Lang.

Bernstein, Basil. 1971. *Class, codes and control.* London: Routledge.

Berthele, Raphael. 1998. *'Und jetzt sprechen alle gleich': eine dialektologisch-soziolinguistische Untersuchung von Primarschulkindern in multilingualem Umfeld.* University of Fribourg: unpublished PhD thesis.

——2004. The typology of motion and posture verbs: A variationist account. In B. Kortmann (ed.) *Dialectology meets typology: Dialect grammar from a cross-linguistic perspective.* Berlin: Mouton de Gruyter, 93–126.

——2006. *Ort und Weg: die sprachliche Raumreferenz in Varietäten des Deutschen, Rätoromanischen und Französischen.* Berlin: de Gruyter.

Bickerton, Derek. 1981. *The roots of language.* Ann Arbor: Karoma.

——1996. *Language and human behaviour.* London: UCL Press.

Biggs, Bruce. 1978. The history of Polynesian phonology. In S.A. Wurm and L. Carrington (eds.) *Second international conference on Austronesian linguistics: Proceedings. Fasc. 2 Eastern Austronesian.* Pacific Linguistics C-61. Canberra: Australian National University, 691–716.

Blakeley, Leslie. 1964. *Old English*. London: English University Press.

Blomkvist, Nils. 1979. Kalmars uppkomst och äldsta tid. In I. Hammarström (ed.) *Kalmar stads historia I: Kalmarområdets forntid och stadens äldsta utveckling*. Kalmar: Kulturnämnden i Kalmar.

Bloomfield, Leonard. 1933. *Language*. New York: Henry Holt.

Blust, Robert. 1999. Subgrouping, circularity and extinction: Some issues in Austronesian comparative linguistics. In E. Zeitoun and P. Li (eds.) *Selected papers from the eighth international conference on Austronesian linguistics*. Taipei: Academia Sinica, 31–94.

——2005. Must sound change be linguistically motivated? *Diachronica* 22: 219–69.

——2007. Òma Lóngh historical phonology. *Oceanic Linguistics* 46: 1–53.

Boas, Franz. 1947. A grammar of Kwakiutl. *Transactions of the American Philosophical Society* 37: 201–377.

Bohnacker, Ute. 2005. Nonnative acquisition of Verb Second: On the empirical underpinnings of universal L2 claims. In Marcel den Dikken and Christina Tortora (eds.) *The function of function words and functional categories*. Amsterdam: Benjamins, 41–77.

Bokamba, Eyamba. 1993. Language variation and change in pervasively multilingual societies: Bantu languages. In S. Mufwene and L. Moshi (eds.) *Topics in African linguistics*. Amsterdam: Benjamins, 207–52.

Bonfante, Giuliano. 1947. The neolinguistic position. *Language* 23: 344–75.

Borg, Alexander. 1985. *Cypriot Arabic: A historical and comparative investigation into the phonology and morphology of the Arabic vernacular spoken by the Maronites of Kormakiti village in the Kyrenia district of north-western Cyprus*. Stuttgart: Deutsche Morgenlandische Gesellschaft.

——and Manwel Mifsud. 2002. Maltese object marking in a Mediterranean context. In P. Ramat and T. Stolz (eds.) *Mediterranean languages: Papers from the* Medityp *workshop*. Bochum: Brockmeyer.

Bowden, John. 1992. *Behind the preposition: Grammaticalisation of locatives in Oceanic languages*. Canberra: Pacific Linguistics.

Bradlow, Ann. 1995. A comparative acoustic study of English and Spanish vowels. *Journal of the Acoustic Society of America* 97: 1916–24.

Braunmüller, Kurt. 1984. Morphologische Undurchsichtigkeit—ein Charakteristikum kleiner Sprachen. *Kopenhagener Beiträge zur germanistischen Linguistik* 22: 48–68.

——2000. Was ist Germanisch heute? *Sprachwissenschaft* 25.2: 271–95.

Braunmüller, Kurt. 2001. Morfologisk typologi og færøsk. In K. Braunmüller and J.L. Jacobsen (eds.) *Moderne lingvistiske teorier og færøsk*. Oslo: Novus, 67–88.

Bremmer, Rolf. 2009. *An introduction to Old Frisian*. Amsterdam: Benjamins.

Browman, Catherine, and Louis Goldstein. 1991. Gestural structures: Distinctiveness, phonological processes, and historical change. In I. Mattingley and M. Studdert-Kennedy (eds.) *Modularity and the motor theory of speech perception*. London: Erlbaum, 313–39.

Brown, Roger, and Alberto Gilman. 1960. The pronouns of power and solidarity. *American Anthropologist* 4.6: 24–39.

Bubenik, Vit. 1993. Dialect contact and koinéization: The case of Hellenistic Greek. *International Journal of the Sociology of Language* 99: 9–23.

——2007. The rise of the koiné. In A. Christidis (ed.) *A history of Ancient Greek: From the beginnings to late antiquity*. Cambridge: Cambridge University Press, 342–5.

Burling, Robbins. 1970. *Man's many voices*. New York: Holt, Rinehart and Winston.

Burridge, Kate. 2002. Changes within Pennsylvania German grammar as enactments of Anabaptist world view. In N.J. Enfield (ed.) *Ethnosyntax*. Oxford: Oxford University Press, 207–30.

Butcher, Andrew. 1994. On the phonetics of small vowel systems: Evidence from Australian languages. In R. Togneri (ed.), *Proceedings of the 5th Australian International Conference on Speech Science and Technology*, vol. I. Canberra: Australian Speech Science and Technology Association, 28–33.

——2006. Australian Aboriginal languages: Consonant-salient phonologies and the 'place-of-articulation imperative'. In J.M. Harrington and M. Tabain (eds.) *Speech production: models, phonetic processes and techniques*. New York: Psychology Press, 187–210.

Bybee, Joan. 1985. *Morphology: A study of the relation between meaning and form*. Amsterdam: Benjamins.

——Revere Perkins, and William Pagliuca. 1994. *The evolution of grammar: Tenses, aspect and modality in the languages of the world*. Chicago: University of Chicago Press.

Bynon, Theodora. 1977. *Historical linguistics*. Cambridge: Cambridge University Press.

Campbell, Lyle. 1997a. Amerindian personal pronouns: A second opinion. *Language* 73: 339–51.

——1997b. On the linguistic prehistory of Finno-Ugric. In R. Hickey and S. Puppel (eds.) *Language history and linguistic modelling: A festschrift for Jacek Fisiak on his 60th birthday*. Berlin: Mouton de Gruyter, 829–62.

Campbell, Lyle and William Poser. 2008. *Language classification: History and method*. Cambridge: Cambridge University Press.

Campbell, Russell N. 1969. *Noun substitutes in modern Thai: A study in pronominality*. The Hague: Mouton.

Carlin, Eithne. 2007. Feeling the need: The borrowing of Cariban functional categories into Mawayan (Arawak). In A. Aikhenvald and R.M.W Dixon (eds.) *Grammars in contact: A cross-linguistic typology*. Oxford: Oxford University Press, 313–32.

Carneiro, Robert. 1973. Scale analysis, evolutionary sequences, and the range of cultures. In R. Naroll and R. Cohen (eds.) *A handbook of method in cultural anthropology*. New York: Columbia University Press, 834–71.

Carstairs-McCarthy, Andrew. 1987. *Allomorphy in inflexion*. London: Croom Helm.

——1994. Inflection classes, gender, and the principle of contrast. *Language* 70: 737–88.

——2010. *The evolution of morphology*. Oxford: Oxford University Press.

Caubet, Dominique. 1993. *L'Arabe marocain*. Leuven: Peeters.

Cauldwell, Richard. 1998. Faith, hope and charity: The vices of listening comprehension. *The Language Teacher* 22.7: 7–9.

Chafe, Wallace. 2002. Masculine and feminine in the Northern Iroquoian languages. In N.J. Enfield (ed.) *Ethnosyntax*. Oxford: Oxford University Press, 99–109.

Chambers, J.K. 1992. Dialect acquisition. *Language* 68: 673–705.

——1995. *Sociolinguistic theory*. Oxford: Blackwell.

——and Peter Trudgill. 1980. *Dialectology*. Cambridge: Cambridge University Press.

Cheshire, Jenny, Sue Fox, Paul Kerswill, and Eivind Torgersen. 2008. Ethnicity, friendship network and social practices as the motor of dialect change: linguistic innovation in London. *Sociolinguistica* 22: 1–23.

Christaller, Walter. 1933. *Die zentralen Orte in Süddeutschland*. Jena: Fischer.

Christiansen, Hallfrid. 1946–48: *Norske dialekter*. Oslo: Tanum.

Cichocki, Piotr, and Marcin Kilarski. 2011. On "Eskimo words for snow": The life cycle of a linguistic misconception. *Historiographia Linguistica* 37: 341–77.

Clackson, James and Geoffrey Horrocks. 2007. *The Blackwell history of the Latin language*. Oxford: Blackwell.

Clahsen, Harald and Pieter Muysken. 1996. How adult second language learning differs from child first language development. *Behavioural and Brain Sciences* 19: 721–23.

Clark, Ross. 1976. *Aspects of proto-Polynesian syntax*. Auckland: Linguistic Society of New Zealand.

——1994. The Polynesian Outliers as a locus of language contact. In T. Dutton and D. Tryon (eds.) *Language contact and change in the Austronesian world*. Berlin: Mouton.

Combrink, Johan. 1978. Afrikaans: Its origin and development. In L. Lanham and K. Prinsloo (eds.) *Language and communication studies in South Africa*. Cape Town: Oxford University Press, 69–95.

Comrie, Bernard. 1978. Ergativity. In W. Lehmann (ed.) *Syntactic typology*. Austin: University of Texas Press, 329–94.

——1980. Morphology and word order reconstruction: Problems and prospects. In J. Fisiak (ed.). *Historical morphology*. The Hague: Mouton, 83–96.

——2008. Inflectional morphology and language contact, with special reference to mixed languages. In P. Siemund and N. Kintana (eds.) *Language contact and contact languages*. Amsterdam: Benjamins.

Cooper, Vincent. 1979. Aspects of St Kitts-Nevis Creole phonology. *Journal of the College of the Virgin Islands* 4: 5–22.

Corballis, Michael. 1999. The gestural origins of language. *American Scientist* 87: 138–46.

Corbett, Greville. 1991. *Gender*. Cambridge: Cambridge University Press.

——1999. Gender and gender systems. In K. Brown and J. Miller (eds.) *Concise encyclopedia of grammatical categories*. Amsterdam: Elsevier, 163–9.

——2005. Systems of nominal classification I: Gender oppositions. In A. Cruse, F. Hundsnurscher, M. Job, and P. Lutzeier (eds.) *Lexicology*. Berlin: De Gruyter, 986–94.

——2006. *Agreement*. Cambridge: Cambridge University Press.

Croft, William. 1994. Semantic universals in classifier systems. *Word* 45: 145–71.

——2000. *Explaining language change*. London: Longman.

Crothers, John. 1978. Typology and universals of vowel systems. In J.H. Greenberg, C.A. Ferguson, and E.A. Moravcsik (eds.), *Universals of Human Language, vol. 2: Phonology*. Stanford, CA: Stanford University Press, 93–152.

Crowley, Terry. 1987. *An introduction to historical linguistics*. Port Moresby: University of Papua New Guinea Press.

Crowley, Terry 2004. Bislama: Phonetics and phonology. In E. Schneider et al. (eds.) *A handbook of varieties of English, vol. 1: Phonology*. Berlin: Mouton de Gruyter, 671–89.

Curnow, Timothy. 2001. What language features can be 'borrowed'? In A.Y. Aikhenvald and R.M.W. Dixon (eds.), *Areal diffusion and genetic inheritance: problems in comparative linguistics*. Oxford: Oxford University Press, 412–36.

Curtis, Edmund. 1936. *A history of Ireland*. London: Methuen.

Cutler, Anne, Maria Luisa Garcia Lecumberri, and Martin Cooke. 2008. Consonant identification in noise by native and non-native listeners: Effects of local context. *Journal of the Acoustical Society of America* 1264–8.

Dahl, Östen. 2004. *The growth and maintenance of linguistic complexity*. Amsterdam: Benjamins.

——2009. Testing the assumption of complexity invariance: The case of Elfdalian and Swedish. In G. Sampson et al. (eds.) *Language complexity as an evolving variable*. Oxford: Oxford University Press.

Dahlbäck, Göran. 1998. Invandring—särskilt tysk—till Sverige under medeltiden. In L. Nilsson and S. Lilja (eds.) *Invandrarna och lokalsamhället*. 11–30.

Dai, John Xiangling. 1992. *Chinese morphology and its interface with the syntax*. Ohio State University PhD thesis.

——1997. Historical morphologization of syntactic structures: Evidence from derived verbs in Chinese. *Diachronica* 7: 9–46.

Dalton, Christiane, and Barbara Seidlhofer. 1994. *Pronunciation*. Oxford: Oxford University Press.

Dauenhauer, Nora, and Richard Dauenhauer. 1998. Technical, emotional and ideological issues in reversing language shift: examples from Southeast Alaska. In L. Grenoble and L. Whaley (eds.) *Endangered languages: language loss and community response*. Cambridge: Cambridge University Press, 57–98.

Dench, Alan. 1994. The historical development of pronoun paradigms in the Pilbara region of Western Australia. *Australian Journal of Linguistics* 14: 155–91.

Derbyshire, Desmond. 1977. Word order universals and the existence of OVS languages. *Linguistic Inquiry* 8: 590–9.

De Vogelaer, Gunther. 2004. Person marking in Dutch dialects. In B. Kortmann (ed.) *Dialectology meets typology: dialect grammar from a cross-linguistic perspective*. Berlin: Mouton de Gruyter, 181–210.

——2005. *Persoonsmarkering in de dialecten in het nederlandse taalgebied*. Ghent: Universiteit Gent.

De Vogelaer, Gunther. 2009. Changing pronominal gender in Dutch; transmission or diffusion? In S. Tsipaklou, M. Karyolemou, and P. Pavlou (eds.) *Language variation: European perspectives II*. Amsterdam: Benjamins, 71–80.

——2010. Morphological change in continental West Germanic: Towards an analogical map. *Diachronica* 27: 1–31.

——and Johan van der Auwera. 2010. When typological rara generate rarissima: Analogical extension of verbal agreement in Dutch dialects. In J. Wohlgemuth and M. Cysouw (eds.), *Rara and rarissima: Collecting and interpreting unusual characteristics of human language*. Berlin: Mouton de Gruyter.

Disner, Sandra. 1984. Insights on vowel spacing. In I. Maddieson (ed.) *Patterns of sounds*. Cambridge: Cambridge University Press, chapter 9.

Dixon, R.M.W. 1972. *The Dyirbal language of North Queensland*. Cambridge: Cambridge University Press.

——1980. *The languages of Australia*. Cambridge: Cambridge. University Press.

——1981. Grammatical reanalysis: An example of linguistic change from Warrgamay (north Queensland). *Australian Journal of Linguistics* 1: 91–112.

——1988. *A grammar of Boumaa Fijian*. Chicago: University of Chicago Press.

——1997. *The rise and fall of languages*. Cambridge: Cambridge University Press.

——2002. *Australian languages: Their nature and development*. Cambridge: Cambridge University Press.

——2003a. Demonstratives: A cross-linguistic typology. *Studies in Language* 27: 61–112.

——2003b. A program for linguistics. *Turkic Languages* 7: 157–80.

——2010a. *Basic linguistic theory I: Methodology*.

——2010b. *Basic linguistic theory II: Grammatical topics*.

——and Alexandra Aikhenvald (eds.). 1999. *The Amazonian languages*. Cambridge: Cambridge University Press.

Dorian, Nancy. 1994. Varieties of variation in a very small place: Social homogeneity, prestige norms, and linguistic variation. *Language* 70: 631–96.

Dressler, Wolfgang U. 1984. Explaining natural phonology. *Phonology Yearbook* 1, 29–51.

——1988. Language death. In F. Newmeyer (ed.) *Linguistics: The Cambridge survey, vol. 4*. Cambridge: Cambridge University Press, 184–91.

Dressler, Wolfgang and Ruth Wodak. 1982. Sociophonological methods in the study of sociolinguistic variation in Viennese German. *Language in Society* 11: 339–70.

——Willi Mayerthaler, Oswald Panagl, and Wolfgang Wurzel. 1988. *Leitmotifs in natural morphology*. Amsterdam: Benjamins 1988.

Dryer, Matthew. 1989. Large linguistic areas and language sampling. *Studies in Language* 13: 257–92.

Durrell, Martin. 1990. Westphalian and Eastphalian. In C. Russ (ed.) *The dialects of Modern German*. London, Routledge, 59–90.

Ebert, Karen Heide. 1971. *Referenz, Sprechsituation und die bestimmten Artikel in einem nordfriesischen Dialekt (Fering)*. Bredstedt: Nordfriisk Instituut.

——1984. Zur grammatischen Differenziertheit des Dialektes (am Beispiel Fering). *Nordfriesisches Jahrbuch* 20: 227–38.

——and Ed Keenan. 1973. A note on marking transparency and opacity. *Linguistic Inquiry* 4: 421–4.

Einarsson, Stefan. 1942. Terms of direction in Modern Icelandic. In H. Larsen and C.A. Williams (eds.) *Scandinavian studies presented to George T. Flom*. Urbana: University of Illinois Press, 37–48.

——1944. Terms of direction in Old Icelandic. *Journal of English and Germanic Philology* 43: 265–85.

Ellis, Alexander. 1889. *On early English pronunciation*, vol. 5. London: Trübner.

Epps, Patience. 2008. *A Grammar of Hup*. Berlin: Mouton de Gruyter.

Eubank, Lynn. 1996. Negation in early German-English interlanguage: More valueless features in the L2 initial state. *Second Language Research* 12: 73–106.

Faarlund, Jan Terje. 2000. *Totenmålet*. Lena: Østre Toten Kommune.

——2001. From Ancient Germanic to modern Germanic languages. In M. Haspelmath et al. (eds.) *Language typology and language universals: An international handbook*. Berlin: de Gruyter, 1706–19.

——2005. Syntactic developments from Old Nordic to Early Modern Nordic. In O. Bandle, K. Braunmüller, and E.H. Jahr (eds.) *The Nordic languages: An international handbook of the history of the North Germanic languages*. Berlin: de Gruyter, 1149–60.

Ferguson, Charles A. 1959. Diglossia. *Word* 15: 325–40.

——1971. Absence of copula and the notion of simplicity: A study of normal speech, baby talk, foreigner talk, and pidgins. In D. Hymes (ed.) *Pidginisation and creolisation of languages*. Cambridge: Cambridge University Press, 141–50.

Feuillet, Jack. 2001. Aire linguistique balkanique. In M. Haspelmath et al. (eds.) *Language typology and language universals: An international handbook*. Berlin: de Gruyter, 1510–28.

Fischer, Olga. 2009. Grammaticalization as analogically driven change? *VIEWZ* 18: 3–23.

Fischer, Steven Roger. 2001. Mangarevan doublets: Preliminary evidence for Proto-Southeastern Polynesian. *Oceanic Linguistics* 40: 112–24.

Flemming, Edward. 2004. Contrast and perceptual distinctiveness. In B. Hayes, R. Kirchner, and D. Steriade (eds.) *Phonetically-based phonology*. Cambridge University Press, 232–76.

Fletcher, Janet, and Andrew Butcher. 2002. Vowel dispersion in two northern Australian Languages: Dalabon and Bininj Gun-wok. In C. Bow (ed.) *Proceedings of the 9th Australian International Conference on Speech Science and Technology*. Melbourne: Australian Speech Science and Technology Association, 343–8.

———— 2003. Local and global influences on vowel formants in three Australian languages. In M.J. Solé, D. Recasens, and J. Romero (eds.) *Proceedings of the 15th International Congress of the Phonetic Sciences*. Barcelona: Causal Productions, 905–8.

——Hywel Stoakes, Deborah Loakes, and Andrew Butcher. 2007. Spectral and durational properties of vowels in Kunwinjku. *International Congress of Phonetic Sciences* 16: 937–40.

Florentine, Mary. 1985. Speech perception in noise by fluent, non-native listeners. *Proceedings of the Acoustic Society of Japan,* 16.

Floricic, Franck. 2003. Notes sur l'accusatif prépositionnel en Sarde. *Bulletin de la société de linguistique de Paris* 98: 247–303.

Fodor, István. 1959. The origins of grammatical gender. *Lingua* 8: 1–41; 186–214.

Foley, William, 1986. *The Papuan languages of New Guinea*. Cambridge: Cambridge University Press.

——and Robert Van Valin. 1984. *Functional syntax and universal grammar*. Cambridge: Cambridge University Press.

Forby, Robert. 1970 [1830]. *The vocabulary of East Anglia*. New York: Augustus Kelley.

Fortune, Reo. 1942. *Arapesh*. New York: Augustin.

Fourakis, Marios, Antonis Botinis, and Maria Katsaiti. 1999. Acoustic characteristics of Greek Vowels. *Phonetica* 56: 28–43.

Frei, Henri. 1944. Systèmes de déictiques. *Acta Linguistica Hafniensia* 4: 111–29.

Gabelentz, Georg von der. 1901. *Die Sprachwissenschaft: ihre Aufgaben, Methoden und bisherigen Ergebnisse* (2nd edn). Leipzig: Weigel.

Gachelin, Jean-Marc. 1991. Transitivity and intransitivity in the dialects of South-west England. In P. Trudgill and J.K. Chambers (eds.) *Dialects of English: Studies in grammatical variation.* London: Longmans, 218–28.

Gaies, Stephen, Harry Gradman, and Bernard Spolsky. 1977. Toward a measurement of functional proficiency: Contextualisation of the noise test. *TESOL Quarterly* 11: 51–7.

Garman, Michael. 1990. *Psycholinguistics.* Cambridge: Cambridge University Press.

Geraghty, Paul. 1983. *The history of the Fijian languages.* Honolulu: University of Hawaii Press.

——1986. The sound system of Proto-Central-Pacific. In P. Geraghty, L. Carrington, and S.A. Wurm (eds.) *FOCAL II: Papers from the fourth international conference on Austronesian linguistics.* Canberra: Pacific Linguistics, 289–312.

Gil, David. 2009. How much grammar does it take to sail a boat? In G. Sampson, D. Gil, and P. Trudgill (eds.) *Language complexity as an evolving variable.* Oxford: Oxford University Press, 19–33.

Givón, Talmy. 1979. *On understanding grammar.* New York: Academic Press.

——1984. *Syntax: A functional-typological introduction.* Amsterdam: Benjamins.

——and Phil Young. 2002. Cooperation and interpersonal manipulation in the society of intimates. In M. Chibatani (ed.) *The grammar of causation and interpersonal manipulation.* Amsterdam: John Benjamins, 23–56.

Goldinger, Stephen, Paul Luce, and David Pisoni. 1989. Priming lexical neighbors of spoken words: Effects of competition and inhibition. *Journal of Memory and Language* 28: 501–18.

——David Pisoni, and Paul Luce. 1991. Speech perception and spoken word recognition: Research and theory. In N.J. Lass (ed.), *Principles of experimental phonetics.* Toronto: B.C. Decker, 277–327.

——Paul Luce, David Pisoni and J.K. Marcario. 1992. Form-based priming in spoken word recognition: The roles of competition and bias. *Journal of Experimental Psychology: Learning, Memory and Cognition* 18: 1211–38.

Gordon, Elizabeth, Lyle Campbell, Margaret Maclagan, and Peter Trudgill. 2004. *The origins of New Zealand English.* Cambridge: Cambridge University Press.

Görlach, Manfred. 1987. Colonial lag? The alleged conservative character of American English and other 'colonial' varieties. *English World-Wide* 8: 41–60.

Grace, George. 1990. The 'aberrant' (vs. 'exemplary') Melanesian languages. In P. Baldi (ed.) *Linguistic change and reconstruction methodology*. Berlin: Mouton de Gruyter, 155–73.

Greenberg, Joseph.1966. Some universals of grammar with particular reference to the order of meaningful elements. In J. Greenberg (ed.), *Universals of language* (2nd edn). Cambridge, MA: MIT Press, 73–113.

——1978. How does language acquire gender markers? In J.H. Greenberg, C.A. Ferguson, and E.A. Moravcsik (eds.) *Universals of human language, vol. 3*. Stanford: Stanford University Press, 47–82.

——1991. The last stages of grammatical elements: Contractive and expansive desemanticization. In E. Traugott and B. Heine (eds.) *Approaches to grammaticalization*. Amsterdam: Benjamins.

Grosjean, François, Jean-Yves Dommergues, Étienne Cornu, Delphine Guillelmon, and Carole Besson. 1994. The gender-marking effect in spoken word recognition. *Perception and Psychophysics* 56: 590–8.

Güldemann, Tom. 2001. *Die Entlehnung pronominaler Elemente des Khoekhoe aus dem !Ui-Taa*. Leipzig University ms.

Haegeman, Liliane. 1992. *Theory and description in generative syntax: A case study in West Flemish*. Cambridge: Cambridge University Press.

——1995. *The syntax of negation*. Cambridge: Cambridge University Press.

Haiman, John. 1980. The iconicity of grammar. *Language* 56: 515–40.

——1988. Rhaeto-Romance. In M. Harris and N. Vincent (eds.) *The Romance languages*. London: Routledge, 315–90.

Hajek, John. 2004. Small consonant inventories as an areal feature of the New Guinea-Pacific region: Testing Trudgill's hypotheses. *Linguistic Typology* 8: 343–50.

Hale, Mark. 1991. Synchronic and diachronic aspects of noun incorporation and related constructions in the Nuclear Mircronesian languages. Harvard University ms.

——2007. *Historical linguistics*. Oxford: Blackwell.

Harley, Heidi. 2006. *English words: A linguistic introduction*. Oxford: Blackwell.

Harlow, Ray. 1982. Some phonological changes in Polynesian languages. In A. Ahlqvist (ed.) *Papers from the 5th international conference on historical linguistics*. Amsterdam: Benjamins, 98–109.

——1987. *A word-list of South Island Maori* (2nd edn). Auckland: Te Reo.

——2001. *A Maori reference grammar*. Auckland: Longman.

Harris, Alice and Lyle Campbell. 1995. *Historical syntax in a cross-linguistic perspective*. Cambridge: Cambridge University Press.

Haspelmath, Martin. 1996. Against markedness (and what to replace it with). *Journal of Linguistics* 42: 25–70.

Haudricourt, André. 1961. Richesse en phonèmes et richesse en locateurs. *L'Homme* 1: 5–10.

Haugen, Einar. 1969 [1957]. The semantics of Icelandic orientation. In S.A. Tyler (ed.) *Cognitive anthropology: readings*. New York: Holt, Rinehart, and Winston, 330–42. First published in *Word* 13 (1957), 447–60.

——1976. *The Scandinavian languages*. London: Faber.

——1984. *Norsk-engelsk ordbok*. Oslo: Universitetsforlaget.

Hawkins, John. 1998. A typological approach to Germanic morphology. In J.O. Askedal (ed.), *Historische germanische and deutsche Syntax*. Frankfurt: Lang.

——2004. *Efficiency and complexity in grammars*. Oxford: Oxford University Press.

Hay, Jennifer, and Laurie Bauer. 2007. Phoneme inventory size and population size. *Language* 83: 388–400.

Heath, Jeffrey. 1975. Some functional relationships in grammar. *Language* 51: 89–104.

Heine, Bernd and Tania Kuteva. 2005. *Language contact and grammatical change*. Cambridge: Cambridge University Press.

——and Mechtild Reh. 1984. *Grammaticalisation and reanalysis in African languages*. Hamburg: Buske.

——Ulrike Claudi, and Friederike Hünnemeyer. 1991. *Grammaticalization: A conceptual framework*. Chicago: University of Chicago Press.

Herbert, Robert and Barbara Nykiel-Herbert. 1986. Explorations in linguistic sexism: A contrastive sketch. *Papers and Studies in Contrastive Linguistics* 21: 47–86.

Hesse, Mary. 1966. *Models and analogies in science*. Notre Dame: Notre Dame University Press.

Hibiya, Junko. 1996. Denasalisation of the velar nasal in Tokyo Japanese. In G. Guy et al. (eds.) *Towards a social science of language: papers in honour of William Labov. Vol. 1: Variation and change in language and society*. Amsterdam: Benjamins, 161–6.

Hickey, Raymond. 2000. On the phonology of gender in Modern German. In R. Matti, T. Nevalainen, and M. Saari (eds.) *Gender in grammar and cognition II: Manifestations of gender*. New York: Mouton de Gruyter, 621–63.

Hoberman, Robert, and Mark Aronoff. 2003. The verbal morphology of Maltese. In J. Shimron (ed.) *Language processing and acquisi-*

tion in languages of Semitic root-based morphology. Amsterdam: Benjamins, 61–78.

Hock, Hans Henrich. 1991. *Principles of historical linguistics* (2nd edn). Berlin: Mouton.

——2003. Analogical change. In B. Joseph and R. Janda (eds.) *The handbook of historical linguistics.* Oxford: Blackwell, 439–60.

Hockett, Charles F. 1958. *A course in modern linguistics.* New York: Macmillan.

Hodge, Carleton T. 1970. The linguistic cycle. *Language Sciences* 13: 1–7.

Hoekstra, Jarich. 2001. Comparative aspects of Frisian morphology and syntax. In H.H. Munske et al. (eds.) *Handbuch des friesischen/ Handbook of Frisian studies.* Tübingen: Niemeyer, 775–86.

Holes, Clive. 1995. *Modern Arabic: Structures, functions and varieties,* Longman: London.

Holm, John. 1988. *Pidgins and creoles: Theory and structure.* Cambridge: Cambridge University Press.

Holman, Eric, Dietrich Stauffer, Christian Schulze, and Søren Wichmann. 2007. On the relation between structural diversity and geographical distance among languages: observations and computer simulations. *Linguistic Typology* 11: 395–423.

Holmqvist, Jonathan. 1991. Semantic features and gender dynamics in Cantabrian Spanish. *Anthropological Linguistics* 33: 57–81.

Hope, Jonathan. 2000. Rats, bats, sparrows and dogs: Biology, linguistics and the nature of Standard English. In L. Wright (ed.) *The development of Standard English 1300–1800.* Cambridge: Cambridge University Press, 49–56.

Hutchisson, Don. 1986. Sursurunga pronouns and the special uses of quadral number. In U. Wiesemann (ed.), *Pronominal systems.* Tübingen: Gunter Narr, 1–20.

Hyltenstam, Kenneth. 1992. Non-native features of near-native speakers: On the ultimate attainment of childhood L2 learners. In R.J. Harris (ed.), *Cognitive processing in bilinguals.* Amsterdam: Elsevier, 351–68.

Hymes, Dell. 1974. Speech and language: On the origins and foundations of inequality among speakers. In M. Bloomfield and E. Haugen (eds.) *Language as a human problem.* New York: Norton, 45–71.

Ihalainen, Ossi. 1976. Periphrastic *do* in affirmative sentences in the dialect of East Somerset. *Neuphilologische Mitteilungen* 77: 608–22.

——1991. On grammatical diffusion in Somerset folk speech. In P. Trudgill and J.K. Chambers (eds.) *Dialects of English: Studies in grammatical variation.* London: Longman, 148–60.

Ingham, Bruce. 1982. *Northeast Arabian dialects*. London: Kegan Paul.

——1994a. *Najdi Arabic: Central Arabian*. Amsterdam: Benjamins.

——1994b. The effect of language contact on the Arabic dialect of Afghanistan. In J. Aguade, F. Corriente, and M. Marugán (eds.) *Actas del Congreso Internacional sobre Interferencias Lingüísticas Arabo-Romances y Paralelos Extra-Iberos*. Zaragoza: Navarro, 105–17.

Jackson, Eric. 2003. Dispersion in the vowel system of Pima. Paper presented at the UCLA LASSO Conference, October 2003.

——2008. Dispersion in the vowel system of Pima. *UCLA Working Papers in Phonetics* 107: 31–55.

Jackson, Jean. 1974. Language identity of the Colombian Vaupés Indians. In R. Bauman and J. Sherzer (eds.) *Explorations in the ethnography of speaking*. Cambridge: Cambridge University Press, 50–64.

Jackson, Kenneth. 1953. *Language and history in early Britain*. Edinburgh: Edinburgh University Press.

Jacobson, Steven. 1984. *Yup'ik Eskimo dictionary*. Fairbanks: Alaska Native Language Center.

Jahr, Ernst Håkon. 1995. Nedertysk og nordisk: språksamfunn og språkkontakt i Hansatida. In E.H. Jahr (ed.), *Nordisk og nedertysk: språkkontakt og språkutvilking i Norden i seinmellomalderen*. Oslo: Novus, 9–28.

——1998. Sociolinguistics in historical language contact: The Scandinavian languages and Low German during the Hanseatic period. In E.H. Jahr (ed.) *Language change: Advances in historical sociolinguistics*. Berlin: Mouton de Gruyter, 119–13.

——2001. Historical sociolinguistics: The role of Low German language contact in the Scandinavian typological split of the late Middle Ages. *Lingua Posnaniensis* 43: 95–104.

Jakobson, Roman. 1929. *Remarques sur l'évolution phonologique du russe comparée à celle des autres langues slaves*. Prague: Travaux du Cercle Linguistique de Prague 2.

Jaworski, Adam. 1986. *A linguistic picture of women's position in society: A Polish–English contrastive study*. Frankfurt: Peter Lang.

——1989. On gender and sex in Polish. *International Journal of the Sociology of Language* 78: 83–92.

Jespersen, Otto. 1894. *Progress in language*. London: Swan Sonnenschein.

——1922. *Language; Its nature, development and origin*. London: Allen and Unwin.

Johnson, Jacqueline, and Elissa Newport. 1989. Critical period effects in second language learning: The influence of maturational state on the acquisition of English as a second language. *Cognitive Psychology* 21: 60–99.

Johnson, Keith. 2000. Adaptive dispersion in vowel perception. *Phonetica* 57: 181–8.

Johnston, Paul. 1997. Regional variation. In C. Jones (ed.) *The Edinburgh history of Scots*. Edinburgh University Press, 433–513.

Jongman, Allard, Marios Fourakis, and Joan Sereno. 1989. The acoustic vowel space of Modern Greek and German. *Language and Speech* 32: 221–48.

Joseph, Brian. 1990. Greek. In B. Comrie (ed.) *The major languages of Eastern Europe*. London: Routledge, 144–73.

——2001. Is there such a thing as "grammaticalization"? *Language Sciences* 23: 163–86.

——2004. Rescuing traditional (historical) linguistics from grammaticalisation "theory". In O. Fischer, M. Norde, and H. Perridon (eds.) *Up and down the cline—the nature of grammaticalization*. Amsterdam: Benjamins, 44–71.

——2009. Review of T. Markopoulos *The future in Modern Greek: From ancient to medieval. Journal of Greek Linguistics* 9: 195–214.

——and Irene Philippaki-Warburton. 1987. *Modern Greek*. London: Croom Helm.

Kabak, Baris. 2004. Acquiring phonology is not acquiring inventories but contrasts: The loss of primary long vowels in Turkic and Korean. *Linguistic Typology* 8: 351–68.

Kato, Masanobu. 1983. Tokyo ni okeru Nenreibetsu Chosa [A study of six age groups in Tokyo]. In F. Inoue (ed.) *A sociolinguistic study of new dialect and language decay*. Tokyo: Minstry of Education, 71–91.

Kay, Paul. 1976. Discussion of papers by Kiparsky and Wescott. In S. R. Harnard, H.D. Steklis, and J. Lancaster. *Origins and evolution of language and speech*. New York: New York Academy of Sciences, 17–19.

Keenan, Ed. 1976. Discussion. In S. R. Harnard, H.D. Steklis, and J. Lancaster. *Origins and evolution of language and speech*. New York: New York Academy of Sciences, 92–96.

Keene, Derek. 2000. Metropolitan values: Migration, mobility and cultural norms, London 1100–1700. In L. Wright (ed.) *The development of Standard English 1300–1800*. Cambridge: Cambridge University Press, 93–114.

Keim, Inken.1978. *Gastarbeiterdeutsch*. Tubingen: Narr.

Keller, Rudi. 1994. *On language change: The invisible hand in language*. London: Routledge.

Kirch, Patrick Vinton, and Roger C. Green. 2001. *Hawaiki, ancestral Polynesia: An essay in historical anthropology*. Cambridge: Cambridge University Press.

Kortmann, Bernd, and Edgar Schneider (eds.) 2004. *Handbook of varieties of English*, vol. I. Berlin: Mouton de Gruyter.

——and Benedikt Szmrecsanyi. 2009. World Englishes between simplification and complexification. In L. Siebers and T. Hoffmann (eds.) *World Englishes: Problems, properties and prospects*. Amsterdam: Benjamins, 265–85.

Kotsinas, Ulla-Britt. 1990. Svensk, invandrarsvensk eller invandrare? Om bedömning av "främmande" drag i "ungdomsspråk"'. In G. Tingbjörn (ed.) *Andra symposiet om svenska som andraspråk i Göteborg 1989*. Gothenburg: Gothenburg University Press, 244–74.

Koutsoudas, Andreas, and Olympia Koutsoudas. 1962. A contrastive analysis of the segmental phonemes of Greek and English. *Language Learning*, 12, 211–30.

Kroch, Anthony. 1978. Toward a theory of social dialect variation. *Language in Society* 7: 17–36.

——Ann Taylor, and Don Ringe. 2000. The Middle English verb-second constraint: A case study in language contact and language change. In S. Herring, P. van Reenen, and L. Schoesler (eds.), *Textual parameters in older language*. Amsterdam: Benjamins, 353–91.

Krupa, Victor. 1982. *The Polynesian languages*. London: Routledge.

Krupnik, Igor, and Ludger Müller-Wille. 2010. Franz Boas and Inuktitut terminology for ice and snow: From the emergence of the field to the *"Great Eskimo vocabulary hoax"*. In I. Krupnik, C. Aporta, S. Gearheard, G.J. Laidler, and L. Kielsen Holm (eds.) *Siku—knowing our ice: Documenting Inuit sea ice knowledge and use*. Heidelberg: Springer, 377–400.

Kruspe, Nicole. 2004. *A grammar of Semelai*. Cambridge: Cambridge University Press.

Küspert, Klaus-Christian. 1988. *Vokalsystem in Westnordischen*. Tübingen: Niemeyer.

Kusters, Wouter. 2003. *Linguistic complexity: The influence of social change on verbal inflection*. Leiden: Leiden University Press.

Kuteva, Tania. 2008. On the frills of grammaticalization. In M.J. López-Couso and E. Seoane (eds.) *Rethinking grammaticalization*. Amsterdam: Benjamins, 189–217.

——2009. Grammatical categories and linguistic theory: Elaborateness in grammar. In P.K. Austin, O. Bond, M. Charette, D. Nathan, and P. Sells (eds.) *Proceedings of the Conference on*

Language Documentation and Linguistic Theory 2. London: SOAS. www.hrelp.org/eprints/ldlt2_03.pdf.

Labov, William. 1972. *Sociolinguistic patterns*. Philadelphia: University of Pennsylvania Press.

——1990[1971]. On the adequacy of natural languages, 1: The development of tense. In J.V. Singler (ed.) *Pidgin and creole tense-mood-aspect systems*. Amsterdam: Benjamins, 1–58.

——1994. *Principles of linguistic change I: Internal factors*. Oxford: Blackwell.

——2007. Transmission and diffusion. *Language* 81: 344–87.

Laing, Lloyd, and Jennifer Laing. 1979. *Anglo-Saxon England*. London: Routledge and Kegan Paul.

Langacker, Ronald W. 1987. *Foundations of cognitive grammar: Theoretical prerequisites*. Stanford, CA: Stanford University Press.

Langer, William. 1987. *An encyclopedia of world history*. London: Harrap.

LaPolla, Randy 2003. Why languages differ: Variation in the conventionalisation of constraints on inference. In D. Bradly, R. LaPolla, B. Michailovsky, and G. Thurgood (eds.) *Language variation: Papers on variation and change in the Sinosphere and in the Indosphere in honour of James A. Matisoff*. Canberra: Pacific Linguistics, 113–44.

——2005. Typology and complexity. In J.W. Minett and W.S.-Y. Wang (eds.) *Language acquisition, change and emergence: Essays in evolutionary linguistics*. Hong Kong: City University Press, 465–93.

Lass, Roger. 1980. *Explaining language change*. Cambridge: Cambridge University Press.

——1990. How to do things with junk: Exaptation in language evolution. *Journal of Linguistics* 26: 79–102.

——1992. Phonology and morphology. In N. Blake (ed.) *The Cambridge history of the English language: Vol. II, 1066–1476*, Cambridge: Cambridge University Press, 23–155.

——1997. *Historical linguistics and language change*. Cambridge: Cambridge University Press.

——2000. Phonology and morphology. In R. Lass (ed.) *The Cambridge history of the English language: Vol. III, 1476–1776*. Cambridge: Cambridge University Press.

Laycock, Donald. 1965. *The Ndu language family*. Canberra: Pacific Linguistics.

——1982. Melanesian linguistic diversity: A Melanesian choice? In R. May and H. Nelson (eds.) *Melanesia: beyond diversity*. Canberra: Research School of Pacific Studies, 33–8.

Lee, Michael. 1988. Language, perception and the world. In J.A. Hawkins (ed.). *Explaining language universals*. Oxford: Blackwell, 211–46.

Lehmann, Christian. 1988. On the function of agreement. In M. Barlow and C.A. Ferguson (eds.) *Agreement in natural language: Approaches, theories, descriptions*. Stanford: CSLI, 55–65.

Lenneberg, Eric. 1967. *Biological foundations of language*. New York: Wiley.

Le Page, Robert, and Andrée Tabouret-Keller. 1985. *Acts of identity: Creole-based approaches to language and ethnicity*. Cambridge: Cambridge University Press.

Levinson, Stephen. 1996. Relativity in spatial orientation and description. In J. Gumperz and S. Levinson (eds.) *Rethinking linguistic relativity*. Cambridge: Cambridge University Press, 133–44.

——(eds). 2003. *Space in language and cognition: Explorations in cognitive diversity*. Cambridge: Cambridge University Press.

——and David Wilkins (eds.). 2006. *Grammars of space: Explorations in cognitive diversity*. Cambridge: Cambridge University Press.

Li, Charles N., and Sandra A. Thompson. 1976. Strategies for signalling grammatical relations in Wappo. *Papers from the twelfth regional meeting of the Chicago Linguistic Society*. Chicago Linguistic Society, 450–9.

Lichtenberk, Frantisek. 1983. *A grammar of Manam*. Honolulu: University of Hawaii Press.

——1991. On the gradualness of grammaticalization. In E. Traugott and B. Heine (eds.) *Approaches to grammaticalization*. Amsterdam: Benjamins, 37–80.

Lightfoot, David. 1979. *Principles of diachronic syntax*. Cambridge: Cambridge University Press.

Liljencrants, Johan, and Lindblom, Björn. 1972. Numerical simulation of vowel quality systems: The role of perceptual contrast. *Language* 48: 839–62.

Lindblom, Björn. 1986. Phonetic universals in vowel systems. In J.J. Ohala and J.J. Jaeger (eds.) *Experimental phonology*. Orlando: Academic Press, 13–44.

——and Ian Maddieson. 1988. Phonetic universals in consonant systems. In L. Hyman and C. Li (eds.), *Language, speech and mind*. London: Routledge, 62–78.

Lively, Scott E., David Pisoni, and Stephen Goldinger. 1994. Spoken word recognition: Research and theory. In M.A. Gernsbacher (ed.) *Handbook of psycholinguistics*. San Diego: Academic Press, 265–301.

Lockwood, W.B. 1955. *An introduction to modern Faroese.* Tórshavn: Føroya Skúlabókagrunnur.

Löfstedt, Ernst. 1968. *Beiträge zu einer nordfriesischen Grammatik. I. Das Substantiv und das Adjektiv, das Zahlwort und der bestimmte Artikel.* Uppsala: Almquist and Wiksell.

Luce, J., and Paul Luce. 1995. An examination of similarity neighborhoods in young children's receptive vocabularies. *Journal of Child Language* 22: 727–36.

Luce, Paul. 1986. Neighbourhoods in the mental lexicon. [Research on Speech Perception Technical Report No. 6.] Bloomington, IN: Dept. of Psychology, Speech Research Laboratory, Indiana University.

——and David Pisoni. 1998. Recognizing spoken words: The neighborhood activation model. *Ear and Hearing* 19: 1–36.

——Stephen Goldinger, Ed Auer, and Michael Vitevitch. 2000. Phonetic priming, neighborhood activation, and PARSYN. *Perception & Psychophysics* 62: 615–25.

Lupyan, Gary, and Rick Dale. 2010. Language structure is partly determined by social structure. PLoS ONE 5.1: e8559. doi:10.1371/journal.pone.0008559.

Lutz, Angelika. 2011. Why is West-Saxon English different from Old Saxon? In H. Sauer and J. Story (eds.), *Anglo-Saxon and the Continent.*

Lynch, John, Malcolm Ross, and Tony Crowley. 2002. *The Oceanic languages.* Richmond: Curzon.

Lyons, John. 1977. *Semantics.* Cambridge: Cambridge University Press.

McWhorter, John. 2007. *Language interrupted: Signs of non-native acquisition in standard language grammars.* Oxford: Oxford University Press.

Maddieson, Ian. 1984. *Patterns of sounds.* Cambridge: Cambridge University Press.

Madvig, Johan Nicolai. 1857. *De grammatische Betegnelser.* Copenhagen.

Mæhlum, Brit. 2000. Social catastrophes as explanation in historical linguistics. In E.H. Jahr (ed.) *Språkkontakt: Innverknaden frå nedertysk på andre nordeuropeiske språk.* Copenhagen: Nordisk Ministerråd, 87–94.

Magga, Ole Henrik. 2006. Diversity in Saami terminology for reindeer, snow, and ice. *International Social Science Journal* 58: 25–34.

Marchese, Lynell. 1988. Noun classes and agreement systems in Kru: A historical approach. In M. Barlow and C. Ferguson (eds.) *Agreement in natural language.* Stanford, CA: CSLI, 323–42.

Marck, Jeff. 1999. Revising Polynesian linguistic subgrouping and its culture history implications. In R. Blench and M. Spriggs (eds.) *Archaeology and language IV*. London: Routledge, 95–122.

——2000. *Polynesian language and culture history*. Canberra: Pacific Linguistics.

Markey, Thomas. 1981. *Frisian*. The Hague: Mouton.

Martin, Laura. 1986. "Eskimo words for snow": A case study in the genesis and decay of an anthropological example. *American Anthropologist* 88: 418–23.

Martinet, André. 1955. *Économie des changements phonétiques*. Berne: Francke.

——1962. *A functional view of language*. Oxford: Oxford University Press.

Martowicz, Anna. 2010. *The origin and functioning of circumstantial clause linkers: A cross-linguistic study*. Edinburgh: University of Edinburgh PhD thesis.

Mathiot, Madeleine (ed.). 1979. *Ethnolinguistics: Boas, Sapir and Whorf revisited*. The Hague: Mouton.

Matras, Yaron. 2009. *Language contact*. Cambridge: Cambridge University Press.

Matthews, Stephen, and Virginia Yip. 1994. *Cantonese: A comprehensive grammar*. London: Routledge.

Mayerthaler, Willi. 1981. *Morphologische Natürlichkeit*. Wiesbaden: Athenaion.

Meador, Diane, James Flege, and Ian Mackay. 2000. Factors affecting the recognition of words in a second language. *Bilingualism: Language and Cognition* 3: 55–67.

Meisel, Jürgen. 1997. The acquisition of the syntax of negation in French and German: Contrasting first and second language development. *Second Language Research* 13: 227–63.

Miller, D. Gary. 1977. Tripartization, sexism, and the rise of the feminine gender in Indo-European. *The Florida Journal of Anthropology* 2: 3–16.

Milroy, James. 1982. Probing under the tip of the iceberg: Phonological normalisation and the shape of speech communities. In S. Romaine (ed.) *Sociolinguistic variation in speech communities*. London: Arnold, 32–48.

——1992a. Middle English dialectology. In N. Blake (ed.) *The history of the English language II: 1066–1476*. Cambridge: Cambridge University Press, 156–206.

——1992b. *Linguistic variation and change*. Oxford: Blackwell.

——and Lesley Milroy. 1985. Linguistic change, social network and speaker innovation, *Journal of linguistics* 21: 339–84.

Milroy, Lesley. 1980. *Language and social networks*. Oxford: Blackwell.

——2000. Social network analysis and language change. *European Journal of English Studies* 4: 2124–7.

Miranda, Rocky. 1975. Indo-European gender: A study in semantic and syntactic change. *Journal of Indo-European Studies* 3: 199–215.

Mithun, Marianne. 1999. *The languages of native North America*. Cambridge: Cambridge University Press.

——2007. Grammar, contact, and time. *Journal of Language Contact* 1: 144–67. www.jlc-journal.org.

Mørck, Endre. 2005. Morphological developments from Old Nordic to Early Modern Nordic. In O. Bandle (ed.) *The Nordic languages: An international handbook of the history of the North Germanic languages, vol. II*. Berlin: de Gruyter, 1128–48.

Mortensen, David. (ms. a) Maladaptive sound change: The emergence of obstruents after high vowels.

——(ms. b) The emergence of dorsal stops after high vowels in Huishu.

Mühlhäusler, Peter. 1977. *Pidginisation and simplification of language*. Canberra: Pacific Linguistics.

——1986. *Pidgin and creole linguistics*. Oxford: Blackwell.

——2001. Typology and universals of pidginisation. In M. Haspelmath et al. (eds.) *Language typology and language universals: An international handbook*. Berlin: de Gruyter, 1648–55.

Musa-Wellens, Ineke. 1994. *A descriptive sketch of the verbal system of the Nubi language, spoken in Bombo, Uganda*. Nijmegen: MA thesis.

Muysken, Pieter. 2001. Creolization. In M. Haspelmath et al. (eds.) *Language typology and language universals: An international handbook*. Berlin: de Gruyter, 1656–67.

Nabelek, Anna, and Amy Donahue. 1984. Perception of consonants in reverberation by native and non-native listeners. *Journal of the Acoustic Society of America* 75: 632–4.

Nesse, Agnete. 2001. *Språkkontakt mellom norsk og tysk i hansatidens Bergen*. Tromsø: Tromsø University PhD thesis.

Nettle, Daniel. 1995. Segmental inventory size, word length, and communicative efficiency. *Linguistics* 33: 359–67.

——1999. *Linguistic diversity*. Oxford: Oxford University Press.

——and Suzanne Romaine. 2000. *Vanishing voices: The extinction of the world's languages*. Oxford: Oxford University Press.

Nevalainen, Terttu. 1998. Social mobility and the decline of multiple negation in Early Modern English. In J. Fisiak and M. Krygier (eds.) *Advances in English historical linguistics*. Berlin: Mouton de Gruyter. 263–91.

Nevalainen, Terttu. 2002. Mobility, social networks and language change in early modern England. *European Journal of English Studies* 4: 253–64.

——2006. *An introduction to Early Modern English*. Edinburgh: Edinburgh University Press.

——and Helena Raumolin-Brunberg. 2003. *Historical sociolinguistics*. London: Longman.

Newman, John. 2002. Culture, cognition, and the grammar of 'give' clauses. In N.J. Enfield (ed.) *Ethnosyntax*. Oxford: Oxford University Press, 74–95.

Newton, Brian. 1968. Spontaneous gemination in Cypriot Greek. *Lingua* 20: 15–57.

——1972. *The generative interpretation of dialect: A study of Modern Greek phonology*. Cambridge: Cambridge University Press.

Nichols, Johanna. 1992. *Linguistic diversity in space and time*. Chicago: University of Chicago Press.

——2007. Review of Ö. Dahl, *The growth and maintenance of linguistic complexity*. *Diachronica* 24.1: 171–8.

——and David Peterson. 1998. Amerind personal pronouns: A reply to Campbell. *Language* 74: 605–14.

Nielsen, Gunhild. 1947. Glidning og lukning i Rømømaalets høje vokaler ('Klusilspring'). *Danske Folkemaal* 15: 41–65.

Nissen, Gunhild. 1945. Konsonaterne i Rømømålet i historisk belysning. *Danske Folkemål* 14: 97–119.

Norde, Muriel. 2001. Deflexion as a counter directional factor in grammatical change. *Language Sciences* 23: 231–64.

Omdal, Helge. 1977. Høyangermålet—en ny dialekt. *Språklig Samling* 1: 7–9.

O'Rahilly, Thomas F. 1946. *Early Irish history and mythology*. Dublin: Dublin Institute for Advanced Studies.

——1976. *Irish dialects past and present*. Dublin: Institute for Advanced Studies.

Orr, Robert. 1999. Evolutionary biology and historical linguistics. *Diachronica* 16: 123–57.

Owens, Jonathan. 1985. The origins of East African Nubi. *Anthropological Linguistics* 27: 229–71.

——1991. Nubi, genetic linguistics, and language classification. *Anthropological Linguistics* 33: 1–30.

——1997. Arabic-based pidgins and creoles. In S. Thomason (ed.) *Contact languages: A wider perspective*. Amsterdam: Benjamins, 125–72.

Owens, Jonathan. 2001. Creole Arabic: The orphan of all orphans. *Anthropological Linguistics* 43: 348–78.

——2006. *A linguistic history of Arabic.* Oxford: Oxford University Press.

Paddock, Harold. 1975. The folk grammar of Carbonair, Newfoundland. In J.K. Chambers (ed.) *Canadian English: Origins and structures.* Toronto: Methuen, 25–32.

——1991. The actuation problem for gender change in Wessex versus Newfoundland. In P. Trudgill and J.K. Chambers (eds.) *Dialects of English: Studies in grammatical variation.* London: Longman, 29–46.

Pawley, Andrew. 1970. Grammatical reconstruction and change in Polynesia and Fiji. In S.A. Wurm and D.C. Laycock (eds.) *Pacific Linguistic Studies in Honour of Arthur Capell.* Canberra: Pacific Linguistics, 301–67.

——1972. Internal relationships of eastern Oceanic languages. *Studies in Oceanic Culture History* 3: 1–142.

——1996a. On the position of Rotuman. In B. Nothofer (ed.), *Reconstruction, classification, description—Festschrift in honour of Isidore Dyen.* Hamburg: Abera Verlag Meyer & Co, 387–410.

——1996b. On the Polynesian subgroup as a problem for Irwin's continuous settlement hypothesis. In J. Davidson, G. Irwin, F. Leach, A. Pawley, and D. Brown (eds.), *Oceanic culture history: Essays in honour of Roger Green.* Dunedin: *New Zealand Journal of Archaeology,* 387–410.

——1999. Chasing rainbows: Implications of the rapid dispersal of Austronesian languages for subgrouping and reconstruction. In E. Zeitoun and P. Li (eds), *Selected papers from the eighth international conference on Austronesian linguistics.* Taipei: Academia Sinica, 95–138.

——2009. The role of the Solomon Islands in the first settlement of Remote Oceania: Bringing linguistic evidence to an archaeological debate. In A. Adelaar and A. Pawley (eds.) *Austronesian historical linguistics and culture history: A festschrift for Robert Blust.* Canberra: Pacific Linguistics, 515–40.

——and Roger Green. 1984. The Proto-Oceanic language community. *Journal of Pacific History* 19: 123–46.

——and Malcolm Ross. 1993. Austronesian historical linguistics and culture history. *Annual Review of Anthropology* 22: 425–59.

Pedersen, Karen Margrethe. 1999. Genusforenkling i Københavnsk. *Danske Folkemål* 41: 79–106.

Pericliev,Vladimir. 2004. There is no correlation between the size of a community speaking a language and the size of the phonological inventory of that language. *Linguistic Typology* 8: 376–83.

Perkins, Revere. 1980. *The covariation of culture and grammar*. Ann Arbor: University of Michigan PhD thesis.

———1995. *Deixis, grammar, and culture*. Amsterdam: Benjamins.

Plank, Frans. 2006. Review of G. Seiler *Präpositionale Dativmarkierung im Oberdeutschen. Linguistic Typology* 10: 441–52.

Post, Mark. 2010. Topographical deixis and the Tani languages of North-East India. In G. Hyslop, S. Morey, and M. W. Post (eds.) *North East Indian linguistics, vol. 3*. New Delhi: Cambridge University Press India, 137–54.

Priestly, Tom. 1983. On 'drift' in Indo-European gender systems. *Journal of Indo-European Studies* 11: 339–63.

Pullum, Geoffrey. 1991. *The great Eskimo vocabulary hoax*. Chicago: University of Chicago Press.

Quirk, Randolph and C.L. Wrenn. 1957. *An Old English grammar* (2nd edn). London: Methuen.

Rambø, Gro-Renée. 2008. *Historiske og sosiale betingelser for språkkontakt mellom nedertysk og skandinavisk i seinmiddelalderen—et bidrag til historisk språksosiologi*. Kristiansand: Agder University PhD thesis.

Raumolin-Brunberg, Helena. 1996. Social factors and pronominal change in the seventeenth century: The Civil War effect? In J. Fisiak and M. Krygier (eds.) *Advances in English historical linguistics* Berlin: Mouton de Gruyter, 362–88.

———1998. Social factors and pronominal change in the seventeenth century: The Civil War effect? In J. Fisiak and M. Krygier (eds.) *Advances in English historical linguistics*. Berlin: Mouton de Gruyter, 361–88.

Reh, Mechthild. 1996. *The Anywa language*. Cologne: Ruediger Koeppe Verlag.

Rice, Keren. 1999. Review of Leonard Faltz (1998) *The Navajo verb: A grammar for students and scholars. Linguistic Typology* 3: 393–400.

———2004. Language contact, phoneme inventories, and the Athapaskan language family. *Linguistic Typology* 8: 321–43.

Rissanen, Matti. 2000. Standardization and the language of early statutes. In L. Wright (ed.) *The development of Standard English 1300–1800: Theories, descriptions, conflicts*. Cambridge: Cambridge University Press, 117–30.

Rivierre, Jean-Claude. 1994. Contact-induced phonological complexification in New Caledonia. In T. Dutton and D. Tryon (eds.)

Language contact and change in the Austronesian world. Berlin: Mouton de Gruyter.

Ross, Malcolm. 1988. *Proto-Oceanic and the Austronesian languages of Western Melanesia.* Canberra: Australian National University Press.

——1992. The sound of Proto-Austronesian: An outsider's view of the Formosan evidence. *Oceanic Linguistics* 31: 23–64.

——1997. Social networks and kinds of speech community events. In R. Blench and M. Spriggs (eds.) *Archaeology and language.* London: Routledge, 209–61.

Rushforth, Scott and James Chisholm. 1991. *Cultural persistence: Continuity in meaning and moral responsibility among Bearlake Athapaskans.* Tucson: University of Arizona Press.

Sampson, Geoffrey. 2009. A linguistic axiom challenged. In Geoffrey Sampson et al. (eds.). *Language complexity as an evolving variable.* Oxford: Oxford University Press, 1–18.

——David Gil, and Peter Trudgill (eds.). 2009. *Language complexity as an evolving variable.* Oxford: Oxford University Press.

Sandøy, Helge. 2001. Færøysk i vestnordisk språkhistorie. In K. Braunmüller and Jogvan i Lon Jacobsen (eds.) *Moderne lingvistiske teorier og færøsk.* Oslo: Novus, 125–54.

——2005. The typological development of the Nordic languages I: Phonology. In O. Bandle, K. Braunmüller, and E.H. Jahr (eds.) *The Nordic languages: An international handbook of the history of the North Germanic languages.* Berlin: de Gruyter, 1852–1861.

Sankoff, Gillian. 2002. Linguistic outcomes of language contact. In J.K. Chambers, P. Trudgill, and N. Schilling-Estes (eds.) *The handbook of language variation and change.* Oxford: Blackwell.

Sapir, Edward. 1963. *Selected writings in language, culture and personality.* Edited by D. Mandelbaum. Berkeley: California University Press.

Sasse, Hans-Jürgen. 2001. Typological changes in language obsolescence. In M. Haspelmath et al. (eds.) *Language typology and language universals: An international handbook.* Berlin: de Gruyter, 1668–77.

Scardigli, Piergiuseppe. 2002. Nordic-Gothic linguistic relations. In O. Bandle, K. Braunmüller, and E.H. Jahr (eds.) *The Nordic languages: An international handbook of the history of the North Germanic languages.* Berlin: de Gruyter, 553–64.

Schlegel, August Wilhelm von. 1846. *Œuvres de M. Auguste-Guillaume de Schlegel.* Leipzig: Weidmann.

Schmalstieg, William. 1980. *Indo-European linguistics: A new synthesis.* University Park: Pennsylvania State University Press.

Schreier, Daniel. 2003. *Isolation and language change: Contemporary and sociohistorical evidence from Tristan da Cunha English.* Basingstoke: Palgrave Macmillan.

Schrijver, Peter. 2006. What Britons spoke around 400 AD. In N.J. Higham (ed.), *Britons in Anglo-Saxon England,* 165–71. Woodbridge: Boydell.

Schwartz, Jean-Luc, Louis-Jean Boe, Nathalie Vallee, and Christian Abry. 1997a. Major trends in vowel system inventories. *Journal of Phonetics* 25: 233–53.

——Louis-Jean Boe, Nathalie Vallee, and Christian Abry. 1997b. The dispersion-focalization theory of vowel systems. *Journal of Phonetics* 25: 255–86.

Sebba, Mark. 1997. *Contact languages: Pidgins and creoles.* London: Macmillan.

Seiler, Hansjakob. 1977. *Cahuilla grammar.* Banning, CA: Malki Museum Press.

Shosted, Ryan. 2006. Correlating complexity: A typological approach. *Linguistic Typology* 10: 1–40.

Siemund, Peter. 2008. *Pronominal gender in English: A study of English varieties from a cross-linguistic perspective.* New York: Routledge.

Siewierska, Anna. 2004. *Person.* Cambridge: Cambridge University Press.

Sinnemäki, Kaius. 2009. Complexity in core argument marking and population size. In G. Sampson, D. Gil, and P. Trudgill (eds.) *Language complexity as an evolving variable.* Oxford: Oxford University Press, 125–40.

Skjekkeland, Martin. 1997. *Dei norske dialektane: tradisjonelle særdrag i jamføring med skriftmåla.* Kristiansand: Høyskoleforlaget.

Sohn, Ho-Min. 1999. *The Korean language.* Cambridge: Cambridge University Press.

Søndergaard, Bent. 1970. Den såkaldte klusilspring, specielt i morsingmål. *Sprog og kultur* 26: 61–8.

Song, Jae Jung. 2001. *Linguistic typology: Morphology and syntax.* London: Longman.

Steinbergs, Aleksandra. 1996. The classification of languages. In W. O'Grady, M. Dobrovolsky, and F. Katamba. *Contemporary linguistics: An introduction.* London: Longman, 372–415.

Stone, Gerald. 1993. Cassubian. In B. Comrie and G. Corbett (eds.) *The Slavonic languages.* London: Routledge, 759–94.

Strang, Barbara. 1970. *A history of English.* London: Methuen.

Sudbury, Andrea. 2000. *Dialect contact and koinéisation in the Falkland Islands: The development of a southern hemisphere English?* Colchester, UK: University of Essex PhD thesis.

Sun, Jackson. 2007. Perfective stem formation in Khalong Tibetan. In R. Bielmeier and F. Haller (eds.) *Linguistics of the Himalayas and beyond.* Berlin: Mouton de Gruyter, 323–40.

Sutton, Douglas (ed.). 1994. *The origins of the first New Zealanders.* Auckland: Auckland University Press.

Swan, Michael. 2007. History is not what happened: The case of contrastive analysis. *International Journal of Applied Linguistics,* 391–6.

Tadmor, Uri. forthcoming. The grammaticalisation of generational relations in Onya Darat. In R. LaPolla (ed.) *The shaping of language: Relationships between the structures of languages and their social, cultural, historical, and natural environments.*

Taeldeman, Johan. 2005. *Oost-Vlaams.* Tielt: Lannoo.

Thomason, Sarah G. 2001. *Language contact: An introduction.* Edinburgh: Edinburgh University Press.

——and Daniel L. Everett. 2005. Pronoun borrowing. *Proceedings of the Berkeley Linguistics Society* 27: 301–15.

——and Terrence Kaufman. 1988. *Language contact, creolisation and genetic linguistics.* Berkeley: University of California Press.

Thrainsson, Höskuldur, Hjalmar Petersen, Jogvan i Lon Jacobsen, and Zakaris Svabo Hansen. 2004. *Faroese: An overview and reference grammar.* Torshavn: Føroya Fróðskaparfelag.

Thurston, William. 1989. How exoteric languages build a lexicon: Esoterogeny in West New Britain. In R. Harlow and R. Hooper (eds.) *VICAL I: Papers in Oceanic linguistics.* Auckland: Linguistic Society of New Zealand, 555–79.

——1994. Renovation and innovation in the languages of north-western New Britain. In T. Dutton and D. Tryon (eds.) *Language contact and change in the Austronesian world.* Berlin: Mouton de Gruyter, 573–609.

Torp, Arne. 2003. Frekvens, trykkletthet, reduksjon. In J.T. Faarlund (ed.) *Språk i endring: indre norsk språkhistorie.* Oslo: Novus, 219–54.

Townend, Matthew. 2002. *Language and history in Viking Age England: Linguistic relations between speakers of Old Norse and Old English.* Turnhout: Brepols.

Trask, R. Larry. 1993. *A dictionary of grammatical terms in linguistics.* London: Routledge.

——1999. *Key concepts in language and linguistics.* London: Routledge.

Traugott, Elizabeth, Rebecca Labrum, and Susan C. Shepherd (eds.).
1980. *Papers from the Fourth International Conference on Historical Linguistics.* Amsterdam: Benjamins.

Tristram, Hildegard. 2004. Diglossia in Anglo-Saxon England, or
what was spoken Old English like? *Studia Anglica Posnaniensia*
40: 87–110.

——2006. Why don't the English speak Welsh? In N.J. Higham
(ed.) *Britons in Anglo-Saxon England*, 192–214. Woodbridge:
Boydell.

Trubetzkoy, Nikolai. 1939. *Grundzüge der Phonologie.* Prague:
Travaux du Cercle Linguistique de Prague 7.

Trudgill, Peter. 1974. *The social differentiation of English in Norwich.*
Cambridge: Cambridge University Press.

——1975. *Accent, dialect and the school.* London: Edward Arnold.

——1978. Creolisation in reverse: Reduction and simplification in
the Albanian dialects of Greece. *Transactions of the Philological
Society 1976–77*: 32–50.

——1983. *On dialect: Social and geographical perspectives.* Oxford:
Blackwell.

——1986. *Dialects in contact.* Oxford: Blackwell.

——1988. Norwich revisited: Recent linguistic changes in an English urban dialect. *English World-Wide* 9: 33–49.

——1992. Dialect typology and social structure. In E.H. Jahr (ed.),
Language contact and language change. Berlin: Mouton de Gruyter, 195–212.

——1995. Grammaticalisation and social structure: Nonstandard
conjunction-formation in East Anglian English. In F.R. Palmer
(ed.) *Grammar and meaning: Papers in honour of Sir John Lyons.*
Cambridge: Cambridge University Press, 136–47.

——1996a. Dialect typology: Isolation, social network and phonological structure. In G. Guy et al. (eds.), *Towards a social science of
language: Papers in honour of William Labov. Vol. 1: Variation
and change in language and society.* Amsterdam: Benjamins, 3–21.

——1996b. Dual-source pidgins and reverse creoloids: Northern
perspectives on language contact. In E.H. Jahr and I. Broch
(eds.) *Language contact in the Arctic: Northern pidgins and contact
languages.* Berlin: Mouton de Gruyter, 5–14.

——1998. Typology and sociolinguistics: Linguistic structure, social
structure and explanatory comparative dialectology. *Folia Linguistica* 31.3–4: 349–60.

——1999a. *The dialects of England* (2nd edn). Oxford: Blackwell.

——1999b. Language contact and the function of linguistic gender.
Poznan Studies in Contemporary Linguistics 35: 9–28.

Trudgill, Peter. 2000. *Sociolinguistics: An introduction to language and society* (4th edn). London: Penguin.

——2001. Greek dialects: Linguistic and social typology. In A. Ralli, B. Joseph, and M. Janse (eds.) *Proceedings of the First International Conference of Modern Greek Dialects and Linguistic Theory*. Patras: Patras University Press, 263–72.

——2002. Sociolinguistic typology. In J.K. Chambers, P. Trudgill, and N. Schilling-Estes (eds.), *The handbook of language variation and change*. Oxford: Blackwell, 707–28.

——2003a. *A glossary of sociolinguistics*. Edinburgh: Edinburgh University Press.

——2003b. *The Norfolk dialect*. Cromer: Poppyland.

——2003c. Modern Greek dialects: A preliminary classification. *Journal of Greek Linguistics* 4: 45–63.

——2004a. *New-dialect formation: The inevitability of colonial Englishes*. Edinburgh: Edinburgh University Press.

——2004b. The impact of language contact and social structure on linguistic structure: Focus on the dialects of Modern Greek. In B. Kortmann (ed.) *Dialect meets typology: Dialect grammar from a cross-linguistic perspective*. Berlin: Mouton de Gruyter, 435–51.

——2004c. Linguistic and social typology: The Austronesian migrations and phoneme inventories. *Linguistic Typology* 8: 305–20.

——2008. The historical sociolinguistics of elite accent change: On why RP is not disappearing. *Studia Anglica Posnaniensia* 44: 1–12.

——2009. Sociolinguistic typology and complexification. In G. Sampson, D. Gil, and P. Trudgill (eds.), *Language complexity as an evolving variable*. Oxford: Oxford University Press.

——2010a. Contact and sociolinguistic typology. In R. Hickey (ed.) *Handbook of language contact*. Oxford: Blackwell.

——2010b. Social structure, language contact and language change. In R. Wodak, B. Johnstone, and P. Kerswill (eds.) *Sociolinguistics handbook*. London: Sage.

——2010c. *Investigations in sociohistorical linguistics: Stories of colonisation and contact*. Cambridge: Cambridge University Press.

Tryon, Darrell (ed.). 1994. *Comparative Austronesian dictionary* Berlin: Mouton de Gruyter.

Tylden, Per. 1956. *2. persons personlege pronomen, dualis og pluralis i gamalnorsk og mellomnorsk diplommål = Universitet i Bergen Årbok*, 4.

Van der Auwera, Johan and Annemie Neuckermans. 2004. On the interaction of predicate and quantifier negation in Flemish. In B. Kortmann (ed.) *Dialectology meets typology: Dialect grammar from a cross-linguistic perspective*. Berlin: Mouton de Gruyter, 453–78.

Van Coetsem, F. 2000. *A general and unified theory of the transmission process in language contact*. Heidelberg: Winter.

Van Haeringen, C.B. 1939. Congruerende voegwoorden. *Tijdschrift voor Nederlandse Taal- en Letterkunde* 60: 126–7.

Vanhove, Martine. 2001. Contacts de langues et complexification des systèmes: le cas du maltais. *Faits de langues* 18: 65–74.

Vennemann, Theo. 2002. On the rise of 'Celtic' syntax in Middle English. In P.J. Lucas and A.M. Lucas (eds.) *Middle English from tongue to text*. Bern: Peter Lang, 203–34.

——2009. Celtic influence in English? Yes and no. *English Language and Linguistics* 13.2: 309–34.

Versteegh, Kees. 1984–6. Word order in Uzbekistan Arabic and universal grammar. *Orientalia Suecania* 33–5: 443–53.

Vogt, Hans. 1948. Dans quelles conditions et dans quelles limites peut s'exercer sur le système morphologique d'une langue l'action du système morphologique d'une autre langue? In M. Lejeune (ed.) *Actes du Sixième Congrès International des Linguistes*. Paris: Klincksieck, 31–45.

——1963. *Dictionnaire de la langue oubykh*. Oslo: Universitetsforlaget.

Wagner, Heinrich. 1959. *Das Verbum in den Sprachen der Britischen Inseln*. Tübingen: Niemeyer.

Wagner, Susanne. 2005. Gender in English pronouns: Southwest England. In B. Kortmann, T, Herrmann, L. Pietsch, and S. Wagner (eds.) *A comparative grammar of British English dialects: Agreement, gender, relative clauses*. Berlin: Mouton de Gruyter, 211–352.

Walker, Alastair. 1990. Frisian. In C. Russ (ed.) *The dialects of modern German: A linguistic survey*. London: Routledge, 1–30.

——and Ommo Wilts. 2001. Die nordfriesichen Mundarten. In H.H. Munske et al. (eds.) *Handbuch des friesischen/Handbook of Frisian studies*. Tübingen: Niemeyer, 284–305.

Wanner, Dieter. 2001. From Latin to Romance languages. In M. Haspelmath et al. (eds.) *Language typology and language universals: An international handbook*. Berlin: de Gruyter, 1691–706.

Weber, Andrea, and Anne Cutler. 2004. Lexical competition in non-native spoken-word recognition. *Journal of Memory and Language* 50: 1–25.

Weiss, Helmut. 2005. Inflected complementizers in Continental West Germanic dialects. *Zeitschrift für Dialektologie und Linguistik* 72: 148–66.

Wells, John. 1982. *Accents of English* (three volumes). Cambridge: Cambridge University Press.

Werner, Otmar. 1984. Morphologische Entwicklungen in den germanischen Sprachen. In J. Untermann and B. Brogyany (eds.). *Das Germanische und die Rekonstruktion der indo-germanischen Grundsprache*. Amsterdam: Benjamins, 181–226.

Wessén, Elias. 1958. *Svensk språkhistoria*. Stockholm: Almqvist and Wiksell.

Whorf, Benjamin Lee. 1956. *Language, thought, and reality: Selected writings of Benjamin Lee Whorf* [edited by John B. Carroll]. Cambridge, MA: MIT Press.

Wichmann, Søren. 2010a. Patterns of migration from early prehistory to the present. Paper presented at The First Conference on ASJP and Language Prehistory (ALP-I), Max Planck Institute for Evolutionary Anthropology, Leipzig, 17–19 Sept. 2010.

——2010b. Neolithic linguistics. In G. Barjamovic, I. Elmerot, A. Hyllested, Be. Nielsen, and B.O. Skaarup (eds.) *Language and prehistory of the Indo-European peoples: A cross-disciplinary perspective*. Budapest: Archaeolingua.

——and Eric W. Holman. 2009a. *Assessing temporal stability for linguistic typological features*. Munich: Lincom Europa.

————2009b. Population size and rates of language change. *Human Biology* 81: 259–74.

——Dietrich Stauffer, Christian Schulze, and Eric Holman. 2008. Do language change rates depend on population size? *Advances in Complex Systems* 11.3: 357–69.

Wierzbicka, Anna. 1986. Does language reflect culture? Evidence from Australian English. *Language in society* 15: 349–74.

——1992. *Semantics, culture and cognition: Universal human concepts in culture-specific configurations*. Oxford: Oxford University Press.

Winford, Donald, and Bettina Migge. 2004. Surinamese creoles: Morphology and syntax. In B. Kortmann et al. (eds.) *A handbook of varieties of English, vol. II: morphology and syntax*. Berlin: Mouton de Gruyter, 482–516.

Winnifrith, Tom. 1987. *The Vlachs: The history of a Balkan people*. London: Duckworth.

Wischer, Ilse. 2006. Grammaticalisation and language contact in the history of English: The evolution of the progressive form. In N. Ritt, H. Schendl, C. Dalton-Puffer, and D. Kastovsky (eds.) *Mediaeval English and its heritage*. Frankfurt: Lang, 165–87.

Wohlgemuth, Jan. 2010. Language endangerment, community size and typological rarity. In J. Wohlgemuth and M. Cysouw (eds.)

Rethinking universals: How rarities affect linguistic theory. Berlin: De Gruyter, 255–77.

Woodbury, Anthony. 1991. Counting Eskimo words for snow. http://www-users.cs.york.ac.uk/susan/bib/nf/_misc/woodbury.htm.

Woolf, Alex. 2007. Apartheid and economics in Anglo-Saxon England. In N. Higham (ed.) *The Britons in Anglo-Saxon England,* 113–29. Woodbridge: Boydell.

Wray, Alison, and George Grace. 2007. The consequences of talking to strangers: Evolutionary corollaries of socio-cultural influences on linguistic form. *Lingua* 117: 543–78.

Wyld, H.C. 1936. *History of modern colloquial English* (3rd edn). Oxford: Blackwell.

Zabrocki, Ludwik. 1963. *Wspolnoty komunikatywne w genezie i rozwoju jezyka niemieckiego* I: *prehistoria jezyka niemieckiego.* [Communicative communities in the origins and development of German I: Prehistory of the German language.] Wroclaw: Zaklad Narodowy imienia Ossolinskich.

Zubin, David, and Klaus-Michael Köpcke. 1981. Gender: A less than arbitrary grammatical category. In R.A. Hendrick, C.A. Masek, and M.F. Miller (eds.), *Papers from the seventeenth regional meeting of the Chicago Linguistic Society.* Chicago Linguistic Society, 439–49.

Index